Alessandra Giorgi and Giuseppe Longobardi's important study of the argument structure of lexical projections, in particular of Noun Phrases, makes substantial advances in this relatively neglected area. Working within a Government and Binding framework, the authors present strong new arguments in favour of the existence of empty categories, and evidence for the correct understanding of word order parameters and of Chomsky's Projection Principle. In particular, they elaborate and discuss a number of tests intended to define under which lexical and syntactic conditions an empty pronominal subject may or must occur in a Noun Phrase. The levels of structural attachment of the arguments of a head noun are carefully established by supporting assumptions made in this domain with independent evidence.

As well as its theoretical advances, this book provides a descriptive analysis of nominal structure in Romance, and compares it with corresponding structure in Germanic languages. It offers a valuable introduction to Italian phrase structure.

CAMBRIDGE STUDIES IN LINGUISTICS

General Editors: B. COMRIE, C. J. FILLMORE, R. LASS,
D. LIGHTFOOT, J. LYONS, P. H. MATTHEWS,
R. POSNER, S. ROMAINE, N. V. SMITH, N. VINCENT

The syntax of Noun Phrases

In this series

Supplementary volumes

THE SYNTAX OF NOUN PHRASES

Configuration, parameters and empty categories

ALESSANDRA GIORGI

Istituto per la Ricerca Scientifica e Tecnologica, Trento, Italy

and

GIUSEPPE LONGOBARDI

Associate Professor of General Linguistics, Università di Venezia, Italy

Foreword by Guglielmo Cinque

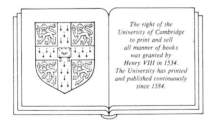

The right of the
University of Cambridge
to print and sell
all manner of books
was granted by
Henry VIII in 1534.
The University has printed
and published continuously
since 1584.

CAMBRIDGE UNIVERSITY PRESS

Cambridge

New York   Port Chester

Melbourne   Sydney

Published by the Press Syndicate of the University of Cambridge
The Pitt Building, Trumpington Street, Cambridge CB2 1RP
40 West 20th Street, New York, NY 10011, USA
10 Stamford Road, Oakleigh, Melbourne 3166, Australia

First published 1991

Printed in Great Britain at the University Press, Cambridge

British Library cataloguing in publication data

Giorgi, Alessandra
The syntax of Noun Phrases: configuration, parameters and empty categories. –
(Cambridge studies in linguistics; 57).
1. Romance languages. Syntax
I. Title. II. Longobardi, Giuseppe
440

Library of Congress cataloguing in publication data

Giorgi, Alessandra
The syntax of Noun Phrases: configuration, parameters, and empty categories /
Alessandra Giorgi and Giuseppe Longobardi: foreword by Guglielmo Cinque.
    p.   cm. – (Cambridge studies in linguistics: 57)
Includes bibliographical references.
ISBN 0-521-37004-3. – ISBN 0-521-37902-4 (pbk.)
1. Grammar, Comparative and general – Noun phrase. 2. Grammar, Comparative
and general – Syntax. 3. Generative grammar.
I. Longobardi, Giuseppe. II. Title. III. Series.
P271.G56 1991
415 – dc20 90-34062 CIP

ISBN 0 521 37004 3 hardback
ISBN 0 521 37902 4 paperback

Contents

Contents

Foreword

Alessandra Giorgi's and Giuseppe Longobardi's articles collected here are not merely a contribution to the syntax of the N(oun) P(hrase). They provide a general and clear introduction to many areas of Romance syntax and of the theory of empty categories in the 'principles and parameters' framework. They should thus be appreciated by both researchers and advanced students interested in these topics.

The specific merits of their contribution are many. For one thing, it is in part as a consequence of these articles, which have been circulating in prepublication form for some years, that the syntax of the NP has become again a central topic of enquiry. In the two decades following Chomsky's fundamental 'Remarks on Nominalizations', the NP had received surprisingly little attention in the literature, despite its centrality and complexity, inferior only to that of the clause itself.

Another important outcome of their work is the unprecedented variety of aspects of the internal structure of NPs which have been brought under analysis and illuminated, often for the first time.

Third and foremost is the quantity of genuine contributions to linguistic theory which emerge from this in-depth analysis of the NP.

In this brief presentation, I will limit myself to mentioning the particular theoretical contributions which, to my mind, are among the most significant results of their detailed work on NP structure. As will become clear, they are quite exceptional in number and quality.

The first concerns the internal articulation of the NP. On the basis of systematic subject/object asymmetries in the domains of Binding Theory and pronominal binding (by a quantifier), Giorgi constructs a solid case for hypothesizing a fully hierarchical structure within the NP.

From these asymmetries she also draws decisive evidence that the notion of c-command relevant to Binding Theory is the one making reference to 'the first branching category' (Reinhart 1976) rather than 'the first maximal projection' (Aoun and Sportiche 1982); an important confirmation of Chomsky's (1986b, 8) conjecture.

Besides motivating the transparency for c-command of NP-internal Case-marking prepositions (in Italian) and the existence of ergative Ns, chapter 1 contains another important theoretical contribution: an *empirical* argument to favour the 'least Complete Functional Complex' of Chomsky (1986a) as the local domain for the Binding principles A and B over previous definitions of that domain.

Longobardi's analysis of extraction from NP in chapter 2 also contains a number of non-trivial implications for linguistic theory. The obligatory movement through Spec in extraction from NP in Romance, motivated on ample empirical grounds, is shown to follow naturally from a fundamental difference in the government properties of Ns and Vs. The analysis also provides a persuasive argument for the conclusion, recently adopted by many investigators, that head government must be satisfied 'over and above antecedent government' for any non-pronominal empty category (cf. Chomsky 1986b, 83).

Longobardi also shows that the Spec of VP-adjoined maximal projections must not be taken to be properly governed (head-governed) although the maximal projections themselves are properly governed.

Two new treatments with wide-range typological implications of Ross's Left Branch Condition and Emonds's and Williams's principles blocking further canonical recursion on the non-recursive side conclude the chapter.

In chapter 3, Giorgi and Longobardi lay out a parametric theory of word-order differences between the Romance and Germanic NP. They show how various apparently unrelated differences can be traced to a single abstract directionality parameter: the different underlying position of the subject (on a left branch under Spec, in Germanic, and on a right branch in Romance). Their analysis opens up the possibility that the directionality parameter extends to the other maximal projections, with very important typological consequences for the analysis of the two language families.

At the end of the chapter, Giorgi and Longobardi single out some further, minor, parameters across Germanic and Romance which concern the categorial status of the possessive.

In this chapter, and more systematically in chapter 4, ample and fine-grained evidence is discussed for another theoretically relevant question: the presence of a PRO subject within NPs; a question often and inconclusively debated in the previous literature. They manage to show that a PRO subject *can* at least be present within the NP, and, for a particular class of Ns, even that it *must* be present.

As this cursory review of only its most important contributions suggests, Alessandra Giorgi and Giuseppe Longobardi's volume will constitute a mandatory reading for anyone interested in the properties of NP structure. But it is also not hazardous to forecast that it will influence many aspects of our current conception of linguistic theory.

Guglielmo Cinque
Venice, 20 April 1989

Acknowledgments

The contents of this book were mostly inspired by the works of N. Chomsky, R. Kayne and G. Cinque; our intellectual debts to them, however, go far beyond the limits of the present work.

Special thanks for judgements, comments and encouragement are due to J. Higginbotham and M. Kenstowicz, who were visiting the Scuola Normale in Pisa at the time this research was being completed.

For the invaluable help provided by their comments and criticism on an earlier draft of the manuscript, we are also grateful to A. Battye, L. Burzio, G. Cinque, D. Lightfoot, N. Vincent and an anonymous referee.

We have also profited from discussions with and received comments and judgements from many friends and colleagues: M. Ambar, M. Anderson, J. Aoun, A. Belletti, P. Benincà, P. M. Bertinetto, H. den Besten, H. Borer, P. Bottari, L. Burzio, A. Cardinaletti, C. Ciociola, D. Delfitto, V. Demonte, V. Deprez, C. Dobrovie Sorin, L. Gràcia, A. Gorecka, G. Graffi, J. Grimshaw, J. Guéron, L. Hellan, M. L. Hernanz, T. Hoekstra, H. Hoji, A. Holmberg, K. Koch-Christensen, H. Lasnik, M. Luján, M. R. Manzini, H. Obenauer, M. Prinzhorn, D. Pesetsky, P. Pica, J. Y. Pollock, T. Reinhart, L. Renzi, E. Reuland, H. van Riemsdijk, E. Ritter, L. Rizzi, I. Roberts, M. Rochemont, T. Roeper, A. Szabolcsi, B. Schein, U. Shlonsky, D. Steriade, T. Stowell, T. Tappe, T. Taraldsen, J. Toman, E. Torrego, G. Webelhut, K. Wexler, E. Williams; to all of them we are much indebted.

Finally, the friendship of Lluïsa Gràcia, Hans Obenauer, Barry Schein and Donca Steriade has supported us throughout the preparation of this book, as well as on many other occasions. We thank them heartily.

Introduction

1   The study of Noun Phrases

The unifying goal of the four chapters contained in this book is that of clarifying how Noun Phrases are internally structured. From a descriptive point of view, we provide an analysis of the structure of Noun Phrases in Romance, especially Italian, and compare the results so obtained to corresponding aspects of nominal structure in the Germanic languages. From a more theoretical point of view, on the other hand, the works assembled here contribute to investigating the notions of c-command and government and the theories of word order and of empty categories adequate to meet the empirical challenges emerging from the study of NPs, therefore providing suggestions of relevance also to the theory of Universal Grammar in general.

Looking back at the history of the formal study of NPs, it seems clear that after Chomsky's (1970) 'Remarks on nominalizations' the topic had not greatly progressed for almost ten years. Actually, no specific work on the internal structure of NPs had appeared, until M. Anderson's (1979) doctoral dissertation 'Noun Phrase Structure'; the year after, G. Cinque, relying also on work on French which later appeared in Milner (1982), opened the way to the investigation of Italian nominal structures, publishing 'On Extraction from NPs in Italian'. Only more recently have other scholars, whose contributions will often be mentioned in these chapters, concentrated their efforts on this topic. It may seem surprising that the subject had not been considered for such a long time, but it is not difficult to find a reason for this: Chomsky, in his 1970 article, made the natural assumption that the structure related to a Verb is the same as that related to the corresponding Noun. There are in fact several obvious selectional similarities which can hardly be captured in any other way. Chomsky, therefore, proposed that lexical heads like V and N belonged to an underspecified category, unifying in a radical way the lexical and, to some extent, syntactic properties of these two categories. This view, however, though very natural, could not be immediately pursued further, since Verbs and Nouns present in the structure they project a number of differences which could not easily fit into the theory at the time and were difficult to reconcile with their similarities. However, as the theory of syntax progressed towards more general principles and developed such notions as Case, government and parameter, the structure of NPs became once again available for theoretical investigation. Both Anderson (1979) and Cinque (1980) developed Chomsky's (1970) original idea that Nouns and Verbs, or more precisely, Noun Phrases and clauses, have many properties in common: in particular their work has suggested that the various 'diatheses' of NPs were related via movement, as is assumed to be the case in sentences, and that the role of 'possessive' elements in NPs closely parallels that of subjects of clauses (I-subjects in Borer's 1986 terms):

(1)   a. The barbarians destroyed the city
       b. The city was destroyed by the barbarians
(2)   a. The barbarians' destruction of the city
       b. The city's destruction by the barbarians

Under this approach (2)a and (2)b are transformationally related in the same sense in which (1)a and (1)b are and the possessive phrases of (2) have the same prominence as the surface subjects of (1); these views are central to our work and are actually generalized into what we may refer to as the 'Configurational Hypothesis', consisting of two clauses:

A.   It is possible to identify, within NPs, definite θ- (and non-θ-) positions at various levels of hierarchical attachment: whenever an element of the N frame appears in a position arguably different from the one where it should be projected at D-structure, its displacement must, then, be governed by the general conditions holding on antecedent–trace relationships created by 'Move α'; moreover the binding of anaphors and pronouns in NPs obeys the same constraints observed in clauses.

B.   The θ-structure of Ns (their θ-grid and the condition on θ-assignment) strictly parallels that of Vs, so that the differences appearing on the surface must be due to the intervention of other modules of grammar which determine some systematic variation.

Among such independently motivated differences, the following three emerge clearly throughout the chapters of this book as the most relevant ones:

(i) The maximal projection of N can be an argument, unlike that of V; hence it need not be licensed by predication, i.e. by externalizing a subject argument. Consequently, the subject of NP is not the predication subject of an Xmax and, as such, is not obligatorily required by Rothstein's (1983) Predication Principle.

(ii) Nouns, unlike Verbs, are non-structural governors and Case-markers (cf. Kayne 1981b; Chomsky 1986a).

(iii) Nouns do not display a special morphology for the passive diathesis; in particular, they present no morpheme analogous to the so-called EN morpheme studied in Roberts (1987).

As a consequence of the assumptions forming the Configurational Hypothesis, it follows that the phrases in (1) and (2) are considered related and, in particular, we will speak of 'passive' NPs, as in (2)b, derived via movement from 'active' ones, like (2)a; in the same spirit, in chapter 1 Giorgi will also introduce and empirically substantiate the concept of 'ergative Nouns', i.e. Nouns derived from ergative Verbs, in the sense of Burzio (1981/1986) and Perlmutter (1978), as in the following case:

(3) a. Tu parti per Parigi
       You are leaving for Paris
     b. La tua partenza per Parigi
       Your departure for Paris

For a variety of empirical reasons, discussed in the text, we believe that the assumptions A and B are correct. However, a conceptual point needs to be stressed as well: the Configurational Hypothesis here adopted should be regarded *a priori* as the null hypothesis, since it does not imply any special stipulation, about the syntax of NPs, which is not independently required in the rest of the grammar. Yet, such a hypothesis has been challenged to various extents in several important contributions to the recent literature: e.g. the valuable and highly detailed study by Zubizarreta (1986) explicitly rejects aspects of the conclusions under point A of the Configurational Hypothesis. Actually, the whole recent debate on Noun Phrases is split into two major tendencies; some researchers following Anderson, Cinque and Milner, have essentially adopted versions of this 'configurational' line of reasoning, most notably Torrego (1984, 1986); others have accepted the burden of proof, arguing that NPs are radically different from clauses and VPs: they have claimed that θ-

positions cannot be identified once and for all and indeed that some arguments of NPs are not assigned θ-roles, but are simply interpreted according to some adjunct-like semantic rule.

This second approach aims to capture the fact that the semantic functions which a Noun is able to assign to its arguments seem much more varied and mutually dependent than the ones assigned by a Verb. Along such guidelines, the domain of relevant observations and generalizations concerning the form and meaning of NPs has been significantly enlarged. Among the most important works, developing variants of this line of research, are the ones by Zubizarreta (1986), Safir (1987) and Grimshaw (1986): they provide arguments and empirical observations that cannot be ignored in any analysis of NPs. We concentrate, however, on certain aspects of NP structure which suggest that the 'Configurational Hypothesis' (essentially the null hypothesis, as we have remarked) is worth maintaining, not only on conceptual and heuristic grounds, but also on empirical ones. In fact, throughout the chapters of this book it will be shown, first, that the structural assumptions following from the 'Configurational Hypothesis' are able to explain a whole variety of phenomena concerning binding, word order and semantic interpretation, and, second, that a substantial portion of these phenomena (especially in chs. 1 and 3) cannot be easily accounted for in a theory not including those assumptions. In particular, the arguments provided in chapter 3 appear to suggest that probably even descriptive adequacy would fail to be attained by a theory of syntax dispensing with empty categories like trace and PRO. Also the structural attachment of arguments and modifiers of Nouns hypothesized in this volume in agreement with the 'Configurational Hypothesis', receives strong support from the data analysed: it must be stressed, in fact, that virtually every assumption made on this topic is independently suggested by more than just one piece of empirical evidence. In conclusion, if the analyses motivated in the chapters which follow prove to be tenable, they will represent indirect but strong proof of the main hypothesis assumed and of the current theory of grammar in general.

Needless to say, our work has been greatly inspired by Cinque's (1980, 1981a), since the empirical generalizations he identifies constitute our starting point, even if we then update and extend his analysis, still maintaining the general approach to the problem.

In the first chapter of this book, Giorgi considers the internal argument structure of NPs, adopting binding phenomena as her major testing ground; from this she draws some conclusions concerning the essentially configurational character of NPs, the definitions of command and locality relevant for the binding principles, and the extension of the ergativity phenomenon across lexical categories.

In the second chapter, Longobardi analyses extraction from NPs, on the basis of the generalizations first proposed by Cinque (1980), and provides the most direct empirical evidence for the idea that any movement out of NP in Romance must be mediated by phrase-internal raising to the Specifier position. In the light of an original suggestion by Kayne (1981b, 1983), it is argued that this peculiar condition on movement can be predicted by an analysis of the nature of N as a governor. In the course of the discussion evidence is suggested in favour of the splitting conjunctive interpretation of the two requirements of head and antecedent government for traces, and a more general constraint on lexical X′ structures, the Consistency Principle, is also proposed.

The third chapter, written jointly by the authors, addresses the question of how to deal, in the framework of a formal theory of syntax, with the problem of crosslinguistic word order variation: it tries to complement the abstract approach and the learnability considerations of generative grammar with insights provided by typological investigation; a methodological attempt also invoked in Hawkins (1985) and made possible especially by R. Kayne's work on comparative syntax of English and Romance in the past fifteen years. In fact, we identify a single parameter of variation between the Romance and Germanic languages, whose consequences affect the shape of NPs in a wide number of more or less directly visible aspects. Some of these phenomena seem to cluster together across languages and to fall very naturally under a parametric theory, even though in a purely logical theory of language acquisition they could easily be regarded as learnable from primary data independently of each other, so as to predict a more random typological variation than the one observed. It is in this sense that a more extensive reliance on empirically founded typologies may prove quite useful to reduce the class of attainable grammars beyond the limits already suggested, abstractly, by learnability considerations. The phenomena we consider in this chapter provide very strong evidence in favour of the leading idea illustrated under points A and B above; in particular they clarify the crucial role played by NP-internally moved phrases and their traces in interaction with empty pronominals, for whose occurrence very strong new evidence is provided.

In the fourth chapter, the two authors try to characterize more formally the nature and the distribution of such empty pronominals, whose existence was strongly suggested by the phenomena analysed in the previous chapter. Special attention is devoted to the subject empty category, about which undeveloped assumptions can often be found throughout the literature, but whose occurrence and properties have never been subjected to the detailed investigation that such a topic deserves. Also the results achieved in this chapter reinforce the general hypothesis that the kinds of structures and the empty categories found in NPs are essentially the same as those identifiable in clauses. Finally, more recent developments of the theory concerning the projections of the Determiner will be briefly discussed.

2   Theoretical background

Before starting the analysis of NP structure, we will briefly provide some theoretical background concerning the Government and Binding framework which will be adopted in the subsequent discussion. Let us first introduce the notion of Universal Grammar (henceforth UG), which is at the core of the theory in question.

Language is viewed as an innate biological faculty, i.e. humans are considered to be endowed from birth with a system of principles predisposed to the acquisition of a grammar under the exposure to linguistic experience; this can be naturally hypothesized just on the basis of the underdetermination and uniformity of the language-learning process (see e.g. Chomsky 1975). Now, such a biological system must also be universal, since no human being displays any particular predisposition to acquire one language rather than another.

However, the most trivial and superficial observation shows that languages differ from each other, i.e. that a particular grammar has different properties from another one: for instance, Italian differs from Chinese. The conceptual problem which arises is then the following: how is it possible that these two opposed challenges can be met by a consistent theory of language acquisition and of language variation? The answer relies to a large extent on the so-called theory of parameters. In the recent past it has been discovered that a cluster of differential properties distinguishing two or more natural languages can often be reduced by an accurate grammatical analysis to a single, more abstract difference, referred to as a parameter of UG. As a consequence, it can be plausibly hypothesized that the superficial differences among languages, apart from the semiotically arbitrary variation in the phonological encoding of concepts in the lexicon, are less numerous than the real ones. The view of the learning process turns out to be much simplified by this discovery: in most cases it can be reduced to the setting of the value of an open parameter, resulting in very substantial surface variation, just on the grounds of exposure to a very restricted sample of sentences; it is only necessary that the latter exemplify clearly at least one consequence of the correct setting of the parameter in question. UG can, thus, be considered to consist of certain fixed principles and several open parameters to be set by the particular linguistic experience of the learner: it gives rise to the various linguistic systems through the choice of the values for the parameters. By means of exposure to a limited *corpus* of data, a child is then able to determine the whole structure of his or her language; for more detailed discussion, see Chomsky (1981: ch. 1).

Several principles of grammar cooperate to define for each language which structures are possible and which are not. The various subparts of the theory of grammar are called 'modules', in that they can operate on the same configuration independently of each other. In the following pages, we will introduce in more detail the most important among them.

A grammar is also modular in the sense that it consists of various levels of representation for each expression that it generates; there is much debate in the actual elaboration of the theory about the empirical content and definition of levels. Traditionally, a grammar is seen as a mapping between the following levels:

(4)

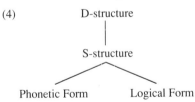

Technically speaking, D-structure is said to be a pure representation of thematic relations, i.e. of the referential roles (such as agent, experiencer, patient and others) which lexical items, conceived of essentially as n-ary logical predicates, assign to their arguments (e.g. a Verb to its subject and object). Such thematic assignment is local, taking place basically under adjacency and, whenever an argument appears away from its normal thematic position (e.g. a direct object not occurring adjacent to its Verb), it is said to have been displaced by a movement rule, leaving behind an empty category or 'trace' in the original position; the mapping to the following level is precisely through the application of this rule of Move α. S-structure, whose linear arrangement of words is most often the one encoded in the phonetic realization, is viewed as an 'annotated' structure, where the history of movement is explicitly recorded by means of traces. The mapping to Logical Form (LF) is essentially performed by the rule of Quantifier Raising (QR). Phonological rules basically intervene in the mapping to the Phonetic Form (PF). In the following chapters, we will never consider PF and we will restrict our attention mainly to D- and S-structure, occasionally referring to certain phenomena which are often claimed to find their origin at LF (e.g. weak crossover effects, quantificational scope). Whether the various levels are really motivated, or are just a notational variant of other ways of expressing the same empirical content by means of just one level is a potentially open question which will not be addressed in this work.

X-bar theory
The first module of grammar to be introduced is the X-bar (X') theory, originally elaborated by Jackendoff (1977; see also Stowell 1981).

As is standard in any syntactic approach, we will admit that words fall into a restricted number of distributionally defined categories. The fundamental categorial types are the following: Noun (N), Verb (V), Adjective (A) and Preposition/Postposition (P). These are called 'lexical categories'; there is also a certain number of non-lexical categories: Inflection (I), which essentially includes verbal auxiliaries and affixes; Complementizer (C), like English *that* or Italian *che*; Determiner (D), i.e. the category of articles and other elements which introduce nominal expressions. A sentence, however, cannot be taken to be simply a concatenation of linearly arranged categories, since adjacent words are grouped together in a systematic way to form larger constituents, or phrases. The resulting structure is often represented by means of tree diagrams, in which each category or phrase corresponds to a so-called 'node', where higher nodes (i.e. larger constituents) are said to dominate (contain) lower ones (smaller constituents). Technically speaking, we will say that every word is a head and every head projects higher constituents of a corresponding categorial type: the highest will be called maximal projection. Thus, among such maximal projections are: Noun Phrase (NP), Verb Phrase (VP), Adjective Phrase (AP), Prepositional Phrase (PP), Inflection Phrase (IP), Complementizer Phrase (CP) (see Chomsky

1986a, 1986b; Radford 1988), and probably Determiner Phrase (DP), on whose precise status see chapter 4 below.

The X-bar approach to constituent structure identifies some invariants in the possible hierarchical configurations. Most importantly, Chomsky (1970) and Jackendoff (1977) observed that, independently of the lexical category which is involved in a particular structure, the way in which a head defines its projections obeys some general constraints. Chomsky (1986b) has extended such an approach to include also the structure projected by non-lexical heads, in particular I and C, which are considered to project clausal constituents, i.e. sentences. X-bar theory establishes that whenever there is a head X, there will also be a maximal projection, referred to as XP or Xmax, and at least one intermediate projection, call it X′. Moreover, X-bar theory defines the levels where the arguments of the head must be attached; the intermediate projection X′ is said to consist of X and its 'Complement'; the following projection of X′, X″ (generally Xmax, in the sense that usually only two projections are hypothesized) is instead said to consist of X′ and its Specifier. Notice, however, that the term 'Specifier', no less than 'Complement', does not identify a category, but only a position which will be alternatively and also simultaneously, in certain cases, filled by different items of various categorial types.

X-bar theory, in other words, defines a skeleton for phrase structure; this, however, is not sufficient, since the branching direction has not yet been specified. In fact, we have only established that a head projects up to a maximal projection, but Complement and Specifier can in principle appear either on the right or on the left of the head. Branching directions are, in fact, parametrized, i.e. they are selected by each language. English, for instance, is a so-called VO language, according to the traditional typological terminology; in the terms of X-bar theory, we can say that the branching direction of V′, containing the complements of V, is to the right. The subject of a sentence, on the contrary, appears in Spec of IP on the left of I, therefore we will say that IP branches to the left. Notice that it is not *a priori* established that all the categories will be consistent, i.e. it could very well happen that in the same language, a given category projects its complements on the left, whereas another one projects them on the right; this option, however, would be a marked case. The actual way in which phrases are linearly ordered with respect to the head of the Xmax immediately containing them could be constrained not by X-bar theory directly, but by the direction of assignment of certain formal and interpretative features, like Case and θ-role, which will be introduced below. Some advantages of this principled treatment of word order, with respect to a more traditional approach to phrase structure have been pointed out by Koopman (1984) and Travis (1984) and will be made clearer in the following analysis, especially in chapter 3. Going back to English, we can reasonably hypothesize that the minimal X-bar skeleton structurally available for each phrase looks as follows, with a very high degree of crosscategorial consistency:

(5)

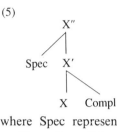

where Spec represents the position of the Specifier, and Compl the position of possible complements of the head.

Thematic theory

Once the structural relations have been established, i.e. the options of X-bar theory have been set, we have not yet provided all the information necessary to project an actual phrase. In fact, to decide how many and which categories can occupy the positions abstractly termed 'Complement', or 'Specifier', we must know something more about the semantic properties of the head. Each lexical head assigns a semantic, i.e. thematic, interpretation to its complements and, for some heads, also to its Spec position.[1] Consider a Verb like *greet*: it projects a VP ($= V''$), it has an intermediate projection V' which also dominates an object NP:

(6)

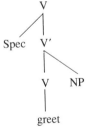

Certain adverbials can appear in preverbal Spec position, for instance *always*, *often* and so on. The NP is interpreted with reference to the thematic grid of the verb: *greet* takes a theme as complement, and requires that it be realized as an NP; we will say, therefore, that the Verb assigns a θ- (thematic) role to its object. The θ-grid of the Verb, however, is not exhausted, since there is another θ-role to be assigned, the so-called external θ-role. Such a θ-role is assigned externally with respect to the maximal projection VP and precisely to the subject position hanging from IP ($= I''$).[2] The structural and thematic relations in a sentence like *John greets Mary* are the following:

(7)

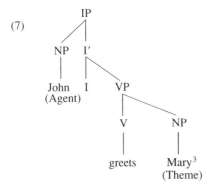

Greets assigns Theme to *Mary* and agent to *John*. θ-assignment is obviously local, as we have anticipated, i.e. each head can specify its semantic relations to phrases 'close' to it: in fact, we do not want the interpretative properties of the object of *greet* ever to be assigned to an element appearing, for instance, in a superordinate sentence, such as *Lucy* in: *I told Lucy that John greeted Mary*. An ideal assumption is that θ-marking always takes place under sisterhood (Chomsky 1986b).[4] The external θ-assignment could seem to be non-local in this sense; locality is, however, restored if we hypothesize that the external θ-assigner is the whole VP and that non-lexical categories such as I or I' are transparent to θ-assignment. We can say, therefore, that all lexical heads assign a thematic interpretation to their arguments; non-lexical heads do not, in the sense that they only permit the θ-roles of another lexical head to be transmitted through their projections. The agent θ-role, in fact, is lexically specified in the θ-grid of the head V, but to be assigned to the Spec of IP, it must pass through I', which, by itself, does not identify any θ-role in the structure.

A given structure can be ungrammatical for lack of θ-assignment. For instance, *John seems to me that Mary is intelligent* is ungrammatical because no θ-role is assigned to *John*. An important principle of UG is called the θ-criterion and can be very roughly formulated as follows:

(8) θ-criterion:
          a. Every argument must be assigned a θ-role
          b. Every θ-role is assigned to an argument

where arguments are essentially referring expressions, a semantic role limited in natural languages to nominal and sentential phrases, like NP and CP (perhaps IP).

Part (b) of the definition needs to be further qualified, since some proviso must be included for intransitivizable Verbs, such as, for instance, *eat*. Notice also that in our definition we have not specified whether θ-assignment must be unique or not. The uniqueness requirement seems to be too strong, since a double thematic specification appears to be available in some cases, such as *John ate the meat raw*; *the meat* receives an interpretation from *eat* and another one from *raw*; both θ-assignments are motivated on an empirical basis. In the following chapters, however, we will not further investigate this problem, so that a formulation of the θ-criterion as in (4) will be sufficient to our purposes.

Finally, let us point out that a position where a θ-role is actually assigned is called a θ-position. An argument (A-)position is a *potential* θ-position, i.e. a site in the tree in which, on structural grounds, a θ-role could be assigned, even though only the choice of the actual lexical item may establish whether this will happen or not. The subject of *seem*, for instance, provides a good example of an A-position which is *not* a θ-position.

On c-command and government

Before proceeding to the explanation of the other modules, we will introduce two crucial structural relations which can be defined on trees and will enter the formulation of most principles subsequently discussed. Such relations are c (i.e. constituent)-command and government; let us illustrate c-command first.

C-command is one particular notion in a family of concepts defining structural relations on a tree: as an abstract schema, we may say that a command relation is instantiated between α and β whenever α does not dominate β and the minimal node of a certain type of dominating α dominates β as well. The more concrete realizations of this schema are obtained specifying the type of 'minimal node' involved: two such notions are of special relevance in the current theory and for the discussion in this book, namely c-command in the strict sense (as originally defined in the first part of Reinhart's 1976 dissertation) and m-command, also called c-command in an extended sense by Aoun and Sportiche (1982). In the strictest version of c-command, α c-commands β if and only if the minimal *branching node* dominating α dominates β; in Aoun and Sportiche's approach this definition is relaxed, yielding a notion which Chomsky (1986b) has more felicitously termed m (i.e. maximal)-command: α m-commands β if and only if the minimal *maximal projection* dominating α dominates β.

It has been debated which of the two notions is more correct with respect to the various modules of grammar. In this book the issue is investigated with respect to Binding Theory; in the first chapter we will try to contribute a possible empirical solution to the problem, in the direction suggested by Chomsky (1986b), i.e. arguing that with respect to such a theory the notion of c-command is the relevant one.

The notion of government can be defined by strengthening that of m-command in various possible ways, adding conditions on the governor and structural conditions of locality; from the latter viewpoint. One abstract schema of definition which is found in several works relies on the concept of reciprocal m-command: α governs β only if α m-commands β and vice versa. Modifications and extensions of this ideally simple definition will be proposed and empirically motivated in detail in chapter 2. It is clear from what we have said that, while command notions define relations between elements at a potentially unbounded structural distance (i.e. crossing an indefinite number of tree nodes), government expresses a much more local kind of relationship.

Case-assignment

An important characteristic of Noun Phrases is constituted by their Case features. Morphologically, several languages distinguish various Cases, as in Latin, Greek, German, Russian and so on. In English, or Italian, the only elements which still appear with an overt Case feature are certain pronouns: e.g. *io* ('I', Nominative) vs *me* ('me', Accusative), English *I* vs *me*, etc. The presence even of a very limited number of visible Case alternations suggests, however, that the grammar must mention all possible NP positions in a sentence, associating each of them with the required Case feature. For instance, we will state that subjects of tensed Is take the nominative form while objects of Vs take the accusative one. In so doing we are also giving a rather exhaustive list of the environments where a lexically realized NP may surface in the language: in English or Italian, next to a tensed Verb or auxiliary, after a Verb or a Preposition.

If we assume now that every lexically filled NP needs to be assigned an abstract Case, even when morphology neutralizes all Case differences, we will obtain a general principle on the distribution of non-empty NPs. We can then formulate the Case Filter (Chomsky 1980, developing a suggestion by J. R. Vergnaud):

> * NP [phonetic matrix]
> if NP has no case

Lexical and non-lexical heads may assign a Case to NPs. Chomsky (1986a) proposes a distinction between two mechanisms of Case-assignment: structural and inherent Case-assignment. Structural Case is assigned by certain heads by virtue of the structural configuration, i.e. with no reference to a corresponding assignment of a θ-role; the structural Cases are basically Nominative and Accusative, assigned by I and V (or P, perhaps) respectively; in fact, between the head I and the NP appearing in the Spec of IP there is no (direct) thematic relation. Between a Verb V and its object usually there is also a thematic relation, but this fact is not necessary in order to trigger Case-assignment. Consider, in fact, the following example:

(9)   Mary believed me to have left

In (9) there is no thematic relation between *believe* and *me*, since this latter gets its semantic interpretation as the argument of the subordinate Verb *leave*; *believe*, however, assigns the pronoun Accusative Case. This phenomenon is known under the name of 'Exceptional Case-marking' (ECM). Notice also that there is no alternative to ECM here, since infinitives cannot Case-mark their subjects; consider, for instance, the following contrast:

(10)   a. * I/Me to leave is desirable
       b. For me to leave is desirable
       c. That I leave is desirable

Example (10)c is grammatical since there is a tensed Inflection which can assign Nominative to the subject; (10)b is also grammatical since *for* has the property, in English, of assigning structural Accusative; (10)a is ruled out by the Case Filter since *me* and *I* cannot have Case.

Let us introduce now the notion of 'inherent Case': such a Case is assigned only to θ-related elements, in a sense as a consequence of θ-marking, and in some languages is often realized through the insertion of a semantically empty Preposition. The Genitive assigned by Nouns and

Adjectives typically belongs to this class; in fact, there is no ECM performed by a Noun or an Adjective. Consider for instance:

(11)   a. * Their belief (of) me to leave
        b. Their belief that I will leave

Sentence (11)a is ungrammatical, with or without *of*, i.e. the prepositional marker for Genitive, since the N *belief* cannot assign Case to an NP without θ-marking it; no similar problem arises in (11)b, given that both Case and θ-marking requirements are satisfied within the subordinate clause.

Case is assigned under government, i.e. in the local domain roughly defined by the structural relation of reciprocal m-command. However, notice that ECM does not meet this condition, if it is formulated in such terms: in fact, there is a maximal projection, IP, intervening between the Verb and the NP in question, which should render Case-marking impossible. An independently needed revision of the notion of government, however, will account for this and related phenomena: for further discussion we refer the reader to the cited references and to chapter 2 below.

Notice finally, that, intuitively, the direction of θ- and Case-marking by the same head can be expected to be consistent: both processes occur locally and often affect the same phrase. Generally this expectation is met; on some cases where the two directions seem to diverge, see Travis (1984) and chapter 3 below.

The Projection Principle and the Full Interpretation Principle

The Projection Principle establishes that lexical structure must be represented categorially at every syntactic level. To be more precise, it requires that the θ-criterion (and in an extended version also the Predication Principle: see directly below) be met at D-structure, S-structure and LF. Such a principle is important because of its predictive power. In fact, if an argument is understood in a certain position, it must be there, even when it is not phonetically realized; if this is the case, then a so-called 'empty category' has to be instantiated in the position in question.

Let us briefly consider the consequences of this principle for movement: the most direct one is that, given the θ-criterion, movement of a maximal projection is admitted only to a non-thematic position. The reason for this constraint should now be clear: in fact, if a position is thematic, at D-structure an argument will have to occupy it. If this argument is moved to a non-thematic position, at S-structure it will continue to meet the θ-criterion by receiving the original θ-role through the so-called chain relating it to its trace. If, instead, it is moved to a thematic position, it will end up with two θ-roles, violating the θ-criterion. If, finally, a position is non-thematic, any argument occurring there at D-structure will violate the θ-criterion before being able to reach a thematic position at S-structure. Recall that the non-thematic positions are the subject position, when it is dethematized, as in passive constructions, or non-thematic at all, as in the case of subjects of so-called raising Verbs (like the already mentioned *seem*), and, trivially, A'-positions, where by definition no θ-role can be assigned. In chapter 3, we will draw some further conclusions about the operation of the Projection Principle.

The Full Interpretation Principle establishes that at LF every maximal projection must be licensed, i.e. it must have an interpretation: a given XP can either be an argument, or a predicate, or an operator. To be an argument an XP must get a θ-role, directly or through a chain (θ-criterion); a predicate must be licensed through predication (see Williams 1980; Rothstein 1983), i.e. by having a subject (Predication Principle), and an operator through the binding of a variable (non-vacuous quantification).[5]

Binding Theory (BT)

The first chapter of this book is specifically concerned with binding phenomena within NPs. The theory of Binding rules the distribution of NPs in coreference relationships, partitioning them in three different classes: anaphors, pronouns and names, otherwise called, less perspicuously, referential (R-) expressions; a different principle of binding applies to each class of items (see Chomsky 1981, 1986a). Such a tripartition of nominal expressions follows from the interaction of two binary features: $\pm$ anaphoric and $\pm$ pronominal. The assignment of the values is based on empirical evidence coming from the result of certain tests. Anaphors are characterized as $+$ anaphoric $-$ pronominal; pronouns as $-$ anaphoric $+$ pronominal; R-expressions as $-$ anaphoric $-$ pronominal; the combination of the positive value for both features cannot correspond to a lexical item, due to independent considerations concerning government and Case theory. There is, however, an empty category which is identified by such values, i.e. the understood subject of most infinitives, usually referred to as PRO. The tests in question are the possibility of having intrinsic reference and the capacity of taking a split antecedent; the first determines the feature $\pm$ anaphoric, i.e. elements with intrinsic reference are classified as $-$ anaphoric, and the second concerns the feature $\pm$ pronominal, i.e. elements which can take a split antecedent are classified as $+$ pronominal. Let us consider them in turn:

(12)   a. * I love himself
        b. I love him
        c. I love John/that man

In (12)a the NP *himself* cannot take a reference directly in the world; in fact, even if from the pragmatic context it might be clear that the speaker is referring to, say, *John*, for instance by pointing to him, there is no way for such a sentence to be considered grammatical. It is simply the case that *himself* cannot be used, without a grammatical antecedent, owing to its intrinsic semantic content. We will say that *himself* and other reflexives select the value $+$ anaphoric. On the contrary, in the same situation, *him* could be used as shown by the fact that (12)b is grammatical: *him*, therefore, has intrinsic reference, which means that it selects the value $-$ anaphoric. As far as (12)c is concerned, obviously, *John* or *that man* have intrinsic reference; we will say thus that they are $-$ anaphoric too. Consider now the following examples:

(13)   a. John$_i$ informed Mary$_j$ that the firm would fire them$_{i+j}$
        b. * John$_i$ restored Mary$_j$ to themselves$_{i+j}$

In (13)a *them* can have *John* and *Mary* as antecedents, taken together as a set; such a possibility is not available for *themselves* in (13)b, even if, taken separately, both *John* and *Mary* could be coreferential with a singular reflexive in the same position:

(14)   a. John restored Mary to herself (through a long psychoanalytic therapy)
        b. John restored Mary to himself (through his patient love)

The conclusion is therefore that *them* is classified as $+$ pronominal and *themselves* as $-$ pronominal. An R-expression will then be specified as $-$ pronominal, just to distinguish it from pronouns like *him* and *them*. The BT includes a principle for each kind of item:

(15)   A: An anaphor is bound in the local domain γ
        B: A pronoun is free in the local domain γ
        C: An R-expression is free

Let us consider principle A first. Since anaphors lack any kind of reference, they will have to be assigned an antecedent or 'binder' from which they can receive one: syntax must constrain their distribution with respect to such antecedents. 'Bound' means 'coindexed (implying "coreferential") with a c-commanding element in argument position'; this way an anaphor inherits (all and only) the reference of its antecedent. The exact specification of the local domain γ, will be discussed at length in chapter 1, section 6. Let us simply point out here that such a locality condition permits the identification of a portion on the tree where the anaphor can look for an antecedent.

Principle B is in some sense a mirror image of principle A, establishing that in a given domain, ideally the same as for the anaphor, a pronoun must be 'free', i.e. not coindexed with a c-commanding element in argument position. The pronoun, in other words, must be locally disjoint in reference.

Finally, an R-expression must be free in the whole structure, i.e. can only corefer with non-c-commanding arguments. So understood, the BT in (15) rules ungrammatical the three following examples, (b) and (c) just under the coreferential readings indicated by the coindexing:

(16)   a. * That man$_i$ thinks I love himself$_i$
        b. * I think that man$_i$ loves him$_i$
        c. * John$_i$ thinks I love that man$_i$

Given that all the principles of the BT make crucial reference to the notion of c-command, a necessary ingredient of the definition of 'bound' and 'free', the binding phenomena constitute an ideal testing ground to establish structural positions in the tree, i.e. to decide whether two phrases are in a c-command relationship or not. In fact, extensive reliance on these heuristic properties of binding effects will be made in chapter 1 below.

Empty categories

As a consequence of the Projection Principle, together with the constraints imposed by X-bar theory on possible trees, an understood element, not lexically represented, must be thought of as an empty category.

Empty categories can be classified according to the same features adopted for lexical expressions. We have already mentioned that PRO, i.e. the subject of many untensed clauses, is specified as +pronominal, +anaphoric; in fact, it has no intrinsic reference and can take a split antecedent. Consider the following examples:

(17)   a. * PRO to behave himself is important[6]
        b. John$_i$ told Mary$_j$ that PRO$_{i+j}$ to behave themselves would be
           important

The trace left by NP-movement in passive, raising and ergative constructions (see below) inherits its reference in the local context by the moved NP, which lands in a c-commanding A-position, therefore it is specified as +anaphoric, −pronominal; the trace of a wh-element, e.g. a fronted relative or interrogative pronoun, is often called 'variable', and might be the empty equivalent of an R-expression, being −pronominal, −anaphoric; in fact, it seems subject to some version of principle C. The definite empty subject of a tensed clause, which is hypothesized in so-called pro-drop languages like Italian, is a pure pronoun, i.e. +pronominal, −anaphoric, and is probably subject to principle B.

Conditions on movement

As we have already mentioned before, if the D-structure position and the S-structure position of a given item differ, their relationship is said to be established by the rule Move α. It is important to distinguish at least two subtypes of movement rules: A-movement, which moves NPs to A-position and A'-movement, which moves various sorts of XPs to A'-positions. One of the best examples of the former type is provided by the traditional passivization process which moves a D-structure object into an S-structure subject position (the Spec of IP, an A-position). A'-movement is instead instantiated by the fronting of so-called 'wh-elements' (e.g. relative and interrogative phrases in English), which can be argued to appear at S-structure in the Spec of CP, a typical A'-position. Either movement is assumed to leave behind a trace, which is represented as t or $[_{XP}\ e]$ often coindexed with the antecedent in most common notations. Thus a passive S-structure could be roughly as in (18):

(18)

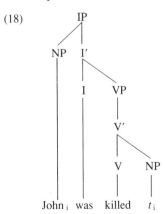

Equivalently, a tree structure like (18) can be replaced by the bracketing notation of (19):

(19) $[_{IP} [_{NP}$ John$]_i [_{I'} [_I$ was$] [_{VP} [_{V'} [_V$ killed$] [_{NP} e]_i]]]]$

In a more incomplete and simplified way, we may also write:

(20)   John$_i$ was killed t_i

In the latter format, an example of S-structure output after A′-movement (wh-movement) can be the following:

(21)   Who$_i$ do you think Mary killed t_i?

For all such structures it has been long debated about which conditions hold on the relation between t and its antecedent (the moved phrase). In this context, we will only point out two conclusions, which are shared by essentially all approaches and are of particular relevance for our treatment of extraction from NP in chapter 2. The first conclusion concerns a condition on the distribution of traces called ECP (Empty Category Principle): Chomsky (1981) proposed that every trace must be properly governed, i.e. either governed by a lexical lead or by a coindexed phrase (basically by its antecedent moved locally). In more recent years it has been suggested that the disjunctive formulation of this principle could be incorrect: it has been argued, in fact, that government by a head is obligatorily required for every trace, even in the presence of a local antecedent. The discussion in chapter 2 below will provide a straightforward argument in favour of the latter, more restrictive, formulation of the ECP and will try to identify an appropriate definition of the relevant notions of government and proper government.

The second remark has to do with the question of so-called intermediate traces of movement. Presently, there is quite general agreement that movement rules may, and in some cases must, displace constituents in a successive cyclic fashion, probably leaving behind a trace at each step. From this point of view a possible derivation of (21) would be better recorded by an S-structure like (22):

(22)   Who$_i$ do you think t_i Mary killed t_i?

The intermediate trace, arguably occurring in the Spec of the subordinate CP, is crucially required in many cases in order to provide a local antecedent to the more embedded one. Exactly this successive cyclic approach will be taken to the question of extraction from NP in chapter 2, showing that no constituent can be removed from inside an NP in the

Romance languages unless it first moves to the Spec of the NP, leaving there an intermediate trace, and then undergoes extraction. Such successive cyclicity of extraction from Romance NPs is forced by a particular constraint, which is formulated in the text and requires that a trace governed by N be bound by an antecedent (in this case, the intermediate trace in Spec) within Nmax.

1* *On NPs, θ-marking and c-command*

A. GIORGI

Introduction

In this chapter we will consider the internal structure of NPs, aiming to provide an answer to three theoretical questions: first, that of the exact notion of command involved in binding, which still poses something of a problem; second, that of the relevance of the notion of ergativity (see Perlmutter 1978; Burzio 1981, 1986) to categories other than V, in this case N; finally, that of the locality domains for principles A and B of the Binding Theory. Throughout the chapter, we will try to present a principled account of how NPs are internally organized, arguing that, despite some superficial freedom of linear order in posthead position, such phrases in Italian are hierarchically structured in a typical configurational manner. Although most of the evidence discussed comes from Italian data, we intend our major claims about configurationality to be part of UG, hence generalizable to other languages. To provide a solution to the theoretical problems, we will basically argue in favour of the following hypotheses:

1.   One of the arguments specified by the θ-grid of a Noun is generated in a structurally prominent position with respect to the others and behaves like the 'subject' of the NP. This hypothesis has already been suggested by Cinque (1980, 1981a) on the grounds of distributional properties of possessive elements in Italian. We will support his original idea with another kind of data which provides clearer evidence for the same conclusion.

2.   An intermediate projection, N', occurs between N and its maximal projection N'', containing the internal (i.e. non-subject) argument positions of the head and defining their c-domain, as if it were a VP. This suggests a definition of c-command which is stricter than that of Aoun and Sportiche (1982), especially

because other properties of N′ confirm its non-maximality in terms of X-bar theory.[1]

3.   Nominalizations corresponding to ergative Verbs only assign their θ-roles under N′, i.e. as internal ones, and can be said to be ergative in the same sense as their verbal counterparts.

Hypotheses 1 and 3 will be shown to follow from the statement of a wider generalization concerning the mapping of the θ-grid of a head X onto the internal structure of lexical phrases, the Thematic Correspondence Hypothesis introduced in section 2.

Our main testing ground will be the distribution of anaphors and pronouns, i.e. phenomena related to the Binding Theory in general, a domain which often proved to be particularly useful for investigating the hierarchical structure of constituents.

In the first section we will show that such Prepositions as adnominal *di* and non-locative *a* do not prevent the NP they govern from c-commanding an external phrase. In section 2 the issue of subject–object asymmetries observable within NPs will be addressed. In the third we will discuss the characteristics of *di* insertion in Italian, which are relevant to an understanding of the mechanisms of complementation of N. We will then take into account certain configurations which constitute a problem for a theory of binding based on too simple a concept of disjointness. Although we do not provide a principled explanation for these facts in the present work, we believe that such data are relevant to the question of the levels of attachment of the various arguments and open the way to further research. Then, we will present the evidence in favour of the existence of ergative Nouns and, finally, the closing section is devoted to the question of the definition of the binding domains.

1   'Dummy' prepositions

In order to address one of the main issues of this chapter, namely c-command within NPs, we will analyse the properties of the semantically 'dummy' prepositions which appear within NPs.

From a descriptive point of view, apart from possessive elements (*suo* ('his/her'), *mio* ('my'), etc.), whose status is further dealt with in chapters 2 and 3 below, all realized lexical NPs which are arguments of a head N are preceded by a preposition. The impossibility of having a preposition-less NP must be related to Case properties of N (see Chomsky 1981, 1986a). According to a literal interpretation of c-command, then, no anaphor should appear, within an NP, bound by another argument of the same N, since c-command by the antecedent should always be prevented by the inevitable PP node. We will see that this is not the case, since many binding relations can indeed be instantiated within NPs. Consider the following examples:

(1)   a. L'opinione di se stesso di Gianni è troppo lusinghiera
          lit.: The opinion of himself of Gianni is too flattering
          Gianni's opinion about himself is too flattering
       b. La paura di se stesso di Gianni è preoccupante
          lit.: The fear of himself of Gianni is worrying
          Gianni's fear of himself is worrying
       c. La descrizione di se stesso di Gianni è troppo lusinghiera
          lit.: The description of himself of Gianni is too flattering
          Gianni's description of himself is too flattering

In all these cases *Gianni*, though governed by the preposition *di*, can bind the anaphor *se stesso*. When a pronoun appears in place of the anaphor, all of these sentences become ungrammatical (we provide here only the literal translation, which is relevant to our purposes):

(2)   a. *L'opinione di lui$_i$ di Gianni$_i$ è troppo lusinghiera
          The opinion of him of Gianni is too flattering
       b. *La paura di lui$_i$ di Gianni$_i$ è preoccupante
          The fear of him of Gianni is worrying
       c. *La descrizione di lui$_i$ di Gianni$_i$ è troppo lusinghiera
          The description of him of Gianni is too flattering

The data in (2) show that the pronoun is bound within its minimal domain, that is, the NP, a domain in which the Binding Theory (henceforth BT) requires that it be free. Assuming that *di* does not head a constituent counting as a relevant c-domain, the contrast between (1) and (2) is actually predicted by a theory of binding under which anaphors and pronouns should have a (more or less) complementary distribution. Note that if all sentences in (1) and (2) were grammatical, a 'weaker' principle could be proposed, namely that the PP headed by *di* in these cases is only optionally considered as a c-domain, so as to increase the total number of acceptable sentences.[2] However, since the two structures clearly contrast, we must conclude that *di* is in no case able to define a c-domain.

We find the same complementary distribution with anaphors and pronouns introduced by the preposition *a* (in the non-locative usage):

(3)   a. la restituzione di Maria a se stessa (da parte dello psicoanalista)
          the restoration of Maria to herself (by the psychoanalyst)

   b. *la restituzione di Maria$_i$ a lei$_i$ (da parte dello psicoanalista)
      the restoration of Maria to her (by the psychoanalyst)

More interestingly, the complementarity of anaphor and pronoun arises
again when it is the antecedent that is introduced by *a*:

(4)   a. la restituzione di se stessa a Maria (da parte dello psicoanalista)
          the restoration of herself to Maria (by the psychoanalyst)
       b. *la restituzione di lei$_i$ a Maria$_i$ (da parte dello psicoanalista)
          the restoration of her to Maria (by the psychoanalyst)

In (4)a *a Maria* can bind an anaphor, suggesting, therefore, that the
properties of *a* with respect to c-command are the same as those of *di*.
They both permit their complement NPs to c-command another argument
of the head N. Notice also that this property is obligatory for *a* as well,
as shown most clearly by the contrast in (5):[3]

(5)   a. *la restituzione a lei$_i$ del figlio di Maria$_i$ (da parte dei rapitori)
          the restoration to her of Maria's son (by the kidnappers)
       b. la restituzione a Maria$_i$ di suo$_i$ figlio (da parte dei rapitori)
          the restoration to Maria of her son (by the kidnappers)

Given the properties of *di*, in fact, one might argue that the ungrammaticality of (4)b is only due to the fact that the pronoun *lei* c-
commands the R-expression *Maria*, so that (4)b would not be an
argument in favour of the hypothesis that *a* is unable to block c-
command; however, the contrast in (5) clearly points to this conclusion.
In (5)a, in fact, the R-expression is more deeply embedded than the
pronoun and, therefore, *Maria* does not c-command *lei*. Since, however,
the structure is ungrammatical, this can be reasonably attributed to the
properties of *a*, which cannot prevent the pronoun from c-commanding
the R-expression, determining a principle C violation.

   Summarizing, the ungrammaticality of (4)b could be attributed to a
violation of either principle B or C, whereas the ungrammaticality of (5)a
can only be due to a principle C violation; (5)b, by contrast, is obviously
grammatical, since the requirements imposed by the BT are satisfied both
by the R-expression and by the pronoun. Moreover, as expected, we also
find the following contrast:

(6)   a. *la (mia) restituzione di lei$_i$ al figlio di Maria$_i$
          the/my restoration of her to Maria's son
       b. la (mia) restituzione di Maria$_i$ a suo$_i$ figlio
          the/my restoration of Maria to her son

The ungrammaticality of (6)a follows from our analysis of the properties
of *di*.

As a conclusion, we can say that *a* and *di*, when they introduce an argument of the head Noun, cannot block c-command of the governed element towards another one and this property renders binding possible within NPs.[4]

2   Subject–object asymmetries

Let us come now to the core of our argumentation; notice that the complementary distribution of anaphors and pronouns we have illustrated in examples (1)–(6) is compatible with different hypotheses about the BT and the notion of c-command: once the proposed assumption about the special properties of *di* and *a* is made, both a definition of c-command which refers to maximal projections, such as the one proposed by Aoun and Sportiche (1982), and one based on branching nodes, such as Reinhart's (1976), make the correct predictions.[5] The question will not remain unanswered, however, since by analysing the internal structure of NPs we will show that using for the BT a definition of c-command inspired by the first of Reinhart's (1976) formulations, we can correctly predict other binding facts, providing further support for the analogous assumption made in Chomsky (1986b).

Consider first that in Italian one can freely invert the order of the postnominal arguments without affecting acceptability. The following phrases, in fact, are all grammatical:

(7)   a. la lettera di Gianni a Maria
          the letter by Gianni to Maria
       b. la lettera a Maria di Gianni
          the letter to Maria by Gianni
       c. la descrizione di Gianni degli avvenimenti
          the description by Gianni of the events
       d. la descrizione degli avvenimenti di Gianni
          the description of the events by Gianni

The presence of an anaphor bound inside the NP does not modify their grammatical status:

(8)   a. la finta lettera di Gianni$_i$ a se stesso$_i$
          the false letter by Gianni to himself
       b. la finta lettera a se stesso$_i$ di Gianni$_i$
          the false letter to himself by Gianni
       c. la descrizione di Gianni di se stesso
          the description by Gianni of himself
       d. la descrizione di se stesso di Gianni
          the description of himself by Gianni

The orders immediately projected by the underlying tree, according to the hypotheses we are going to develop here will be the ones in the (b) and (d) examples. To obtain the other ones too we assume the intervention of a stylistic rule, operating at a level which does not affect syntactic operations such as binding. This proposal is analogous to the one made by Burzio (1986, ch. 1, p. 66) concerning the free ordering in Italian of the complements of the Verb; he calls the relevant rule 'complement shifting rule'. This rule permutes the order of DO and IO, as well as the relative order of the inverted subject and other non-clausal complements.

Consider now the following examples:

(9)   a. L'opinione di lui$_i$ della madre di Gianni$_i$ è troppo lusinghiera
           lit.: The opinion of him of Gianni's mother is too flattering
           Gianni's mother's opinion about him...
           *His opinion about Gianni's mother...
        b. *La sua$_i$ opinione della madre di Gianni$_i$ è troppo lusinghiera
           lit.: His opinion of Gianni's mother is too flattering

(10)   a. La paura di lui$_i$ della madre di Gianni$_i$ è eccessiva
           lit.: The fear of him of Gianni's mother is excessive
           Gianni's mother's fear of him...
           *His fear of Gianni's mother...
        b. *La sua$_i$ paura della madre di Gianni$_i$ è eccessiva
           lit.: His fear of Gianni's mother is excessive

(11)   a. La descrizione di lui$_i$ della madre di Gianni$_i$ è troppo lusinghiera
           lit.: The description of him of Gianni's mother is too flattering.
           Gianni's mother's description of him...
           *His description of Gianni's mother...
        b. *La sua$_i$ descrizione della madre di Gianni$_i$ è troppo lusinghiera
           lit.: His description of Gianni's mother is too flattering

To explain these contrasts, it is impossible to rely on a definition of c-command referring to maximal projections, since under standard assumptions such a theory could not distinguish between the (a) and (b) sentences of each pair. In fact, provided that *di* can never block c-command, both the (a) and (b) sentences should be ruled ungrammatical by a violation of principle C, because the pronoun would c-command the R-expression. Then, if the notion of c-command remained unvaried, the incorrect results would be obtained independently of any assumption about the internal structure of NPs: the first c-domain would correspond to the whole NP, both in case the latter is assumed to be 'flat' (i.e. a structure in which the head and the complements are immediately dominated by the maximal projection) and in case it is viewed as more hierarchically layered.

Under any current theory of binding, in fact, the contrasts of (9)–(11) can be straightforwardly accounted for only if (i) there exists an intermediate N projection containing *di lui* but not *della madre di Gianni* in the (a) examples and also crucially excluding the possessive pronoun in the (b) ones; and (ii) it counts as a c-domain.

We will propose here, then, that there must exist an N′, i.e. that NPs are so internally organized that it is possible to identify a structurally prominent phrase, the 'subject' of the NP as distinguished from the 'objects' or 'internal' arguments. As a further step, we will argue that N′, conceived of as the domain of such 'internal' arguments, is also their c-domain.

Notice that, as far as we know, the necessity of intermediate projections of N has rarely been argued for with sufficient detail (a remarkable exception is Lightfoot 1982, ch. 4), although its existence follows from a concept of simplicity and uniformity applied to the X-bar theory; rather, the possibility of a flat structure has been advocated by Travis (1984).

Actually, the first part of the hypothesis is in agreement with a formulation already proposed by Cinque (1980, 1981a) to accommodate the phenomena of possessivization in Italian NPs. Let us briefly introduce his argument: essentially, he identifies a *thematically* prominent argument, that is, a 'subject' in the thematic (semantic) sense, attributing to it *structural* prominence as well. In our argumentation, however, we will substantiate the hypothesis of such structural prominence of the subject of NP on the basis of the binding evidence. Cinque observes that only a particular type of argument can be expressed by a possessive pronoun:[6]

(12)   a. la descrizione degli avvenimenti di Gianni
            lit.: the description of the events of Gianni
            Gianni's description of the events
        b. la sua descrizione degli avvenimenti
            his description of the events
        c. la loro(= degli avvenimenti) descrizione di Gianni
            their (= of the events) description of Gianni

Example (12)a (partially) realizes the θ-grid of the Noun *descrizione* ('description'), with the agent *Gianni*, and the theme *gli avvenimenti* ('the events'). The θ-roles expressed here are the same as those which can be assigned to the arguments of the corresponding Verb *descrivere* ('describe'). Both the Noun and the Verb identify an internal θ-role (theme) and an external one (agent). Therefore, we will adopt the terminology used for sentences, speaking of internal and external arguments, even if the latter in NPs do not seem to occur *outside* the maximal projection of the head. In Italian NPs both the argument expressing the internal θ-role and that expressing the external one are usually preceded by the preposition *di* ('of'), which can be taken to be a semantically empty realization of Genitive Case; but the external θ-role can always be expressed also by means of a possessive pronoun, as shown by the fact that (12)b can have the same meaning as (12)a. By contrast, (12)c is ungrammatical under the interpretation assigned to (12)a; the internal θ-role, in fact, cannot be expressed by a possessive pronoun, unless the argument bearing the external one is not overtly realized, or appears in a *by*-phrase, as in (13):

(13)   la loro (= degli avvenimenti) descrizione (da parte di Gianni)
        their (= of the events) description (by Gianni)

(In Italian the *by*-phrase of NPs is expressed by means of a locution *da parte di*, more literally *on the part of*.) In this case the NP has undergone 'passivization', as Cinque proposed, i.e. the element identifying the external argument appears in a *by*-phrase and an internal argument can display the properties previously typical of the external one replacing it as the 'subject' of the NP.[7] The parallelism with the subject position of a sentence is immediate, justifying Cinque's terminology. His interpretation of these facts can be summarized, then, as follows: possessives must hang from Nmax; only one of the two overt Genitive arguments of a Noun, namely the external one, may hang from Nmax, hence may be expressed as a possessive; the other must hang from a lower projection (N'). Now, these conclusions arrived at by Cinque to derive the possessivization phenomena are those that we noticed were required, even more directly, to attempt an account of the binding data of (9)–(11).

In other words, the examples in (13) point to the existence of a subject–object asymmetry within NPs, with respect to the process of possessivization. Analogously, the data in (9)–(11) suggest the existence of such an asymmetry with respect to binding phenomena.

In order to obtain in a principled way the levels of attachment suggested by this argumentation, we may propose a 'Thematic Correspondence Hypothesis', actually an idea already contained in Chomsky's (1970) lexicalist hypothesis and developed in many subsequent works by other authors, stating that Verbs and corresponding Nouns define the same θ-role from their grid as the external one. Moreover, such an external θ-role is the only one assigned outside N', in NPs, or outside VP (or perhaps V' if subjects are always generated in VP; see Fukui and Speas 1986 and Koopman and Sportiche 1988) in clauses; the other θ-roles will be assigned internally, within N′ and VP (V′) respectively.[8] This approach will automatically apply to the examples in (9)–(11). Recall, in fact, that there is only one reading available for the (a) sentences of the pairs given in (9)–(11), as indicated in the glosses, in spite of the fact that both arguments are introduced by *di*, and that, therefore, in principle either one could be interpreted as subject: *di lui* ('of him') can only be attributed the θ-role usually associated with the internal argument, and *della madre di Gianni* ('of Gianni's mother') is understood as the external one, that is, it receives the θ-role which is assigned to the external element in the corresponding sentential case. The other interpretation, the one obtained by switching the θ-roles, is impossible, even if, as we have illustrated in examples (7)–(8), this possibility is in principle available in Italian. In the (b) sentences, on the other hand, the possessive pronoun can only be interpreted as the agent, or the experiencer, i.e. with those semantic values assigned to the external argument in the corresponding clause; whereas *della madre di Gianni* ('of Gianni's mother') receives the internal θ-role. No other interpretation is possible and the sentence constitutes a principle C violation under coreference of *suo* ('his') and *Gianni*. Once again these facts are highly reminiscent of the well-known subject–object asymmetries and, as we anticipated above, it is possible to formalize this parallelism in terms of syntactic structure. More specifically, it can be concluded that there is actually an N′ and that this node plays a crucial role in defining the c-domain for binding. We may thus assign such examples the following structure:[9]

(14)

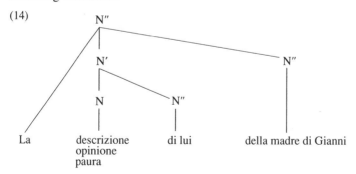

The claim that N′ prevents an element it dominates from c-commanding another one immediately dominated by N″ achieves the desired results: for example, the NP (*di*) *lui* ('of him') cannot c-command *Gianni*, which is contained in a phrase attached under N″ in (14). Conversely, in the (b) sentences of examples (9)–(11), the presence of a coreferential possessive pronoun will result in a violation of principle C due to the fact that it must in any event appear outside N′, both because it bears an external θ-role, and because possessives can only surface under a higher projection, if we accept Cinque's proposal.

The notion of c-command to be adopted on the grounds of the binding facts presented here is then the following:[10]

(15) α c-commands β iff
        the first branching node dominating α also dominates β

Such a definition leaves open the question of what happens when the relevant node does not branch, but since the matter is irrelevant to the present purpose, we will not pursue it here.

This proposal, in conjunction with the stipulation that possessives are excluded from N′ (which will be empirically substantiated later: see ch. 3) accounts for both the binding facts presented here and Cinque's observations on possessive elements. Both potential binders and possessives can only be attached outside N′ and therefore they can only express the external θ-role, or an internal one if the NP has undergone passivization (see also ch. 2).[11]

Another argument in the same vein comes from the distribution of *proprio* ('self's'), which can either behave as a so-called long-distance anaphor, or as a clause-bound one (see Giorgi 1983):

(16)   la descrizione di Mario$_i$ della propria$_i$ madre
        lit.: the description of Mario of self's mother

In this sentence the phrase containing *proprio* must be interpreted as the theme of the description. The impossibility for *della propria madre* ('of self's mother') of being interpreted as the agent shows that, if so, *proprio* would remain unbound. Our reasoning runs as follows: *proprio* can either be a subject-orientated anaphor, or a clause-bound one (see Giorgi 1983). If *Mario* is interpreted as a theme, it cannot function as a subject and, therefore, it cannot be available as an antecedent for a subject-orientated anaphor. On the other hand, if *proprio* is used as a clause-bound anaphor, lack of c-command can explain the impossibility of the reading in which *Mario* is interpreted as a theme.

The distribution of epithets can be analysed in the same way:

(17)   la paura della madre di Gianni$_i$ di quello stupido$_i$
        lit.: the fear of Gianni's mother of that stupid

Quello stupido ('that stupid'), in fact, must be understood as the experiencer of the fear and cannot be understood as the theme. Again, this fact can be explained by the BT, and precisely by principle C, if we hypothesize that the theme role is assigned to the 'object' position under N′, and the agent role to the hierarchically higher 'subject' position.

Notice also that, as predicted by the Thematic Correspondence Hypothesis, the subject, introduced by the preposition *di*, is higher also with respect to an indirect object, introduced by *a*. This is expected also on the grounds of examples (3)–(6) above, which suggest the existence of mutual c-command between direct and indirect objects in Italian (see sect. 4 below for discussion). Thus, (18)a and b are ungrammatical, independently of linear order, as a consequence of principle A:

(18)   a. *la telefonata di se stesso$_i$ a Gianni$_i$
            lit.: the phone call of himself to Gianni
         b. *la telefonata a Gianni$_i$ di se stesso$_i$
            lit.: the phone call to Gianni of himself
(19)   la telefonata di Gianni$_i$ a se stesso$_i$
            the phone call of Gianni to himself

Example (19), on the other hand, is grammatical, since the binding requirements can be satisfied.

The following examples show the same point as (9)–(11):

(20)   a. la telefonata della madre di Gianni$_i$ a lui$_i$
            the phone call of Gianni's mother to him
         b. la telefonata a lui$_i$ della madre di Gianni$_i$
            the phone call to him of Gianni's mother
(21)   *la sua$_i$ telefonata alla madre di Gianni$_i$
            his phone call to Gianni's mother

Examples (20)a and b show that the indirect object *a lui* does not c-command the subject *di Gianni*, independently of linear order, so that no principle C violation arises. Example (21), conversely, shows that a possessive in subject position cannot be coindexed with an R-expression in the indirect object position, owing to principle C requirements.

Consider now the following examples:

(22)   a. la telefonata di Gianni$_i$ alla propria$_i$ madre
            the phone call of Gianni to self's mother
         b. la telefonata alla propria$_i$ madre di Gianni$_i$
            the phone call to self's mother of Gianni
(23)   a. *la telefonata a Gianni$_i$ della propria$_i$ madre
            the phone call to Gianni of self's mother
         b. *la telefonata della propria$_i$ madre a Gianni$_i$
            the phone call of self's mother to Gianni

The ungrammaticality of (23)a and b shows that *proprio* can only be bound by the subject, as in (22)a and b. Again, ungrammaticality arises in (23)a and b, independently of linear order.

The same reasoning holds with respect to epithets:

(24)   a. la telefonata della madre di Gianni$_i$ a quello stupido$_i$
          the phone call of Gianni's mother to that stupid
    b. la telefonata a quello stupido$_i$ della madre di Gianni$_i$
          the phone call to that stupid of Gianni's mother

In (24)a and b, there is no violation of principle C. As expected, however, coindexation is not possible in the following phrases:

(25)   a. *la telefonata di quello stupido$_i$ alla madre di Gianni$_i$
          the phone call of that stupid to Gianni's mother
    b. *la telefonata alla madre di Gianni$_i$ di quello stupido$_i$
          the phone call to Gianni's mother of that stupid

In (25)a and b, *quello stupido* would anyway c-command the other R-expression, yielding a violation of principle C.

In addition to the principles of the BT, there exist other well-known processes in natural languages identifying a c-command relationship between two arguments. In order for our basic structural hypothesis to become more plausible, it must be shown that such processes also single out, inside NPs, the same subject–object asymmetries presented above. One of these processes is binding of a pronoun by a quantified NP:

(26)   La descrizione di ogni ragazzo$_i$ di sua$_i$ madre è troppo lusinghiera
    lit.: The description of every boy (agent) of his mother (theme) is too flattering
    i. *His mother's description of every boy...
    ii. Every boy's description of his mother...

(27)   La descrizione di Mario$_i$ di sua$_i$ madre è troppo lusinghiera
    i. The description of Mario (theme) of his mother (agent) is too flattering
    ii. The description of Mario (agent) of his mother (theme) is too flattering

We may notice that (27) is ambiguous in that it can mean either 'his mother's description of Mario' or 'Mario's description of his mother'. Crucially, in (26) there is no ambiguity, i.e. the presence of a quantified antecedent for the pronoun inhibits one of the two readings. In the only possible interpretation, the quantified NP receives the external (agent) θ-role because the NP containing the bound pronoun has to be c-commanded by the quantified antecedent in order to avoid a weak crossover violation (see Reinhart 1976; Koopman and Sportiche 1982). In fact, under the other interpretation of (26), the pronoun would not be c-commanded by the quantified NP, yielding a violation of the relevant principles of grammar.

Comparable results are expectedly obtained with a dative internal argument:

(28)   a. la telefonata di ogni ragazzo$_i$ a sua$_i$ madre
             the phone call of every boy to his mother
        b. ?*la telefonata di sua$_i$ madre a ogni ragazzo$_i$
             the phone call of his mother to every boy

Another piece of evidence in favour of the conclusion illustrated above comes from sentences with the 'sloppy' reading of a pronoun. This too is a phenomenon where, according to Reinhart (1983), a pronoun, in order to receive the 'sloppy' interpretation, must be treated as a bound variable, hence must be c-commanded by the NP understood as its antecedent:

(29)   Ti ho esposto l'opinione di Gianni di sua moglie, non quella di Franco
        lit.: I revealed to you the opinion of Gianni of his wife, not that of Franco
        i. I revealed to you Gianni$_i$'s opinion about his$_i$ wife, not Franco$_j$'s opinion about his$_j$ wife
        ii. *I revealed to you his$_i$ wife's opinion about Gianni$_i$ not his$_j$ wife's opinion about Franco$_j$

Sentence (29) has, of course, a number of non-sloppy interpretations; but here we are concerned only with the two sloppy ones which are *a priori* conceivable.[12] Now, the only possible sloppy reading is (29)i, once again, if the intended antecedent of the pronoun receives the internal θ-role; i.e. according to our hypothesis it is immediately dominated by N′, while the possessive pronoun is embedded within the external argument outside N′, so it cannot qualify as a possible binder.

Consider finally another test which yields the same results. It is already known (Burzio, 1981, 1986) that the Italian quantifier *ciascuno* ('each') in the floating usage has to be c-commanded by the NP it quantifies on. Therefore, we correctly predict the following facts:

(30)   a. (?)la descrizione di un bandito ciascuno dei poliziotti
             lit.: the description of a gangster each of the policemen
        i. *the description by a gangster each of the policemen
        ii. the description of a gangster each by the policemen
        b. (?)la descrizione di un bandito ciascuno ai poliziotti

lit.: the description of a gangster (theme) each to the policemen
i. *the description by a gangster each (agent) to the policemen
ii. the description of a gangster each (theme) to the policemen

These examples confirm once again that the theme and the goal do not c-command the agent, i.e. internal arguments do not c-command the external one, as predicted by our hypothesis.[13] Let us return now to examples (1) and (2) repeated below as (31) and (32):

(31)   a. L'opinione di se stesso di Gianni è troppo lusinghiera
         Gianni's opinion about himself is too flattering
      b. La paura di se stesso di Gianni è preoccupante
         Gianni's fear of himself is worrying
      c. La descrizione di se stesso di Gianni è troppo lusinghiera
         Gianni's description of himself is too flattering
(32)   a. *L'opinione di lui$_i$ di Gianni$_i$ è troppo lusinghiera
         The opinion of him of Gianni is too flattering
      b. *La paura di lui$_i$ di Gianni$_i$ è preoccupante
         The fear of him of Gianni is worrying
      c. *La descrizione di lui$_i$ di Gianni$_i$ è troppo lusinghiera
         The description of him of Gianni is too flattering

It is easy to see that this theory makes the correct predictions there; if in (31) (*di*) *Gianni* is attached under N″, it binds the anaphor under N′; if (*di*) *se stesso* were higher than the R-expression, principles A (and C) should be violated, contrary to fact. In the sentences in (32), if (*di*) *Gianni* hangs from the higher level, principle B is violated, because the pronoun is c-commanded by the R-expression, whereas it should be free. On the other hand, if it is *di lui* which hangs from the higher projection, principle C is violated; therefore, coindexing is anyway impossible.[14]

With respect to the status of the category we analysed as N′, notice that if it were a maximal projection there would be no need to refute Aoun and Sportiche's notion of c-command as the one involved in binding. However, a couple of counter-arguments to this view immediately come to mind: first, this category does not seem to be subject to movement rules, whereas essentially all maximal projections may move (see Chomsky 1986b); second, according to Rothstein's (1983) predication theory, non-argument maximal projections require predication of an external argument, whereas non-maximal projections do not. Now, while VP requires a subject, the constituent identified as N′, which certainly is not an argument, does not (see Zubizarreta 1986; see also this vol. ch. 4); therefore, maximality cannot be claimed for N′ in the same way as for VP.[15]

3   On Case-marking

Cinque (1980, 1981a) has also shown that the phrase *di* + pronoun is not possible as the expression of an external θ-role in Italian, except under specific conditions:

(33)   a.   *la descrizione degli avvenimenti di te
             the description of the events of you
       b.   la tua descrizione degli avvenimenti
             your description of the events

There is an equally strong preference for expressing in the form of a possessive a pronominal realizing the semantic function of 'possessor', i.e. one of those Genitive-marked expressions bearing to the head Noun a more generic relationship that Higginbotham (1983) has called R-relation:

(34)   a.   *l'automobile di te
             the car of you
       b.   la tua automobile
             Your car

Cinque proposes a filter to block realization of *di* + pronoun phrases hanging from N″. However, the situation seems to be more complex, since in some cases such attachment is permitted, as, for example, in contrastive environments:

(35)   Ho apprezzato la descrizione degli avvenimenti di lui, ma non quella di lei
            lit.: I appreciated the description of the events of him, but not that of her
            I appreciated his description of the events, but not hers

Here the stressed third person pronoun *lui*, contrasting with *lei*, expresses the gender distinction, which is focused in this sentence (see also Belletti 1978). Since the Italian possessive pronoun does not distinguish genders, the use of the latter form would yield a pragmatically uninterpretable utterance (unless the use of deixis could render it understandable):

(36)   *Ho apprezzato la sua descrizione degli avvenimenti, ma non la sua
            I appreciated his/her description of the facts, but not his/hers

A *di* + pronoun phrase is also permitted, and a possessive is not, when there is an AP, or a relative (or pseudo-relative) clause, modifying the pronoun:[16]

(37)   a. Ricordo il racconto di lui orgoglioso della promozione
           I remember the story of him proud of the promotion
        b. *Ricordo il suo racconto orgoglioso della promozione
           I remember his story proud of the promotion
(38)   a. Ricordo il racconto di lui che partiva per l'Africa
           I remember the story of him who was leaving for Africa
        b. *Ricordo il suo racconto che partiva per l'Africa
           I remember his story who was leaving for Africa

Descriptively speaking, it appears that the possessive is obligatorily used whenever possible. This generalization also extends to structures in which the pronominal argument is the internal one and there is no overt external argument (ignoring the *by*-phrase, which functions more as an adjunct than as an argument; see Jaeggli (1986), and the references cited in n. 13 above). In the latter case the position under N″ is not lexically filled and the internal argument can be realized as a possessive pronoun:

(39)   a. ?*La descrizione di me (da parte della polizia) non corrispondeva a
           verità
           The description of me (by the police) did not correspond to reality
        b. La mia descrizione (da parte della polizia) non corrispondeva a
           verità
           My description (by the police) did not correspond to reality

Example (39)a is not as bad as (37)b and (38)b, showing that the constraint violated in the latter cases is more central to the grammar than the principle violated in (39).

What makes the crucial difference between *di* + pronoun and the possessive, accounting for the alternation in their use? One obvious difference lies in the realization of Case on the two forms. In order to appear within an NP, a regular pronoun must be Case-marked by means of *di*, whereas the possessive does not need this support. In fact, a possessive can be assumed to satisfy the Case-requirements imposed by Chomsky's (1986a) theory by realizing its inherent (Genitive) Case by means of Case-agreement with the head N, as suggested by many languages with overt Case inflection.[17] The relevant principle can be expressed as follows:

(40)   A Case-marking Preposition is licensed iff
        the assigned Case cannot be directly realized

(where 'directly realized' means without the introduction of a Preposition). In this sense, *di* insertion is a 'last resort'.

Given the tendential uniqueness of possessivization (see chs. 2 and 3 below), (40) correctly predicts that *di* insertion will be better tolerated when another argument is already realized as a possessive:

(41)   a. la mia descrizione di te
            my description of you
        b. ?*la mia descrizione tua
            my description yours

The same is true with respect to the class of Ns which, according to Cinque's (1980, 1981a) analysis, may only have the 'active' form (see ch. 2 below for a presentation of Cinque's N classes in Italian):

(42)   a. il desiderio di cioccolata di Maria
            lit.: the desire of chocolate of Maria
            Maria's desire for chocolate
        b. il desiderio di te
            lit.: the desire of you
            the desire for you (you = theme/*experiencer)
        c. il tuo desiderio
            your desire (your = exp/*theme)

A Noun like *desiderio* cannot be passivized, as we have already mentioned; i.e., if the possessive form is present it can only be interpreted as the experiencer and not as the theme. This fact explains why (42)b is not ruled out by principle (40): Case cannot be directly realized, given that the intended reading of (42)c is ungrammatical. Let us now consider some additional correct consequences of our principle (40): first, it also accounts for the following contrasts, which apparently are beyond the scope of Cinque's original account, because the latter only makes reference to the internal structure of an NP:

(43)   a. *Il libro è di me
            lit.: The book is of me
        b. Il libro è mio
            The book is mine

The form which is realized as a possessive is admitted, while the other one is not.[18]

Let us note, in addition, that the form *di* + anaphor is also subject to principle (40). Consider, in fact, the following contrasts involving the reflexive *se stesso* and its possessive counterpart *proprio* (whose more complex behaviour is analysed in Giorgi, 1984):

(44)   a. *Gianni considera il libro di se stesso il migliore di tutti
            Gianni considers the book of himself the best of all

    b. Gianni considera il proprio libro il migliore di tutti
       Gianni considers self's book the best of all
    c. ?Gianni conserva ancora molte foto di se stesso in partenza per
       l'Africa
       Gianni still keeps many pictures of himself leaving for Africa
    d. *Gianni conserva ancora molte proprie foto in partenza per
       l'Africa
       Gianni still keeps many self's pictures leaving for Africa

Finally, another piece of evidence in favour of our reformulation of Cinque's filter will be presented after discussing the structure of ergative Nouns in section 5.

In the light of the behaviour of *proprio*, consider also some data coming from a totally different phenomenon: Chomsky (1986a, p. 117) analyses the paradigm concerning the distribution of *one* in the arbitrary impersonal interpretation. Here we will reproduce his examples as well as the Italian paradigm:

(45)   a. One should not do such things
       b. Uno non dovrebbe fare queste cose
       c. One's friend should not do such things
       d. *L'amico di uno non dovrebbe fare queste cose
       e. *One was here yesterday
       f. *Uno era qui ieri
       g. *They ought to meet one
       h. *Dovrebbero incontrare uno

(Chomsky also discusses some structures involving ECM, which are independently excluded in Italian.)

The paradigms seem to be identical in Italian and English, except for the ungrammaticality of (45)d, which contrasts with the acceptable English example, (45)c. Given the affinity of the rest of the paradigms, such a difference is surprising: however, principle (40) seems to be independently able to account for it. In fact, the same (generic) meaning in Italian can be expressed precisely by means of the anaphoric possessive *proprio*, under the arbitrary interpretation, as shown by example (46):

(46)   I propri$_{arb}$ amici non dovrebbero fare queste cose
       lit.: One's friend should not do such things

In other words, the presence of *di uno* ('one's') in this case is impossible, given the availability of a form which realizes Case directly.

Briefly summarizing the results of this section, it was suggested here that the preference of Italian for using the possessive form whenever possible, both inside NPs and in predicative constructions, is due to a more general constraint on Case-realization by means of a Preposition.[19]

4   On some expected principle C and B violations

Consider now the examples (3)–(6) again. On the grounds of such examples, in section 1, we claimed that *a* has to be treated on a par with *di* in that it does not delimit the c-domain of the NP it governs. Pursuing the discussion in sections 1 and 2, these sentences raise some interesting problems for the BT as usually understood. In (3)a and (4)a, in fact, we have to hypothesize a structure like the following (we also include forms with pronouns as antecedents, which behave in the same way as R-expressions):

(47)

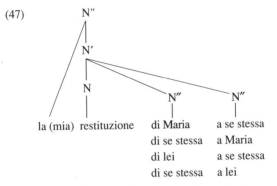

la (mia) restituzione	di Maria	a se stessa

la (mia) restituzione   di Maria   a se stessa
                         di se stessa a Maria
                         di lei   a se stessa
                         di se stessa a lei

The R-expression (or the pronoun) and the anaphor are both internal arguments and therefore hang from N′. If it is true that *di* and *a* never block c-command, in (47) we should expect a violation of principle C or B, analogous to that found in (5)a and (6)a. However, as has already been shown, such sentences are grammatical and therefore raise a problem for this analysis. *A priori* there are two possible solutions; the first one consists in claiming that such structures are grammatical because there is no configuration typical of a principle C or B violation, i.e. that representation (47) is incorrect. The second accepts the view that there is such a configuration and explains the fact that the violation does not arise, rejecting the above interpretation of the BT as incorrect. Here it will be demonstrated that the first possibility cannot be pursued and, although we will not give a complete reformulation of the BT to deal with these data, we discuss a generalization concerning them that should be derivable from a proper formulation of the BT.

According to the first alternative, it would be possible to account for

(3)a and (4)a as follows: assume crucially that N′ blocks c-command, in agreement with our claim, but that the level of attachment can be chosen arbitrarily, i.e. in violation of the Thematic Correspondence Hypothesis. To obtain the grammaticality of (3)a, one could claim that (*di*) *Maria* is attached under N″ and *a se stessa* under N′:

(48)

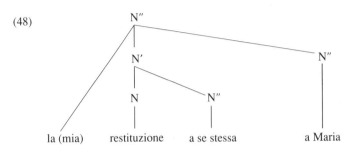

Here *Maria* would c-command and bind the anaphor *se stessa*, but the latter would not c-command the R-expression; similarly in (4)a:

(49)

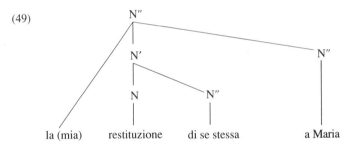

However, this approach seems untenable, since it would also rule in phrases like (5)a and (6)a above which are clearly ungrammatical. In fact, in such cases the pronoun would always have the option of attaching at a lower level in order not to c-command the R-expression. Moreover, this solution undermines our distinction between internal and external position, which seems to be necessary to explain other cases of binding. Recall also, as was pointed out in section 1, that *a* never blocks c-command, as shown by the contrast given in (5), and, therefore, no alternative theory based on the assumption that it does can be proposed to explain the data given above.

In conclusion, the structural configuration given in (47) turns out to be the only appropriate hypothesis. Notice, incidentally, that exactly the same pattern can be found in sentential structures, i.e. within VPs, raising an identical problem:

(50) a. Una lunga terapia psicoanalitica ha restituito Maria$_i$/lei$_i$ a se
      stessa$_i$
      A long psychoanalytic therapy restored Maria/her to herself
      b. Una lunga terapia psicoanalitica ha restituito se stessa$_i$ a
      Maria$_i$/lei$_i$
      A long psychoanalytic therapy restored herself to Maria/her
(51) a. *Una lunga terapia psicoanalitica ha restituito lei$_i$ all'affetto del
      fratello di Maria$_i$
      A long psychoanalytic therapy restored her to the love of Maria's
      brother
      b. *Una lunga terapia psicoanalitica ha restituito a lei$_i$ l'affetto del
      fratello di Maria$_i$
      A long psychoanalytic therapy restored to her the love of Maria's
      brother

As in the nominal examples discussed earlier, these data can be taken to
show that the two complements must always c-command each other and
therefore in (51)a and (51)b one should expect again a principle C, or B,
violation which does not arise. Before suggesting a tentative explanation
for the theoretical problems it poses, let us complete the paradigm by
revealing further data which motivate at least the weaker hypothesis,
namely that direct and indirect objects *may* c-command one another.
Consider, in fact, the distribution of the possessive anaphor *proprio*:

(52) a. la restituzione di Gianni$_i$ alla propria$_i$ famiglia da parte dello
      psicoanalista
      the restoration of Gianni to self's family by the psychoanalyst
      b. la restituzione della propria$_i$ moglie a Gianni$_i$ da parte dello
      psicoanalista
      the restoration of self's wife to Gianni by the psychoanalyst

These phrases again show that direct and indirect object must be able to
mutually c-command. *Proprio*, in fact, behaves here as a clause-bound
anaphor and must be assumed to obey c-command, given that it is not
subject-orientated (see Giorgi 1983); as expected, it can appear in either
position.
   The same pattern holds with respect to the distribution of *proprio* in
VPs:

(53) a. Una lunga terapia psicoanalitica ha restituito Gianni$_i$ alla propria$_i$
      moglie
      A long psychoanalytic therapy restored Gianni to self's wife
      b. Una lunga terapia psicoanalitica ha restituito la propria$_i$ moglie a
      Gianni$_i$
      A long psychoanalytic therapy restored self's wife to Gianni

The conclusion is reinforced by the binding of a pronoun by a quantifier:

(54)   a. Una lunga terapia psicoanalitica restituì ogni ragazzo$_i$ alla sua$_i$ famiglia
        A long psychoanalytic therapy restored every boy to his family
    b. Una lunga terapia psicoanalitica restituì sua$_i$ madre ad ogni ragazzo$_i$
        A long psychoanalytic therapy restored his mother to every boy

Both sentences in (54) yield correct examples of pronominal binding. Consider also the corresponding nominals:

(55)   a. la restituzione di ogni ragazzo$_i$ alla sua$_i$ famiglia
        the restoration of every boy to his family
    b. la restituzione di sua$_i$ madre ad ogni ragazzo$_i$
        the restoration of his mother to every boy

Similar results are obtained under the sloppy-identity reading of a pronoun, again both in sentences and in nominals:

(56)   a. Il preside presentò Gianni al suo nuovo professore, ma non Maria
        The dean introduced Gianni to his new professor, but not Maria
    b. Il preside presentò il suo nuovo professore a Gianni, ma non a Maria
        The dean introduced his new professor to Gianni, but not to Maria
(57)   a. la presentazione al suo nuovo professore di Gianni, ma non di Maria
        the introduction to his new professor of Gianni, but not of Maria
    b. la presentazione del suo nuovo professore a Gianni, ma non a Maria
        the introduction of his new professor to Gianni, but not to Maria[20]

In (56) and (57) the sloppy reading is always possible, showing that even in these cases c-command is reciprocal.[21]

    Consider now the theoretical issue raised by structure (47): notice that in all the unexpected examples of binding, we have been concerned with the c-command relation of an anaphor toward its antecedent. This is crucial for the structure to be grammatical, because, if the c-commanded element is not the antecedent of the anaphor, the structure is regularly unacceptable:

(58)   a. Gianni$_i$ ritiene se stesso$_i$ un bravo ragazzo
        Gianni believes himself to be a nice boy
    b. Gianni$_i$ ritiene Maria molto contenta di lui$_i$
        Gianni believes Maria very happy with him
    c. *Gianni$_i$ ritiene se stesso$_i$ molto contento di lui$_i$
        Gianni believes himself very happy with him

In (58)c the antecedent of the anaphor, i.e. the coindexed c-commanding element, must be *Gianni* and cannot be the equally coindexed pronoun, since the latter does not c-command *se stesso*; therefore a principle B violation presumably arises. In fact principle A should be as satisfied as in (58)a, and the pronoun could not be directly disjoint from *Gianni*, as shown by (58)b. The descriptive generalization can thus be formulated as follows:

(59)   If an anaphor and its antecedent mutually c-command, no
         disjointness effect arises[22]

Generalization (59) can hardly be a theorem of a classical BT based on symmetric relations such as coindexing and coreference; instead, it could follow directly from a theory in which principles B and C were understood in terms of Higginbotham's (1983) antisymmetric notion of 'linking', essentially as conditions imposing referential non-dependence, roughly in the sense of Evans (1980), but not straight non-coreference in the sense of Lasnik (1976). Under this approach, in fact, in the cases discussed above, the anaphor would be (correctly) referentially dependent on the antecedent (name or pronoun) and the latter, given the antisymmetric nature of the relation, would never be dependent on the anaphor, though coreferring with it. As a consequence, if interpreted in these terms, the BT is not violated; if principle A as well is understood as requiring that an anaphor be *dependent* on the antecedent (linked), not just *bound* in the traditional sense, a problem complementary to the one addressed so far can also be solved:

(60)   a. *la mia restituzione di se stessa a se stessa
           my restoration of herself to herself
       b. *Ho restituito se stessa a se stessa
           I restored herself to herself

In these cases, provided that a structure of the type of (47) is correct, the anaphors should bind each other, literally satisfying principle A in the classical definition, but only one could link the other, determining a violation in the antisymmetric reinterpretation of the BT. Thus, although other cases still raise unsolved issues, the latter formulation appears to be at first sight more capable of dealing with the anaphoric properties displayed by Italian double-object constructions.[23]

Consider in this light the argument proposed by Chomsky (1986b) for claiming that N′ defines a c-domain; such an argument relies on the assumption that the trace left by NP movement would cause a principle C violation, were N′ not a block for c-command. He discusses the following example:

(61)

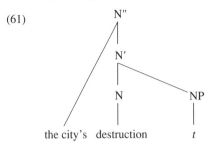

If N′ were to permit c-command, the trace would c-command *the city*; Chomsky (1986b) argues that, since the phrase is grammatical, N′ must be the c-domain of the trace. From our discussion, on the one hand it turns out that N′ does not allow further extension of c-command; but, on the other, given the evidence that has just been examined, Chomsky's observation cannot be taken as an argument in favour of this conclusion. Recall, in fact, that the trace of 'passivization' is usually considered an anaphor, and as such, even in the case in which *t* and its antecedent, *the city*, mutually c-command, the binding requirements should still be satisfied, as captured by generalization (59). Consider now the following examples:

(62)   a. *La propria opinione di Gianni è troppo lusinghiera
          Self's opinion of Gianni is too flattering
       b. *La propria paura di Gianni è eccessiva
          Self's fear of Gianni is excessive
(63)   a. *La propria$_i$ restituzione a Maria$_i$ da parte dello psicoanalista era improbabile
          Self's restoration to Maria by the psychoanalyst was unlikely
       b. La restituzione dei propri$_i$ gioielli a Maria$_i$ da parte di Gianni era improbabile
          The restitution of self's jewels to Maria by Gianni was unlikely

In sentences (62) and (63) the third person (singular or plural) possessive anaphor, *proprio* ('self's') (see Giorgi 1983), has to be bound by a c-commanding NP. Such a condition is actually satisfied in (63)b, where, as predicted, the NP governed by *a* c-commands another complement in its thematic position under N′. However, as shown by the ungrammaticality of the other examples, *proprio* cannot be bound by an argument of the same head N. The traditional interpretation of the BT could attribute this fact just to a principle C violation. However, according to the arguments presented above, it is binding principle A that must be primarily violated, since principle C can only be indirectly violated, as a consequence of *Gianni* not being an antecedent of the anaphor. Given the structural hypotheses of the previous sections, as far as (62) is concerned, the c-command asymmetry is straightforward, in the case in which *di Gianni* receives the internal θ-role. If it receives the external one, Cinque's generalization about possessivization rules the structure out, given that an internal argument would be possessivized over an external one, overtly expressed in Genitive Case. The same holds with respect to an NP governed by *a*, as shown in (63)a, which contrasts with (63)b.[24]

5   On ergative Nouns

An interesting question concerns nominal heads related to 'ergative' Verbs (Perlmutter 1978; Burzio 1981, 1986). Within the hypothesis of a strict parallelism between Verbs and corresponding Nouns (the Thematic Correspondence Hypothesis), we are led to the prediction that, since ergative Verbs can only assign internal θ-roles, the same should be true for derived Nouns. Let us examine the behaviour of the head N *apparizione* ('appearance'), which is lexically related to the ergative verb *apparire* ('to appear'). Consider the following examples:[25]

(64)   la restituzione di se stessa$_i$ a Maria$_i$ da parte dello psicoanalista
         the restoration of herself to Maria by the psychoanalyst

(65)   a. *la finta telefonata di se stesso$_i$ a Gianni$_i$
            the false phone call of himself to Gianni
         b. *la finta telefonata di Gianni$_i$ a se stesso$_i$
            the false phone call of Gianni to himself

(66)   a. l'apparizione di Maria$_i$ a se stessa$_i$, in sogno
            the appearance of Maria to herself, in her dreams
         b. l'apparizione di se stessa$_i$ a Maria$_i$, in sogno
            the appearance of herself to Maria, in her dreams

The grammaticality of (66)a is not surprising, since *di*, as we have already discussed, does not block c-command and, whichever the level of attachment of the phrase *di Maria* may be, we expect it to be able to bind an anaphor in internal position, exactly as *di Gianni* does in (65)b. More interesting is the grammaticality of (66)b, which contrasts with (65)a and parallels, on the other hand, (64). In (66)b, an R-expression, bearing an internal θ-role and therefore hanging from N', can bind the anaphor governed by *di*. As required by our Thematic Correspondence Hypothesis in conjunction with Burzio's (1981, 1986) ergative theory, we are led to the conclusion that the phrase containing the anaphor in this case hangs from N'. Both (64) and (66) are grammatical for the same reason, i.e. in both cases the internal position is the relevant one for the assignment of the theme θ-role, and, given that the theme NP is inherently Case-marked, it can even surface there. Notice also that nothing prevents such an argument from moving as a possessive into a position under N", but in this case no NP-internal coreference relation with other non-anaphoric arguments may hold (see the previous section for discussion):

(67)   a. la sua$_{j/*i}$ restituzione a Maria$_i$/lei$_i$ da parte dello psicoanalista
            her restoration to Maria/her by the psychoanalyst
     b. la sua$_{j/*i}$ apparizione a Maria$_i$/lei$_i$
            her appearance to Maria/her

(68)   a. (cf. (63)a) *la propria$_i$ restituzione a Maria$_i$/lei$_i$ da parte dello psicoanalista
            self's restoration to Maria/her by the psychoanalyst
     b. *la propria$_i$ improvvisa apparizione a Maria$_i$/lei$_i$
            self's sudden appearance to Maria/her

Another important piece of evidence comes from the distribution of *proprio*:

(69)   a. *la telefonata della propria$_i$ madre a Gianni$_i$
            the phone call of self's mother to Gianni
     b. la telefonata di Gianni$_i$ alla propria$_i$ madre
            the phone call of Gianni to self's mother

(70)   a. l'apparizione della propria$_i$ madre a Gianni$_i$, in sogno
            the appearance of self's mother to Gianni, in his dreams
     b. l'apparizione di Gianni$_i$ alla propria$_i$ madre, in sogno
            the appearance of Gianni to self's mother, in her dreams

(71)   la restituzione della propria$_i$ moglie a Gianni$_i$ (da parte di un bravo psicoanalista)
            the restoration of self's wife to Gianni (by a good psychoanalyst)

As we have already discussed in section 2 above, (69)a and b contrast with respect to the binding properties of *proprio*, since in (a) the latter is not c-commanded by the intended antecedent *Gianni*. Again, within an NP headed by *apparizione*, such contrast does not arise, paralleling the distribution we observe with *restituzione* and confirming the internal nature of the genitive argument.

The now familiar condition on the distribution of the floating quantifier *ciascuno* ('each') provides additional evidence for the claim (see Burzio 1981, 1986):

(72)   a. *la telefonata di un professore ciascuno agli studenti
            the phone call of a professor each to the students

> b. la restituzione di un libro ciascuno agli studenti
>   the restitution of a book each to the students
> c. l'apparizione di un fantasma ciascuno agli studenti
>   the appearance of a ghost each to the students

As expected, the NP bearing the agent θ-role in *telefonata* ('phone call') cannot be in a position such that *ciascuno* ('each') is c-commanded by *gli studenti* ('the students'), whereas this is possible both with *restituzione* ('restitution') and *apparizione* ('appearance'). Once again, *apparizione* patterns together with *restituzione* and not with *telefonata*, due to the availability of the internal θ-position. Consider next the following contrasts based on the c-command requirement for bound pronouns:

(73)   a. *la telefonata di sua$_i$ madre a ogni studente$_i$
          the phone call of his mother to every student
       b. la restituzione dei suoi$_i$ documenti a ogni studente$_i$
          the restitution of his documents to every student
       c. l'apparizione, in sogno, di un suo$_i$ antenato a ogni studente$_i$
          the appearance, in (his) dreams, of his ancestor to every student

In this case too the genitive argument of such Nouns as *apparizione*, which we may term 'ergative', behaves like the object of 'transitive' ones.

A fourth argument comes from the distribution of what we may call 'referential Adjectives', i.e. Adjectives which express an argument of the head Noun. Consider for instance the following examples:[26]

(74)   a. the Russian invasion of China
       b. *the Chinese invasion of Russia
       c. Russia's invasion of China
       d. China's invasion by Russia

The contrast between (74)a and (74)b, pointed out in Kayne (1984), suggests that an Adjective which does not identify a quality, but discharges an actual θ-role, can only express the external one of the Noun it modifies; a possible account of this generalization is suggested by Kayne himself and an extension of the analysis is attempted in chapter 3 below. If the generalization is correct, it provides us, in any event, with an interesting test: it should be impossible for an ergative Noun to express any θ-role by means of an Adjective. We predict, therefore, that the grammaticality of a phrase containing an ergative Noun and a referential Adjective should be comparable to that of phrases like (74)b. This seems to be correct (see, however, n. 27):

(75)   a. l'entrata del governo in parlamento
        the entrance of the government in the parliament
    b. *l'entrata governativa in parlamento
        the governmental entrance in the parliament

(76)   a. l'apparizione dei tedeschi di fronte alla linea Maginot
        the appearance of Germans in front of the Maginot line
    b. ?*l'apparizione tedesca di fronte alla linea Maginot
        the German appearance in front of the Maginot line

The examples in (75) and (76) show that the Adjective *governativa* and *tedesca* cannot be used to express a θ-role, which, according to our hypothesis, is assigned internally. Examples (75)b and (76)b, in fact, contrast with (77)b and (78)b:

(77)   a. l'appello del governo al parlamento
        the appeal of the government to the parliament
    b. l'appello governativo al parlamento
        the governmental appeal to the parliament

(78)   a. l'assalto dei tedeschi alla linea Maginot
        the assault of the Germans on the Maginot line
    b. l'assalto tedesco alla linea Maginot
        the German assault on the Maginot line

Appello ('appeal') and *assalto* ('assault'), in fact, appear to be non-ergative Nouns: they assign an agent θ-role, hence an external one, to their genitive argument and, thus, regularly permit it to be replaced by an Adjective.[27]

A further test to distinguish the internal or external nature of a genitive argument of N is provided by a property of English nominal syntax which is most relevant to the theoretical argumentation of chapter 3 below; consider the following examples:

(79)   a. The description of Mary
        i. *Mary = agent
        ii. Mary = theme
    b. The entrance of Mary into the room was sudden
    c. The appearance of Mary was sudden

In English Noun Phrases, a non-heavy (in a morphosyntactic sense made more precise in ch. 3) animate *of NP* can be assigned the internal θ-role, but not the external one, so that the first interpretation of (79)a is ruled out, although not the second one. Going now to ergative nominalizations, since neither (79)b nor (79)c is ruled out, we can conclude, as expected, that the θ-role assigned in these cases is not an external one.

Finally, let us remark that the data concerning ergative Nouns provide additional evidence about the mechanisms of *di* insertion in Italian. In section 3, we claimed that the form *di* + pronoun (or anaphor) is excluded whenever it is possible to adopt the possessive (see principle 40 above), irrespectively of the level of attachment of the *di* phrase. This generalization seems to compare favourably with that proposed by Cinque (1980, 1981a), which relies instead only on the differences in level of attachment. Even if ergative Nouns, in fact, only have internal arguments, therefore not hanging from N″, the form *di* + pronoun (or anaphor) is normally prohibited:

(80)   a. la mia partenza
           my departure
        b. *la partenza di me
           the departure of me
(81)   a. la tua entrata in parlamento
           your entrance in the parliament
        b. *l'entrata di te in parlamento
           the entrance of you in the parliament

Partenza ('departure') and *entrata* ('entrance') are related to the ergative Verbs *partire* ('to leave') and *entrare* ('to enter') and therefore must admit a θ-position under N′. Nevertheless, they do not permit the expression of this θ-role in the form *di* + pronoun, suggesting that this property is not dependent on structural distinctions.

6   Evidence from NPs for the notion of Complete Functional Complex

In this final section we will discuss two types of evidence, related to the structure of NPs, which can support the view recently developed by Chomsky (1986a) concerning the definition of the domain relevant for the binding principles A and B. We will first consider the binding properties of those NPs whose heads project an argument structure, but which, being names for objects, can also be completed by a 'possessor', or, more generally, by a genitive element having with the head a relation looser than a strictly thematic one (Higginbotham's (1983) R-relation). As we will see, such Ns include, among others, items like *letter*, *book* and so on. The second piece of evidence will have to do with NPs in predicative contexts.

Chomsky (1986a) restates principles A and B of the Binding Theory; one reason for this move is, as far as we can see, highly theory-internal, namely that, by eliminating the notion of i-within-i, it becomes impossible to define the concept of 'accessible' subject, as was crucial for the previous definitions of binding domains, so that some reformulation is in order. However, in so doing, Chomsky also eliminates any direct use of the term 'subject', introducing the new notion of Complete Functional Complex (CFC). Here we discuss some data which can also provide an empirical basis in favour of a definition of CFC able to express in a natural way certain generalizations, hardly captured by previous frameworks. The relevant parts of the definitions given in Chomsky (1986a, pp. 171–2) are the following:

(82)   i. The indexing I and the pair (α, β) are *compatible* with respect to the BT if α satisfies the BT in the local domain β under indexing I:
I is BT compatible with (α, β) if:
(A) α is an anaphor and is bound in β under I
(B) β is a pronominal and is free in β under I
       ii. Licensing condition for a category α governed by γ in the expression E with indexing I:
For some β, I is BT-compatible with (α, β):
α is an anaphor or pronominal and β is the least Complete Functional Complex containing γ for which there is an indexing J BT-compatible with (α, β)

A CFC is informally defined in Chomsky (1986a, p. 169) as the domain in which 'all the grammatical functions compatible with the head are realized; the complements necessarily, by the Projection Principle, and the subject, which is optional unless required to license a predicate, by definition'.

To identify the binding domains, these definitions mention neither an accessible subject, nor a SUBJECT, nor specific projections, such as NP or S, as in Chomsky (1981, 1982). The fact that it is the presence of a subject which usually defines a binding domain is derived from the requirement that the Functional Complex be 'complete'. At first sight, then, it seems that for the identification of the binding domains the notion of CFC is extensionally equivalent to an explicit mention of an accessible subject or to a list of the categories which have subjects.

Consider now the structure related to Nouns such as *book* and *letter*. As we pointed out above, they can identify both an element having with the head a rather generic semantic relation, for instance a 'possessor', and a specific θ-grid (argument structure), represented by the agent of the writing and the addressee in the case of *letter*, by the agent and a topic of the writing in the case of *book*.

(83)   a. la lettera a Maria di Gianni
           Gianni's letter to Maria
        b. il libro su Maria di Gianni
           Gianni's book about Maria

Examples (83) are in principle ambiguous in that the *di* + NP phrase can function either as a thematic argument or as a 'possessor'.

The two genitive structures can also cooccur, and the resulting NP displays interesting properties with respect to binding phenomena. For instance, in (84) *Museo Pallavicini* identifies the possessor:

(84)   la preziosa lettera di Leonardo agli Sforza del Museo Pallavicini
        the valuable letter of Leonardo to the Sforzas of the Pallavicini
        Museum

Now let us analyse the following data:

(85)   a. la finta lettera di Gianni a se stesso
           Gianni's false letter to himself
           la sua$_i$ finta lettera a se stesso$_i$
           his false letter to himself
(86)   a. il libro di Moravia$_i$ su se stesso$_i$
           Moravia's book about himself
        b. il suo$_i$ libro su se stesso$_i$
           his book about himself

In (85) and (86) with the genitive argument interpreted as bearing a specific θ-role (namely agent) the presence of an anaphor is always admitted. This follows no matter which version of the BT is adopted; i.e. it follows either from a BT that makes reference to subjects or from the version given in Chomsky (1986a). Following Cinque's (1980, 1981a) definition of subject-of-NP in Italian, in fact, in (4) and (5), it is the whole NP which qualifies both as a CFC and as the domain made opaque by a subject. In these cases, according to what we said above, the subject, which expresses the agent of the writing, hangs from a higher level with respect to the other argument. We also correctly expect, under any definition of the binding domains, that (in the same meaning) the examples in (87) will be ungrammatical:

(87)   a. *la sua$_i$ lettera a lui$_i$
           his letter to him
        b. *il suo$_i$ libro su di lui$_i$
           his book on him

However, if we add another genitive phrase the picture changes in an interesting way:

(88)   a. *la sua$_i$ lettera di Maria a se stesso$_i$
           his (possessor) letter of Maria (agent) to himself
       b. la sua$_i$ lettera di Maria a lui$_i$
           his (possessor) letter of Maria (agent) to him

(89)   a. *il suo$_i$ libro di Moravia su se stessa$_i$
           her (possessor) book of Moravia (agent) about herself
     .   il suo$_i$ libro di Moravia su di lei$_i$
           her (possessor) book of Moravia (agent) about her

The same happens if the genitive phrase expressing the possessor is realized in the form *di* + NP:

(90)   a. *le lettere di Picasso a se stessa$_i$ di Peggy Guggenheim$_i$
           The letters of Picasso to herself by Peggy Guggenheim
       b. (?) le lettere di Picasso a lei$_i$ di Peggy Guggenheim$_i$
           the letters of Picasso to her of Peggy Guggenheim

Thus, when a possessor is present, the distribution of anaphors and pronouns is not literally predicted by any present theory. However, it will be suggested here that the notion of 'least Complete Functional Complex' could be accommodated to account for these facts much more naturally than any other current notion for defining the binding domains.[28]

Let us consider how the various alternatives may face the empirical challenge proposed by the data in (88)–(90). Notice, first, that the correct generalization seems to be that the binding category for a complement of N includes the thematic subject but excludes the genitive phrase expressing the possessor.[29] The version of the BT which stipulates that NP and S are binding domains is plainly inadequate in this light. If possessors are, under either form (possessive or *di* + NP – see the following chapters for an analysis of the relation between the two structures), included in the NP projection, it is clear that this version of the BT will fail to capture the generalization above. Consider now a definition singling out the notion of 'minimal category with a subject'. Under this approach, (88)–(90) might be accounted for if the notion of 'subject' relevant for the definition were restricted to 'thematic subjects', i.e. subjects specified by the θ-grid of the head. This move would apparently yield the correct results, in particular if possessors, under any form, are higher in the tree than thematic arguments, separated from subject and complements by a further N projection, a structural hierarchy which will be independently shown to be correct in chapter 2 below (see also Milner 1982 for French). However, the limitation to 'thematic subjects' seems rather stipulative and probably hard to extend from NPs to clauses, given the well-known opacizing effect of raised subjects and of various expletives. Moreover, a simple further observation raises a conceptual problem for such an approach: in fact, even if bearing just a generic R-relation (in Higginbotham's sense) to the head such as the interpretation as 'possessor', a pronominal possessive can be bound from outside the NP (in other words, it is never disjoint):

(91)   Gianni$_i$ mi mostrò la sua$_i$ preziosa lettera di Leonardo agli Sforza
        Gianni showed me his valuable letter by Leonardo to the Sforzas

This suggests that the whole NP node must still constitute a binding domain; that is, it must qualify as a second larger CFC, formed by the first one (i.e. the θ-grid) plus the R-related genitive phrases.

Other approaches to the problem would lead to incorrect predictions. As we have already pointed out, an approach in terms of maximal projections would be unsatisfactory. Moreover, defining the domain relevant for the application of the principles of binding exclusively in terms of the domain of the thematic *subject*, i.e. the agent, incorrectly rules out (91). To predict the occurrence of the pronoun in (91), one has to say that the possessor too is a subject relevant for the definition of the binding domain. This point of view, however, contradicts the basic intuition originally due to Cinque (1980, 1981a) and, that NPs only have one subject, which is structurally identifiable as the element which can occur in Spec as a possessive (see sect. 2 above and ch. 2). It seems, therefore, that there are empirical and conceptual arguments against the two best-known previous formulations. Let us examine, in turn, a definition in terms of CFC.

The whole NPs in (88)–(90) are CFCs: according to the definition given by Chomsky (1986a), in fact, the possessor is included in the CFC, certainly representing a function of the head (the structural subject, following Cinque). As was noticed, this is correct but insufficient: such a CFC cannot be the least one containing the anaphor or the pronoun in (88)–(90). However, the concept of CFC is flexible enough to tolerate the slight extension needed to achieve the correct result. Let us try to define CFC as it emerges from what we have said here:

(92)   β is a Complete Functional Complex iff it meets at least one of the
        following requirements:
        a. it is the domain in which all the θ-roles pertaining to a lexical head
        are assigned

b. it is the domain in which all the grammatical functions pertaining
to that head are realized (where the R-relation counts as the
structural subject of the NP)

As far as we can see, such a definition can account both for the
traditional binding phenomena and for the data just discussed. In the case
of a verbal head, conditions (a) and (b) are simultaneously satisfied, in
that the same constituent minimally includes the complements and the
subject, that is, the realization of all the θ-roles and the grammatical
functions pertaining to it.[30] In the case of a referential NP, the *least* CFC
will thus be the minimal projection (even non-maximal) which satisfies
either (a) or (b).[31] In the rest of the section we will present a piece of
independent evidence for the proposed definitions coming from an
analysis of predicative NPs. Consider the following sentences:

(93) a. Gianni$_i$ è il miglior giudice di suo$_i$ padre
         Gianni is the best judge of his father
      b. Gianni$_i$ è il miglior giudice di se stesso$_i$
         Gianni is the best judge of himself
      c. *Gianni$_i$ è il suo$_i$ miglior giudice
         Gianni is his best judge
      d. ?Gianni$_i$ è il proprio$_i$ miglior giudice
         Gianni is self's best judge

(94) a. Reputo Gianni$_i$ il miglior giudice di suo$_i$ padre
         I consider Gianni the best judge of his father
      b. Reputo Gianni$_i$ il miglior giudice di se stesso$_i$
         I consider Gianni the best judge of himself
      c. *Reputo Gianni$_i$ il suo$_i$ miglior giudice
         I consider Gianni his best judge
      d. Reputo Gianni$_i$ il proprio$_i$ miglior giudice
         I consider Gianni self's best judge

(95) a. Gianni$_i$ sembra il miglior giudice di suo$_i$ padre
         Gianni seems the best judge of his father
      b. Gianni$_i$ sembra il miglior giudice di se stesso$_i$
         Gianni seems the best judge of himself
      c. *Gianni$_i$ sembra il suo$_i$ miglior giudice
         Gianni seems his best judge
      d. Gianni$_i$ sembra il proprio$_i$ miglior giudice
         Gianni seems self's best judge

In the case of predicative structures, such as those exemplified here, the
subject is not thematically autonomous with respect to the predicative NP.
In fact, it must constitute the external argument of the latter in order to
satisfy Rothstein's (1983) and Chomsky's (1986a) Predication Principle.
We will not analyse the precise mechanism of θ-role assignment here, since

the only aspect we have to focus on now is that the subject of the clause receives the external θ-role (agent) of the predicate 'judge' and that the argument of the postcopular NP receives the internal θ-role (patient). In addition, the external argument of the predicative NP may be taken to instantiate one grammatical function of the head Noun, that of predication subject of Nmax. Therefore the least Complete Functional Complex defined by the head 'judge' is the whole sentence or small clause, which simultaneously satisfies the two conditions of (92). Once again, the anaphor is admitted, as in (93)b, (94)b and (95)b and, what is especially relevant, the pronoun is not as in (93)c, (94)c and (95)c.[32] A possessive pronoun coreferential with the precopular NP is perfectly acceptable, provided just that it is more deeply embedded (that is, inside another CFC), as shown by (93)a, (94)a and (95)a.

The possessive anaphor *proprio* is acceptable (93d, 94d, 95d) and clearly contrasts with the pronoun. This fact, however, is not significant *per se*, given that the CFC should be extended anyway, due to the absence inside the predicative NP of an index BT compatible with the anaphor (see Chomsky 1986a).

Once again, the slightly revised notion of CFC seems to be superior with respect to the other ones. In fact, a definition simply referring to the category NP or to *structural* subjects would incorrectly rule in the coindexing of sentences (c). Notice, finally, that we correctly distinguish the behaviour of possessives in predicative and in referential NPs, like (87) or the following:

(96)   Gianni$_i$ ama la sua$_i$ casa
          Gianni loves his house

which is obviously grammatical. The crucial difference between (93)c, (94)c and (95)c on one hand, and (96) on the other, is that in our terms the NP is a CFC in (96), but not in the (c) sentences above.

2* Extraction from NP and the proper notion of head government

G. LONGOBARDI

Introduction

The purpose of this chapter is twofold: on the one hand we want to propose a new theory of extraction from NP; we claim that the restrictions on this phenomenon found in Italian and, in general, in Romance and best summarized in Cinque (1980) are a consequence of the fact that the only grammatical extractions from NP are necessarily mediated by a previous NP-internal movement to Spec.[1] In sections 4 to 7, we will provide various sorts of empirical arguments which appear to support the proposed account: such arguments also favour it over previous theories, either the ones formulated in terms of binding conditions (Specified Subject Condition: SSC) or those acknowledging the relevance of Spec for extraction, without, however, admitting that an actual trace of the extracted phrase is left in that position.

Our second goal is more broadly theoretical: developing a suggestion in Chomsky's (1986b) *Barriers* and a hypothesis already embodied in the definition of government proposed in Longobardi's (1985b) 'The Theoretical Status of the Adjunct Condition', we will argue that a proper relationship to a head (head government) must obligatorily hold of every trace, probably already at S-structure, independently of the presence of a local antecedent (antecedent government); in section 6 we provide a direct empirical argument in favour of such independence of the head-government requirement with respect to the one imposing antecedent government.[2]

From a more technical standpoint, we also explore some of the requirements for an adequate general definition of government and proper government. Following current formulations (particularly the framework developed in Longobardi 1985b), we will assume, as a point of departure, that a head α governs a phrase β iff α and β mutually m-command and either α is lexical (N, V, A, P) or is coindexed with β, and that, further, some accessibility of the Spec and head of an Xmax to an external governor must be allowed.[3] In order to develop these ideas we will first investigate some differences among lexical heads as governors, especially between Verbs and Nouns (section 8). Then, we will try to make precise the scope and limits of the phenomenon of Spec accessibility to a governor external to the maximal projection, pointing out a number of facts which bear on the proper formulation of the Minimality Condition on government in Chomsky's (1986b) sense (see in particular sections 5 and 9–11). The major conclusions arrived at on this subject are the following:

(i)   Spec accessibility to an external governor is recursive (i.e. government may cross more than one maximal projection)

(ii)   A head may govern a maximal projection which is its external argument but may not govern across it into Spec

(iii) A head protects the categories in its Spec from external government iff
       1. It is lexical and
       2. It selects their Case (through Case-making or Case-agreement)

(iv)   The canonical direction of government (in Kayne's 1983 sense) is a necessary component of proper government by a head, in addition to the selectional relation between the latter and the governee advocated in Longobardi (1985b).

Finally, the results achieved are built into a more formal restatement of the definition of government in section 12.

1   Cinque's generalization

A basic generalization, first proposed by Cinque (1980), states that in Italian no member of the argument or adjunct frame of a head Noun may be extracted by wh-movement or cliticization unless it is the 'subject' of the NP. Cinque provides a partially independent definition of what counts as a 'subject' in various N classes; for a more detailed analysis we refer the reader to his work (Cinque 1980, 1981a) and to Giorgi's extension of it in chapter 1; for our present purposes it is sufficient to say that the subject of an NP is roughly that argument which may be expressed in prenominal position, with the typical morphology of possessive Adjectives in Italian (see ch. 3).

As noted in Zubizarreta (1979), Cinque's generalization may thus be rephrased as follows:

(1)   Among the phrases belonging to the frame of a head N, only that which represents the argument expressible by a possessive can be extracted from Nmax.[4]

Generalization (1) is equivalent to Cinque's original formulation in terms of 'subjects', notably with one exception, which supports such a reformulation in a way that we consider later, in section 4. First, (1) captures the subgeneralization that only genitive arguments, meaning thereby PPs of the form *di*-NP ('of NP'; see ch. 1 above), may be extracted out of NPs. In fact, only such PPs can be pronominalized through a possessive. In addition, (1) summarizes some further restrictions.

For example, the PP *di Gianni* in the following sentence is ambiguous between an interpretation as the theme of the desire and one as the experiencer of it:

(2)   Abbiamo ricordato il desiderio di Gianni
        We remembered the desire of Gianni

But the wh-extracted and cliticized counterparts preserve only the second reading:

(3)   a. Gianni, di cui abbiamo ricordato il desiderio
           Gianni, of whom we remembered the desire
        b. Ne abbiamo ricordato il desiderio
           We of-him remembered the desire[5]

In fact, it is only such an experiencer reading (i.e. the same θ-role as the subject of the corresponding active Verb) which is available to the possessive form pronominalizing *di Gianni* in (4):

(4)   Abbiamo ricordato il suo desiderio
        We remembered his desire

Similar facts arise in the other NP classes identified by Cinque: with so-called 'intransitive' head Nouns, like e.g. *telefonata* ('phone call'), and 'inherently passive' ones, like *cattura* ('capture'), the unique genitive argument can both become a possessive (hence it is a subject in Cinque's sense) and be extracted:

(5)   a. la telefonata di Gianni
           the call of Gianni
        b. la sua telefonata
           his call
        c. Ne intercetterò la telefonata
           I of-him will intercept the call

       d. Gianni, di cui intercetterò la telefonata . .
          Gianni, of whom I will intercept the call

(6)   a. la cattura del soldato (da parte del nemico)
          the capture of the soldier (by the enemy)
       b. la sua cattura (da parte ...)
          his capture (by ...)
       c. Ne annunceranno la cattura
          They of-him will announce the capture
       d. il soldato di cui annunceranno la cattura
          the soldier of whom they will announce the capture

The most interesting cases for generalization (1) are, however, those of head Nouns like *descrizione* ('description'), ambiguous between an active and a passive reading, or like *libro* ('book'), or *foto* ('picture'), designating a material object for which a 'possessor' can be expressed in addition to the author (the agent). Consider, in fact, that (7)a and b are both ambiguous between the theme and agent reading of the argument:

(7)   a. la descrizione di Gianni
          the description of Gianni
       b. la sua descrizione
          his description

However, in (8)a the possessive can only be the agent, and in (8)b it can only be the theme; accordingly, the extracted element must express the agent in (9) and the theme in (10):

(8)   a. la sua descrizione di Maria
          his description of Maria
       b. la sua descrizione da parte di Maria
          hi description by Maria

(8)   a. Ne interruppi la descrizione di Maria
          I of-him interrupted the description of Maria
       b. Gianni, di cui interruppi la descrizione di Maria
          Gianni, of whom I interrupted the description of Maria

(10)   a. Ne interruppi la descrizione da parte di Maria
          I of-him interrupted the description by Maria
       b. Gianni, di cui interruppi la descrizione da parte di Maria
          Gianni, of whom I interrupted the description by Maria

As examples (9) and (10) show, Cinque's generalization extends uniformly (in many instances even more clearly) to nominalizations in the event interpretation, like *descrizione* here. Cinque (1980) also argues convincingly that the cases in which the generalization he proposes appears to be superficially violated can be independently shown to concern a PP reanalysed as external to the NP, perhaps after extraposition, a process rare in Romance and governed by some lexical idiosyncrasies.

    Analogous to the cases of (7)–(10) is (11): while (11)a is in principle ambiguous, with either PP interpretable as the possessor (and the other as the theme, or, if human, also as the author), only the possessor can be expressed through a possessive in (11)b, and, thus, extracted in (c) and (d):[6]

(11) a. Ho ammirato tutte le foto di Gianni/di mia sorella/della
        fondazione
        I admired all the pictures of Gianni/of my sister/of the foundation
      b. Ho ammirato tutte le sue foto di Gianni
        I admired all her pictures of Gianni
      c. Ne ho ammirato tutte le foto di Gianni
        I of-it admired all the pictures of Gianni
      d. mia sorella/la fondazione, di cui ho ammirato tutte le foto di
        Gianni
        my sister of whom/the foundation of which I admired all the
        pictures of Gianni

Accordingly, the following examples are marginal in the (pragmatically plausible) reading where *suoi*, *ne* and *di cui* are understood as referring to the author (i.e. as agents):

(12) a. Ho rovinato tutti i suoi dischi di mio padre
        I damaged all his records of my father
      b. Ne ho rovinato tutti i dischi di mio padre
        I of-it damaged all the records of my father
      c. l'orchestra di Vienna, di cui ho rovinato tutti i dischi di mio padre
        the Vienna Orchestra, of which I damaged all the records of my
        father

Finally, let us note that, as also pointed out in Zubizarreta (1979), the appearance of the 'opacity' effect is not sensitive to the type of categorial realization of the 'subject', e.g. whether it is expressed as a bare Adjective, and not as a PP or a possessive:

(13) a. Ricordo la progressiva distruzione tedesca della repubblica
        cecoslovacca, nel 1938–9
        I remembered the gradual German destruction of the Czech
        republic in 1938–9
      b. *Ricordo la sua progressiva distruzione tedesca nel 1938–9
        I remember its stepwise German destruction in 1938–9
      c. *la repubblica cecoslovacca, di cui ricordo la progressiva
        distruzione tedesca nel 1938–9
        the Czech republic, of which I remember the gradual German
        destruction in 1938–9

Once again, what really counts is that when no possessivization for an argument is allowed, no extraction is possible either. Instead, if the subject AP *tedesca* ('German') is replaced by *da parte della Germania* ('by

Germany'), both (13)b and (13)c become perfectly grammatical, since *by*-phrases do not count as 'subjects', as Cinque observed. In fact, evidence that *by*-phrases in NPs are rather adverbial in status and do not strictly belong to the argument frame of the head Noun is also brought in Jaeggli (1986) and Longobardi (1985).[7]

It can also be added, in support of the generalization, that some *di* + NP sequences, which are adverbial in nature, fail at the same time to be possessivized and extracted, giving rise to minimal contrasts like the following:

(14)   a. In quel museo si possono vedere opere di tre pittori fiamminghi
           In that museum it is possible to see works of three Flemish painters
        b. In quel museo si possono vedere opere di 300 anni fa
           In that museum it is possible to see works of 300 years ago

(15)   a. In quel museo si possono vedere loro opere (dei pittori fiamminghi)
           In that museum it is possible to see their works (of the Flemish painters)
        b. In quel museo si possono vedere loro opere (*di 300 anni fa)
           In that museum it is possible to see works of theirs (* of 300 years ago)
        c. Di quanti pittori fiamminghi si possono vedere opere, in quel museo?
           Of how many Flemish painters is it possible to see works, in that museum?
        d. *Di quanti anni fa si possono vedere opere, in quel museo?
           Of how many years ago is it possible to see works, in that museum?

Limiting ourselves to these examples, we will refer the reader to Cinque (1980) for further data and for an account of some apparent lexical exceptions to the proposed generalization. The latter extends not only to Italian, but to a number of other Romance languages, as is clear from the original work of Ruwet (1972a) and the research reported in Steriade (1981), Milner (1982), Zubizarreta (1979), Aoun (1985), which are especially concerned with French (and, as far as Steriade's is concerned, also with Rumanian), and by Torrego (1986, on Spanish), and it is likely to hold for Romance in general. In his paper, Cinque proposed to derive such a generalization from the opacity induced by the subject of the NP to the trace of other arguments and internal constituents (i.e. from the SSC or, in more recent terms, from principle A of the Binding Theory).

Such a proposal implies, of course, two assumptions: first, certain NPs must always contain a phonetically unrealized but syntactically functioning subject able to induce opacity to the other arguments (such is the case, e.g. of *desiderio* ('desire') in (3)); secondly, the trace of wh-movement must be subject to opacity (principle A) as well as that of clitic-movement. The first assumption seems quite reasonable. In fact, such a supposed 'invisible' subject induces opacity also to lexical anaphors; consider the following sentences with the head Noun *paura* ('fear'), which belongs to the same class as *desiderio* (but is pragmatically more appropriate for some of our examples):

(16)   Gianni ricorda la paura di se stesso
          Gianni remembers the fear of himself

In (16) *Gianni* and *se stesso* may corefer only if the 'subject' of the fear is understood as the same as *Gianni*. That this phonetically undetectable subject is obligatory here is also suggested by the fact that the pronoun is necessarily disjoint from *Gianni* if the latter is the understood experiencer of the fear in (17):

(17)   La paura di lui ha reso Gianni ansioso
          The fear of him made Gianni anxious

Detailed evidence in favour of the existence of such an empty 'subject' of NPs is presented in chapters 3 and 4, along with an investigation of the far-reaching typological consequences of this hypothesis, based on work by Roeper (1984) and Chomsky (1986a). Unfortunately, the second assumption required by Cinque's theory, i.e., that wh-traces are subject to principle A of the Binding Theory, although widely held in the 1970s, seems now to be less tenable (cf. Chomsky 1980 and Rizzi 1982a, ch. 2, for discussion and motivation), as noticed in fact by Cinque (1980) himself.[8] We will thus try to derive generalization (1) from more abstract principles without resorting to the notion of opacity and to principle A.

2   On deriving Cinque's generalization

Consider first that the fact that only phrases allowed to appear as possessives in Spec can undergo extraction may be interpreted as suggesting that it is precisely in Spec that the relevant trace of constituents extracted from NPs must lie.[9] How can this interpretation of (1) be theoretically derived? In order to do so in a satisfactory way, we will try to develop a theory embodying the three following assumptions and to explore both its empirical consequences and the possibility of deducing it from more general conditions:

(18)   a. There exists a general principle determining which phrases may
            appear in the Spec of an NP
        b. Every trace must be properly governed by a head and if a trace is
            properly governed by N it must have an antecedent within Nmax
        c. A trace in the Spec NP can be governed by an external head

Let us comment on these three assumptions, starting from the last one. As is known from the case of exceptionally Case-marked subjects and from the classical Comp-trace phenomenon, the Spec position of some IPs must be accessible to proper government from outside; similar arguments are likely to be reproducible for the Spec of CP (see Lasnik and Saito 1984; Chomsky 1986b; Longobardi forthcoming) when it contains traces of extracted adjuncts. From the definition of government and proper government that we gave e.g. in Longobardi (1985b), it already follows, actually, that the Spec position of any Xmax should be accessible to proper government from the outside. There is some empirical evidence suggesting that this hypothesis is correct also in the specific case in which the Xmax in question is precisely an NP. It concerns the extraction of QPs which are usually assumed to occupy the Spec position of NP, i.e. French *combien* or *beaucoup* (cf. Obenauer (1976; Kayne 1981a):

(19)   ?Il faut beaucoup qu'il rencontre *e* d'amis
        It is necessary many that he meets friends

The crucial role of proper government of the trace by the Verb *rencontre* is confirmed by the ungrammaticality of (20), whose contrast with (19) is likely to represent a typical ECP-based subject–object asymmetry:

(20)   *Il faut beaucoup que *e* d'amis le recontrent
        It is necessary many that friends meet him

Now consider (18)b: in order to restrict extractions just to elements in the Spec position we must combine the already established theory of government with a further idea, namely that Nouns are not themselves sufficient governors, in a sense to be made precise, for the trace of an extracted constituent. Notice that if the Spec position is reached by some arguments of the head Noun through movement (see Anderson 1979; see also ch. 3 below, where it is argued that actually all prenominal possessive arguments bind a postnominal trace in Romance, although not in Germanic), it becomes necessary to assume that Nouns are insufficient governors only for the trace of extracted constituents, but not for that of NP-internally preposed ones. It is precisely this assumption that we will try to derive from general principles in section 8 below. The structure of sentences with extractions from NP in Romance would, under this analysis, be like that represented in (21):

(21)   a. il soldato di cui ho visto la *t* cattura *t*
          the soldier of whom I saw the capture
    b. ne ho visto la *t* cattura *t*
          of-him I saw the capture

Structures like (21) bear an obvious and, we would like to claim, theoretically significant resemblance to the one assumed by van Riemsdijk (1978) for P-stranding in Dutch (and other Germanic languages), exemplified in (22)a, and also a theoretically less significant one to English extractions from complements of *believe* after passivization and ECM, as in (22)b:

(22)   a. Waar heb je *t* op *t* gerekend?
          What did you count on?
    b. Who do you believe *t* to have been captured *t*?

Our descriptive hypothesis can then be summarized in the following way: for each class of head Nouns one of the genitive arguments, chosen according to independent principles of structural prominence, hinted at in (18)a and carefully formulated below on the basis of previous discussions by Cinque (1980, 1981a) and Giorgi (1986) (see for English, Hornstein 1977, Anderson 1979; for French Milner 1982, Aoun 1985), is allowed to occupy the Specifier position: there, it can be either superficially realized as a possessive (only if it is pronominal or anaphoric in Romance, any NP with 's in English) or moved away by cliticization or wh-extraction, leaving a trace properly governed from outside the NP.

    If such an approach is on the right track, it will provide strong additional evidence for the accessibility of Spec to proper government from outside and thus a formulation of Chomsky's (1986b) Minimality Condition allowing lexical heads, at least in some cases, not to protect categories in their Spec from external governors.

    Consider now another consequence: if we want to adopt the proposed framework to capture Cinque's opacity-like effect on non-subjects, it becomes quite implausible to try to extend it to cover restrictions on extractions from NP with P-stranding in English, however similar the phenomena may be on the surface:

(23)   a. Who did you see a picture of?
    b. *Who did you see my picture of?

In fact, since the fundamental insight behind our analysis is precisely that of restricting extraction to arguments independently able to appear in

Spec as possessives (the so-called 'subjects', either bearing an internal or external θ-role), then, no extraction-through-Spec should be expected for (23)a, since no overt movement to Spec can ever strand a P:

(24)   *I saw John's picture of

Trying to reduce the ungrammaticality of (23)b to a theory of extraction-through-Spec is, then, likely to weaken seriously the empirical motivation which suggests such an approach.[10] The same reasoning obviously applies to extraction of non-genitive PPs which is claimed to be sometimes possible in English (for further remarks on this point see n. 58).

3   The Possessivization Principle

Let us try, now, to be more precise about the principles governing the appearance of an argument of N as a possessive, the only form that can occur in Spec (see also ch. 3), i.e. about point (18)a above.

The cited works about Romance and English NPs have shown that the phenomenon seems to be crosslinguistically governed by the following conditions:

(25)   a. A non-genitive phrase may never be expressed as a possessive
        b. A genitive phrase bearing a possessor role may be expressed as a possessive
        c. A genitive phrase bearing an external θ-role may be expressed as a possessive only if no possessor is *overtly* present
        d. A genitive phrase bearing an internal θ-role may be expressed as a possessive only if no possessor or external argument is *overtly* present
        e. No more than one phrase may appear as a possessive
        f. With some head Nouns (e.g. *desiderio* 'desire') no internal argument may ever be expressed as a possessive even if no other genitive phrase is overtly realized

The specification 'overtly' is required since in chapter 3 below evidence will be provided that an empty subject may cooccur in Romance NPs with possessivization of an internal argument: thus, in Italian the structure (26)b can be argued to underlie the corresponding string, which is obviously perfectly acceptable and contrasts in grammaticality with (26)a, where possessivization 'crosses over' a lexical subject overtly realizing Genitive Case:

(26) a. *[la sua$_i$ [descrizione t_i] di Maria]
         her/his/its (theme) description of Maria (agent)
      b. [la sua$_i$ [descrizione t_i][$_{NP}e$]]
         her/his/its (theme) description (+ understood agent)

Consider now the possibility of collapsing these conditions into a formally more appealing principle. To do so, we must first examine a new piece of empirical evidence concerning the argument structure of NPs. Recall that Giorgi has argued in chapter 1 that the internal arguments of head Nouns and the external one are separated by an intermediate projection N′ which constitutes the c-domain of the internal ones. The main empirical consequences motivating such a proposal are a number of binding asymmetries concerning both anaphors and bound pronouns when used with internal or external roles. A similar approach we may take to distinguish two different levels of attachment for possessors (more generally, R-related phrases in Higginbotham's (1983) sense) and thematic external arguments (generally agents or experiencers) is the following: non-possessive anaphors and pronouns are normally not very natural outside N′ (cf. ch. 1, n. 28), but more deeply embedded possessives may provide the desired argument; consider, in fact, that in (27), with the possessive pronoun *sua* referentially dependent on *Gianni*, the two genitive phrases may freely exchange their interpretations as the possessor and the agent (i.e. the author of the letters), owing to the usual relative freedom of surface order for postnominal arguments (see ch. 1):

(27)   Tutte le lettere di Gianni di sua madre sono state sequestrate
         All the letters of Gianni of his mother were confiscated

But, if we either replace *sua* by a possessive anaphor, like *propria*, bound to *Gianni* or this latter by a quantified NP binding the pronoun as a variable, the interpretation tends to be unique: the genitive phrase containing the bound anaphor or pronoun must be understood as the agent and the antecedent phrase as the possessor:

(28) a. Tutte le lettere di Gianni della propria madre sono state
         sequestrate
         All the letters of Gianni (possessor) of self's mother (agent) were
         confiscated
      b. Tutte le lettere di ogni soldato di sua madre sono state sequestrate
         All the letters of every soldier (possessor) of his mother (agent)
         were confiscated

As expected, restricting our attention to the sloppy-identity reading of the possessive pronoun in (29), the latter is only possible if *Piero* and *Gianni* are understood as possessors and *sua madre* ('his mother') as the author:

(29)   Le lettere di Piero di sua madre sono state sequestrate, quelle di Gianni no
The letters of Piero of his mother were confiscated, those of Gianni were not
i. Piero's letters written by Piero's mother were confiscated, Gianni's letters written by Gianni's own mother were not
ii. *Piero's mother's letters written by Piero were confiscated, Gianni's mother's letters written by Gianni were not

Under current assumptions on binding, these data suggest that agents are in the c-domain of possessors and not vice versa.[11] Slightly generalizing Giorgi's proposal (ch. 1), we may assume that genitive arguments of Nouns may appear at three different levels depending on their interpretations – internal arguments as sisters of N, external ones as sisters of N′, and possessors as sisters of N″ – and that each projection of N identifies a c-domain. Thus we have evidence to assert that the internal structure of an NP may be three-tiered as in the following case (or even in its stylistically rearranged variants, where the linear order of arguments no longer reflects constituency):[12]

(30) $[_{NP}$Il celebre $[_{N''}[_{N'}$ ritratto della regina] di Lord Snowdon] di quel famoso collezionista]
The renowned portrait of the queen of (= made by) Lord Snowdon of (= belonging to) that famous collector

Now we are finally in a position to make complete sense of the various observations found in the literature and to collapse (25)a–e into the simpler and more explanatory (31) (as for (25)f, however, a partial explanation will be provided in ch. 3, sect. 9):

(31)   Possessivization Principle:
The unique phrase allowed to appear as a possessive is the hierarchically highest genitive argument of an NP

Accordingly, the following judgements hold with respect to possessivization, as exemplified for the sake of clarity through the use of the possessive relative anaphor *cui* (see Cinque, 1981b):

(32)   a. Quel famoso collezionista, il cui celebre ritratto della regina di
           Lord Snowdon è un capolavoro della fotografia
           That famous collector, whose renowned portrait of the queen of
           Lord Snowdon is a masterpiece of photography
        b. ??Lord Snowdon, il cui celebre ritratto della regina di quel famoso
           collezionista
           Lord Snowdon, whose renowned portrait of the queen of that
           famous collector
        c. *La regina, il cui celebre ritratto di Lord Snowdon (di quel famoso
           collezionista)
           the queen, whose renowned portrait of Lord Snowdon (of that
           famous collector)

(The diacritics obviously refer to the relevant interpretations.)[13] It is clear
from the brief discussion of examples (26) that the Possessivization
Principle (31) cannot be derived from an intervention constraint or
opacity-like condition on antecedent–trace relationships: in other words
if the overt genitive subject of (26)a induced opacity to the trace of the
possessivized object or created a 'minimality' barrier (roughly in
Chomsky's 1986b sense) to its relationship to the antecedent, it would be
unclear why the same effect is not yielded by the phonetically unrealized
one in (26)b. Therefore, let us attempt to suggest another kind of plausible
structural encoding for principle (31). The difference between lexical
subjects (blocking possessivization of the lower arguments) and empty
ones (not blocking it) suggests a possible account in terms of Case theory.
Suppose, with Chomsky (1986a), that Genitive Case is assigned at D-
structure to all non-inherently prepositional arguments of N (except,
perhaps, clauses, owing to Stowell's (1981) Case Resistance Principle) and
that its realization, as distinct from assignment, takes place at S-structure
in possibly different forms; one form is *of* insertion (*di* insertion in Italian,
see ch. 1) for postnominal genitive phrases, others are superficial Case
agreement with the head N, as is presumable in the case of referential
Adjectives (e.g. *German* in (13) above; for these see especially ch. 3, sect.
4) or of possessive pronouns in many languages, insertion of a phrase-final
morpheme like English *'s*, of a head-final one like German *-s*, of inflected
word endings, as e.g. in Latin or Greek.[14] Among such realizations of
genitive there is a subset defining the class of elements that can be termed
'possessive NPs', in the sense of being subject to our Possessivization
Principle (31); this subset is essentially represented by two main types: on
the one hand we find realizations of genitive in Spec (i.e. on the left side
of NPs with basically postnominal complements), like English *'s*, German

-*s* when realized prenominally, on the other, those more indirect realizations of genitive arguments which obtain when the argument in question surfaces as an inflected element which may be argued to Case-agree with the head N (e.g. Romance referential Adjectives, like those of (13)). Of course, the two types have an intersection, formed by those elements which agree in surface Case with the head N and may (e.g. Italian possessive pronouns like *mio* ('my') etc.) or must (English, French, German pronouns like *my*, *mon*, *mein*, etc.) occur prenominally.[15] Technically speaking, the constraints on the interpretation of the possessive elements summarized in the Possessivization Principle (31) could be derived from the following structural assumptions:[16] suppose that an additional feature [Poss], determining the future realization of the genitive assigned at D-structure, can be attributed to one of the arguments. As a matter of fact, such a formalism will be independently motivated later on (see ch. 3, sect. 12 again). Suppose also, now, that this feature [Poss] percolates down from Nmax, stopping at the first level where an argument which has genitive to realize occurs. This makes it automatically sensitive to the independently attested structural hierarchy and, since [Poss] is a realization feature, it will naturally skip an empty argument, whose assigned Case is not realizable.[17]

At this point we may wonder whether the parallelism between extraction from NP (clitic movement or wh-movement) and possessivization cannot be captured in an alternative way, i.e. without taking movement to Spec as a necessary intermediate step toward extraction. Suppose, in fact, that we claimed that a head Noun is a proper governor only for the trace of the phrase uniquely identified as possessivizable by principle (31) above: under a theory requiring a proper head governor for every trace, no other phrase could move, either to the Spec position, to become a possessive, or outside, under extraction. Thus the two identical patterns would each follow independently from the same principle (the head-government requirement).

Such an account is, however, based on a not so obvious empirical assumption, namely that all possessives (except, possibly, those bearing a possessor role), even in postnominal position, are necessarily related to a trace, so that the generalization embodied in (25)a–e can be captured by reformulating (31) as a condition on movement. No conclusive evidence has been provided to establish such a claim, however plausible it may be in some cases (see ch. 3 below).

Furthermore, the suggested alternative account seems hardly tenable on theoretical grounds: a principle like (31) looks idiosyncratic and unparalleled, hence very suspicious, as a condition on proper government by a lexical category, whereas it is quite natural as a condition on possessivization if we understand the latter, *à la* Cinque, as a process uniquely assigning an argument of N the same surface prominence as subjects of clauses.

For these conceptual reasons the theory of two-step movement through Spec seems the correct account for extraction from NP in Romance, i.e. the one which best expresses the systematic parallelism between extractability and possessivization. However, there exists also a good amount of direct empirical evidence supporting this hypothesis. Examining such evidence will be our task in the next few sections.

4   Movement through Spec vs opacity

In addition to solving the conceptual problem posed by the appeal to opacity for wh-traces, our hypothesis is likely to display also a slight empirical advantage over Cinque's original approach. Consider, in fact, that, in Italian, pied piping under wh-movement of heavy constituents, even of sentential ones, is relatively well tolerated at a certain formal stylistic level:

(33)   (?)Mario, che tu abbia visto il quale proprio non credo
            Mario, that you saw whom I really do not believe.

We may, then, wonder whether sentential complements of Nouns can be so wh-extracted. Let us first consider the sentential object of an 'active' Noun, like *idea* ('idea'):

(34)   a. *Mario, che tu possa sposare il quale io disapprovo l'idea
            Mario, that you may marry whom I disapprove the idea
        b. (?)Mario, l'idea che tu possa sposare il quale io disapprovo
            Mario, the idea that you may marry whom I disapprove

As can be seen, pied piping of the whole NP is acceptable, but extraction of the sentential complement alone is out.

The ungrammaticality of (34)a follows both from the opacity theory and from our approach. In the former we may, in fact, appeal to the presence of an opacizing empty subject of the Noun *idea*, in the latter to the impossibility for the complement of such a Noun to raise to the Spec position, as evidenced by the fact that (35)b cannot be understood as the pronominalized version of (35)a, but rather only with the possessive bearing the experiencer role:

(35)   a. l'idea di un matrimonio con Mario
            the idea of a marriage with Mario

    b. la sua idea
       her/his/*its idea

There are certain cases, however, where the opacity theory fails to predict the ungrammaticality of extraction; consider the following structures:

(36)   a. La probabilità di una guerra appare molto bassa
        The probability of a war appears very low
    b. La probabilità che ci sia una guerra appare molto bassa
        The probability that there will be a war appears very low
(37)   a. Una guerra, di cui non so valutare la probabilità, sarebbe
        catastrofica
        A war, of which I cannot evaluate the probability, would be
        catastrophic
    b. *Una guerra, che ci sia la quale non so valutare la probabilità ...
        A war, that there will be which I cannot evaluate the probability

In (37)a, extraction is possible under the opacity theory, since the genitive phrase, being the only conceivable argument of the head Noun *probabilità* ('probability'), which does not assign other θ-roles in these structures (cf. *La mia probabilità di una guerra/che ci sia una guerra*), cannot be induced opacity by any subject (actually, it should, perhaps, itself count as the subject). By parity of argument, the opacity theory, without specific stipulations, would allow (37)b. The extraction-through-Spec hypothesis may, instead, draw the crucial distinction on independent grounds; the genitive phrase may, in fact, be extracted, since, unlike sentences, it can be moved to Spec as a possessive; consider the following contrast:

(38)   a. Una guerra, la cui probabilità è molto bassa, sorprenderebbe tutti
        A war, whose probability is very low, would surprise everyone
    b. *Che ci fosse una guerra in Italia, la cui probabilità è molto bassa,
        sorprenderebbe tutti
        That there could be a war in Italy, whose probability is very low,
        would surprise everyone

The possessive relative anaphor *cui* may express a nominal argument but not a sentential one, suggesting that sentential arguments may never appear in Spec under any circumstance; that sentential constituents are generally unable to move to Spec can be more directly concluded on the grounds of English contrasts like the following:[18]

(39)   a. the probability that Mary will come
    b. *that Mary will come's probability
    c. the probability of this event
    d. this event's probability

Such a property of clausal arguments is not simply due to their 'heaviness', as shown by (40), where the Spec contains an NP with a relative clause inside:

(40)   a. The man who just left's idea
        b. The bakery I like's best cake

Rather, it can be more plausibly attributed to a failure to be marked for Genitive Case, the latter being a prerequisite to possessivization, hence for movement to Spec, as suggested above (see our formulation 31).[19] If movement to Spec is independently forbidden for clausal constituents, our approach to extraction predicts precisely that no such constituent will ever be able to move out of an NP, hence correctly predicts the ungrammaticality of sentences like (37)b, as opposed to (37)a.

5   Government into Spec

In this and the following sections we will try to provide a more elaborate and persuasive argument in favour of our hypothesis that extraction from NP always occurs through Spec. Consider that our proposal crucially requires a trace in the Spec of any NP which has undergone extraction of one of its arguments; we have also suggested before that every trace must be properly governed by a head and that Nouns are not sufficient as proper governors for a trace antecedent-free in the NP (see (18)b above). If both these premises are correct and if such a head-government requirement must be fulfilled at S-structure (or anyway before intermediate traces of extracted arguments may be deleted, as suggested in Lasnik and Saito (1984) and in Chomsky (1986b), under a possible interpretation of the Projection Principle), we must expect the trace in the Spec of an NP always to require proper government by an external head (see (18)c above), a possibility independently allowed, as we have seen in section 2.

Suppose, now, that we can find a head which properly governs for the CED (see Huang 1982; Longobardi 1985b; i.e. L-marks, hence removing barrierhood, in Chomsky's 1986b terms) one of its arguments, so as to allow regular extraction from it, when it is sentential, without, however, being able to govern a trace into the Spec of this argument (disallowing, thus, strict successive cyclicity). Our prediction is that when the argument in question is an NP, extraction will be totally impossible. If the test can be constructed and the prediction turns out to be correct, this will represent strong evidence in favour of the hypothesis of extraction through Spec and, more generally, in favour of the set of theoretical premises that we have assumed. Identifying such a case requires, however, a preliminary refinement of the notion of accessibility of Spec to an external governor, which we will achieve in this section, starting from the analysis of the following paradigm in Italian:

(41)   a. ??Gianni, a cui parlare *e* sarà difficile
           Gianni, to whom talking will be difficult
        b. ??Gianni, a cui temo/penso/credo che parlare *e* sarà difficile
           Gianni, to whom I fear/think/believe that it will be difficult to talk
        c. Gianni, a cui temo/penso/credo che sarà difficile parlare *e*

Examples (41)a and b represent instances of extraction from a preverbal subject, a typical CED violation, which is completely rescued, as expected, when the subject appears postverbally in a properly governed position, as in (41)c (cf. Longobardi 1985b). However, the effect of the violations in (41) is incomparably milder than that displayed by other purported CED violations involving an extracted PP; consider, in fact, the following extractions of PPs out of the most common types of adjuncts:

(42)   a. *Gianni, al quale sapevo molte cose anche prima di parlare *e*
           Gianni, to whom I knew many things even before talking
        b. *Gianni, al quale ho saputo molte cose avendo parlato *e*
           Gianni, to whom I learned many things having talked

In order to understand exactly what is going on in (41)a and b we must also consider (43):

(43)   a. *Gianni, a cui mi chiedo quando parlare *e* sarà possibile
           Gianni, to whom I wonder when talking will be possible
        b. *Gianni, a cui non so proprio di che cosa parlare *e* sarà possibile
           Gianni, to whom I don't know of what talking will be possible

In (43) the CED violation manifests itself with all the expected force. Again, inversion of the subject makes the sentences acceptable in a language allowing extraction from simple wh-islands, like Italian:

(44)   a. Gianni, a cui mi chiedo quando sarà possibile parlare *e*
        b. Gianni, a cui non so proprio di che cosa sarà possibile parlare *e*

A comparison between (43) and (41)a and b immediately suggests that the weakening of the expected CED violation in the latter crucially hinges on the accessibility of the Spec of the intermediate CP to the extracted wh-phrase (in (41)a) or to its trace (in (41)b). Our theoretical proposal will then be the following: assume that in (41)a the wh-phrase *a cui* has first moved to the Spec of the subject infinitival CP; at that point further extraction should be prevented by the CED. Suppose, however, that the CED (or, more generally, island constraints) is so formulated as to establish a constituent (when non-properly governed or, equivalently, non-L-marked as one) as a barrier for a certain empty category only if it also contains the governor of the latter. Such a hypothesis actually follows directly from a Connectedness Condition approach of the kind proposed in Kayne (1983) and modified in Longobardi (1985b): in fact, if the governor of the trace is external to the island, it will start a new set of g-projections immune from its effects. We suggest, then, that either the wh-phrase itself or its trace in the Spec of the intermediate CP are somehow required to trigger government of the other trace trapped within the island, forming structures like (45)a and b, respectively:

(45)   a. $[_{CP1}$ a cui $C[_{IP}[_{CP2}$ t $[_{IP}$ PRO parlare $t]]...]]$
          b. ...penso $[_{CP1}$ t che $[_{IP}$ $[_{CP2}$ t $[_{IP}$ PRO parlare $t]]...]]$

In order to satisfy the head-government requirement we must suppose that what governs the embedded trace in (45) is not just the antecedent (wh-phrase or intermediate trace), but rather the head of CP1, empty in (45)a and expressed by *che* in (45)b. Why, then, is the presence of an antecedent in the Spec of CP1 required? We must suppose that a non-lexical head, like a complementizer, only governs under coindexing with the governee, an assumption independently made in Longobardi (1985b) (see the introduction to this chapter). Such a coindexation with the more embedded trace can be ensured through the antecedent in CP1 via Spec–head agreement in pre-IP position (see Chomsky 1986b), so as to end up with structures like (46):[20]

(46)   a. ...a cui_i C_i $[_{IP}$ $[_{CP}$ t_i $[_{IP}...]]...]$
          b. t_i che_i $[_{IP}$ $[_{CP}$ t_i $[_{IP}...]]...]$

We are thus hypothesizing that a head, namely C, may govern not only the Spec of its own complement IP, i.e. the subject infinitival CP2 of (45), but also the Spec of the latter containing the lower trace.[21] This will be a case for an unbounded interpretation of the notion of Spec accessibility, as expressed in the following statement:

(47)   If α governs Xmax, then α governs the Spec of Xmax

The still dubious acceptability of (41)a and b suggests that either such a recursive interpretation or the Spec–head coindexing process must yield a certain degree of marginality (see below for a brief discussion). Let us put aside for the moment any further formalization of (47) and rather consider the evidence supporting our account of (41).[22] First, notice that the contrast with (43) immediately follows from the fact that in the latter, given some version of the doubly filled Comp filter, no relevant wh-trace may be present in the Spec of CP1 to trigger the required indexing of the head C. Second, consider that the same explanation applies to the French contrast between (48) and (20) repeated below:

(48)   ??Combien faut-il que *e* d'amis le rencontrent?
          How many is it necessary that friends meet him?
(20)   *Il faut beaucoup que *e* d'amis le rencontrent
          It is necessary many that friends meet him

Such a contrast, pointed out by Obenauer (1976), has been traced back by Kayne (1981a) to the fact that *combien*, a wh-word unlike *beaucoup*, can overcome an ECP violation through successive cyclic movement, i.e. through government from Comp. The configuration is analogous to that of (41) and can be easily rephrased in our terms: an intermediate trace of *combien* indexes, via Spec–Head agreement, the complementizer *que*, which then governs the original trace in the Spec position of the NP subject of IP (i.e. of the Spec of its complement).[23]

Consider, further, that if an intermediate trace is necessary to rescue (41)b from a much more severe violation, such a trace will itself have to be properly head-governed, i.e. in our framework will have to be governed across CP by a higher predicate, e.g. *pensare* ('think') in (41)b, another case of government into Spec. We know, however, that sentential complements to a factive Verb, like e.g. *rimpiangere* ('regret'), do not allow (perhaps for lack of proper government by such a Verb[24]) a trace in their Spec; this is shown very clearly in French, in fact, by the impossibility, under *regretter*, of Stylistic Inversion and of the application of the *que-qui* rule, two processes arguably requiring a wh-trace in pre-IP position (see Rouveret 1980 and Kayne 1981a). Our prediction is, then, that substituting *rimpiangere* for *pensare*, or for other Verbs, in (41)b should tend to restore the full ungrammaticality due to the CED, which is, in fact, true:

(49)   *Gianni, a cui rimpiango che parlare *e* sia così difficile
          Gianni to whom I regret that talking is so difficult

No contrast appears, however, between (41)c and (50), since with the subject inverted, an intermediate trace is no longer required:

(50)　　　Gianni, a cui rimpiango che sia così difficile parlare *e*
　　　　　Gianni, to whom I regret that it is so difficult to talk

Our analysis receives further considerable support from yet another fact: notice that we are crucially assuming not only that the extracted wh-phrase or its trace must occur in the Spec of CP1 of (45), but also that another trace must be able to appear in the Spec of CP2, in order to be accessible to external government: in more traditional terms, no Comp can be skipped. This correctly leads us to predict also the following contrasts:

(51)　　　a.　??Gianni, a cui parlare *e* non è facile
　　　　　　　Gianni, to whom speaking is not easy
　　　　　b.　*Gianni, a cui quando parlare *e* non è chiaro
　　　　　　　Gianni, to whom when to speak is not clear
(52)　　　a.　??Maria, a cui temo che parlare *e* mi darà fastidio
　　　　　　　Maria to whom I fear that speaking will bother me
　　　　　b.　*Maria, a cui temo che come parlare *e* sia un problema ancora irrisolto
　　　　　　　Maria, to whom I fear that how to speak is still an unresolved problem

Extraction from a subject wh-island in postverbal position is instead possible, as, for instance in the inverted version of (51)b:

(53)　　　Gianni, a cui non è chiaro quando parlare *e*

In the light of the analysis so far provided consider now some other cases:

(54)　　　a.　??Gianni, con cui accade spesso che parlare *e* non sia possibile
　　　　　　　Gianni, with whom it often happens that talking is not possible
　　　　　b.　??Gianni, con cui era prevedibile che parlare *e* non sarebbe stato facile
　　　　　　　Gianni, with whom it was foreseeable that talking would not be easy
(55)　　　a.　*Gianni, con cui l'ha impressionata che parlare *e* non fosse possibile
　　　　　　　Gianni, with whom it impressed her that talking was not possible
　　　　　b.　*Gianni, con cui ci dà fastidio/preoccupa che parlare *e* non sia ancora possibile
　　　　　　　Gianni, with whom it bothers/worries us that talking is not yet possible

    c. *Gianni, con cui era fastidioso/preoccupante che parlare *e* non
       fosse possibile
       Gianni, with whom it was bothersome/worrying that talking was
       not possible

In (54) extraction always takes place from an 'inverted' subject that seems
to be an internal argument of the head of the predicate, namely an
unaccusative Verb, an Adjective derived from a transitive Verb and a
passive verbal complex. In all these cases the acceptability of the CED
violation is comparable to that found with Verbs such as *pensare* and the
like. We conclude, then, that the heads of such predicates allow a trace in
the Spec of the embedded CP, arguably by properly governing it. In (55),
by contrast, we find inverted subjects with Verbs which do not assign
accusative case (call them 'unergative' Verbs) and with Adjectives or
participles related to such Verbs. Here the judgement on the relevant
extraction tends to be the same as in the *rimpiangere* case, which we have
analysed before (see (49)). We can hypothesize, therefore, that in such
cases the predicate is not able to have access to the Spec of CP as a proper
governor of the trace. The difference must be related to the fact that here
the relevant CP does not have the position and the role of an internal
argument of the predicate. Notice that it is very plausible that such an
inverted subject of unergative predicates is itself properly head-governed,
if that position is the extraction site for wh-movement in languages like
Italian (see Rizzi 1982a). According to standard analyses (see Burzio 1981,
1986; Chomsky 1981), we will assume that such subjects are included in,
or at least not excluded from (see Chomsky 1986b), the VP. Crucially for
us, it also appears that sentential subjects of this sort do usually allow for
extractions, i.e they are properly governed for the CED as well (L-marked
in Chomsky's 1986b sense), as shown by the immediate improvement of
examples (55), when the infinitival CP is inverted into a properly governed
position:[25]

(56)   a. Gianni, con cui l'ha impressionata che non fosse possibile parlare *e*
       b. Gianni, con cui ci preoccupa che non sia ancora possibile parlare *e*
       c. Gianni, con cui era fastidioso che non fosse possibile parlare *e*

Notice that the non-accessibility or only marginal accessibility to external
government of the Spec of the CP following these predicates is not likely
to be too directly related to the factive semantics of most of these clauses;
in fact, the phenomenon extends to instances of these constructions where

no factivity presupposition comes into play, owing to the conditional mood of the Verb:

(57) a. *Gianni, a cui mi preoccuperebbe che parlare *e* non fosse facile
          Gianni to whom it would worry me that talking was not easy
      b. *Gianni, con cui potrebbe impressionare Maria che parlare *e* non fosse permesso
          Gianni, with whom it might impress Maria that talking was not allowed

Moreover, other Verbs, belonging to the same class of potentially factive and 'psychological' (in Postal's 1971 and Ruwet's 1972b sense) predicates, but displaying *essere* auxiliary and no direct object, so as to be classed among Burzio's unaccusatives, allow the construction we are discussing much more easily. Consider (58), minimally contrasting with (55) or (57):

(58) a. ?Gianni, con cui le è dispiaciuto che parlare *e* non fosse facile
          Gianni, with whom it displeased her that talking was not easy
      b. ??Gianni, con cui era spiacevole che parlare *e* non fosse ancora possibile
          Gianni with whom it was unpleasant that talking was not yet possible
      c. ?Gianni, con cui mi dispiacerebbe che parlare *e* non fosse più possibile
          Gianni, with whom it would displease me that talking was no longer possible

although the judgements are somewhat subtle, the performed test seems thus to systematically distinguish inverted subjects of unergative predicates from others.

We will then suppose that such predicates properly govern (or, equivalently, L-mark) their inverted subjects but do not have access to their specifiers. In other words, externally θ-marked phrases represent a barrier to government of their Spec but not to movement. This would follow if we restricted external government by a category α into Spec to specifiers contained within the complement of α: for a more formal elaboration see section 12 below. For now, let us just recall the two generalizations we have argued for in the course of this section:

(59) a. If α governs β and γ, where γ is the Spec of β, then α also governs the Spec of γ
      b. α governs δ across an Xmax boundary only if δ is contained within an internal argument of α.

From the latter it follows that

(60)   Unergative predicates, although properly governing their inverted
        subjects, do not govern into the Spec of the latter

In the next section we will exploit generalization (60) to construct the desired argument in favour of extraction from NP through the Spec position.

6   Extraction from inverted subjects

In the preceding section we have gained some further insight into the mechanism of Spec accessibility to an external governor and we have laid the basis for the explanation of the phenomena we are going to present in this section. Inverted subjects of unergative predicates (Verbs or Adjectives) seem in fact to provide the case required to perform the test sketched at the beginning of the last section: they allow for extraction, when they are CPs, but not for extraction through Spec (successive cyclicity). If extraction from NP always takes place through Spec (i.e. is successive-cyclic) our prediction is, then, that extraction will not be possible at all from NPs which are inverted subjects of unergative predicates.[26]

The prediction is obviously correct for *ne* extraction, as is known mainly from Burzio's (1981, 1986) work (see also Belletti and Rizzi 1981):[27]

(61)   a. (Ci) ha telefonato un complice dell'assassino
           (To-us) has phoned an accomplice of the murderer
        b. *(Ce) ne ha telefonato un complice
           (To-us) of-him has phoned an accomplice
(62)   a. E'scomparso un complice dell'assassino
           Has disappeared an accomplice of the murderer
        b. Ne è scomparso un complice
           Of-him has disappeared an accomplice
(63)   a. E' stato arrestato un complice dell'assassino
           Was arrested an accomplice of the murderer
        b. Ne è stato arrestato un complice
           Of-him was arrested an accomplice

Our framework permits us now to derive these facts in a principled way, relating them to the observation that the prediction turns out to be correct also with respect to wh-extraction: in fact, the phenomenon has long failed to be discussed in the literature, perhaps because it gives rise, in a few cases, to slightly weaker, yet clear, contrasts:[28]

(64)   ?*Di quale assassino ha telefonato un complice?
         Of which murderer has phoned an accomplice?
(65)   Di quale assassino è scomparso/è stato arrestato un complice?
         Of which murderer has disappeared/was arrested an accomplice?

Other ungrammatical examples are listed below:

(66)   a. *Gianni, di cui mi ha ricattato un vecchio amico
          Gianni, of whom blackmailed me an old friend
       b. *la nuova legge, di cui ha movimentato l'attività parlamentare la
          semplice proposta
          the new law, of which has stirred up the parliamentary activity the
          mere proposal
       c. ?*Maria, di cui mi hanno fatto riflettere le parole finali
          Maria, of whom made me reflect the final words
       d. *il nostro complice, di cui mi ha danneggiato un interrogatorio
          our accomplice, of whom damaged me an interrogation
       e. *di quale parlamentare ti hanno presentato a Maria certi
          collaboratori?
          of which congressman have introduced you to Maria certain aides?

Minimal pairs exhibiting sharp object vs inverted subject contrasts are the
following:

(67)   a. Maria, di cui ha conosciuto una sorella
          Maria, of whom he has met a sister
       b. *Maria, di cui lo ha conosciuto una sorella
          Maria, of whom has met him a sister
(68)   a. Non ho capito di chi vuoi invitare a cena un fratello
          I didn't understand of whom you want to invite for dinner a
          brother
       b. *Non ho capito di chi ti vuole invitare a cena un fratello
          I didn't understand of whom wants to invite you for dinner a
          brother[29]

In the preceding section we have suggested that some Adjectives tend to
share the 'unergative/unaccusative' value of the related Verb with
respect to government into the Spec of their inverted subject. We can thus
expect to find those contrasts carrying over to *ne* and wh-extraction.
Cinque (forthcoming) has already shown that extraction of *ne* from an
inverted subject classifies Adjectives as well as Verbs:

(69)   a. Ne è certa la condanna
          Of-him is certain the conviction
       b. *Ne è alto il fratello
          Of-him is tall the brother

The following paradigms show that the facts tend to pattern in the way suggested by the analysis of the examples of the last section:

(70)   a. Ne è chiara l'origine
           Of-it is clear the origin
        b. Ne era prevedibile la condanna
           Of-him was foreseeable the conviction[30]
(71)   a. ?*Ne è fastidiosa l'origine
           Of-it is bothersome the origin
        b. ?*Ne è preoccupante la condanna
           Of-him is worrisome the conviction

Here too, wh-movement sometimes yields slightly less sharp contrasts (depending on lexical choices and informational structure), which, however, seem to go in the same direction:

(72)   a. una situazione di cui è chiara l'origine
           a situation of which is clear the origin
        b. Gianni, del quale era prevedibile la condonna
           Gianni, of whom was foreseeable the conviction
(73)   a. ??una situazione di cui è fastidiosa l'origine
           a situation of which is bothersome the origin
        b. ??Gianni, del quale era preoccupante la condanna
           Gianni, of whom was worrisome the conviction

In all the ungrammatical cases the sentence can be rescued through pied piping of the whole NP, as shown below, since the inverted position is itself properly governed, as we recalled (see Rizzi 1982a; Longobardi 1985a):

(74)   Gianni, un amico del quale credo che voglia ricattarmi
                Gianni, a friend of whom I believe wants to blackmail me

We said that some of the violations with wh-movement appear to be less strong than expected: it is true, for instance, that the adjectival cases of (71) and (73) are more acceptable, a phenomenon perhaps related to the fact that unaccusativity is less clearly distinguishable for As than for Vs (no Case or auxiliary tests seem to be available), which, arguably, might lead to a marginal reanalysis of some unergative As into the other class. With Verbs, however, it seems that the basic violation is quite strong, hence we will assume that the representative case to be considered is that of *ne* extraction, and that extraneous factors intervene to produce apparent counter-examples with a subclass of the wh-moved cases. To consider only a single, but crucial, such factor, notice that some of the structures reviewed above can be improved by substituting the definite article for the indefinite one, as in the following, which contrasts with (68)b:

(75)   ?Non ho capito di chi ti vuole invitare a cena il fratello
          I didn't understand of whom wants to invite you for dinner the
          brother

Consider also the following contrast:

(76)   a. *quell'uomo politico, di cui ci ha telefonato un segretario
             that politician, of whom has phoned us a secretary
          b. ?quell'uomo politico, di cui ci ha telefonato il segretario
             that politician, of whom has phoned us the secretary

A straightforward interpretation of these facts can be based on the observation that the definite article in Italian (and, apparently, in other Romance languages) may have a 'possessive' interpretation in the case of inalienable possession and with certain 'rational' Nouns, like *fratello* ('brother') and other kinship expressions or like *segretario* ('secretary'), *presidente* ('president'), etc. (see Guéron 1986; see also Azoulay 1978). As an exemplification, consider contrasts like the following:

(77)   a. A proposito di Maria, ci ha telefonato il/un segretario per
             rimandare l'appuntamento
             Speaking of Maria, has called us the/a secretary to postpone the
             appointment
          b. Quanto a Maria, siamo riusciti a parlare con il/un fratello
             As for Maria, we were able to speak with the/a brother

The examples with the indefinite article sound quite inappropriate if the secretary (or brother) that we are referring to is meant to be Maria's, which, on the other hand, is by far the most natural interpretation, for it provides a resumptive position for the otherwise unlinked topic *Maria* and satisfies the intrinsically 'relational' valence of the head Nouns in question. If *Maria* has more than one brother or secretary it would be natural to use the partitive construction (*uno dei fratelli* 'one of *the* brothers') in contexts like (77), so as to preserve an instance of the definite article. In all examples like (77) it is also obviously possible to use an overt possessive referring back to *Maria*, essentially expressing the same reading as the definite article.

   This property of definite articles immediately suggests, then, that the unexpectedly mild violations of constraints on extraction in the case of certain NPs with the definite article is likely to be due to a marked interpretation of the genitive wh-phrase as a dislocated constituent (essentially as a topic), with the article marginally acting as a resumptive position for it.[31]

The marginality still displayed in sentences like (73) easily relates to the overlapping of the two strategies of normal wh-interpretation (for question and relative phrases, etc.) and of topic/resumptive interpretation, a phenomenon whose at best marked status has been independently noticed by Cinque (1984).[32]

After this digression, let us now examine some other consequences of the movement-through-Spec analysis that we have proposed and that appears to be directly supported by its ability to predict the impossibility of extraction from NPs when they are inverted subjects of unergative predicates (i.e. from postverbal external arguments). To summarize our reasoning, consider that these subjects instantiate a constituent, call it αmax, in a position such that for αmax $= CP$ we can show that straight extraction is possible, but successive cyclicity through Spec is not, as sketched below:

(78)   a. $X_i \, [\alpha\text{max} \dots \alpha \dots t_i \dots]$
        b. $*X_i \, [\alpha\text{max} \, t_i \dots \alpha \dots t_i \dots]$

If α is now NP, our hypothesis that movement through Spec is always obligatory assimilates extraction from NP to case (78)b, immediately explaining its ungrammaticality and capturing the relevant generalization.

The analysis so far provided for the impossibility of extraction from nominal external arguments crucially bears on the exact formulation of the requirement of proper government in at least two respects. Chomsky (1981), introducing the notion of proper government in part on the grounds of work by Pesetsky (1978), presented it as a disjunction of requirements: proper government for a category is a local relationship (government) either with a coindexed phrase (essentially antecedent government) or with a lexical head (head government). An extreme use of the disjunctive approach was made by Lasnik and Saito (1984), along with a particular relaxation of the locality condition for antecedent government. In Chomsky (1986b) the possibility was suggested, however, that government by a head might be an independent requirement for every trace, never dispensable even in the presence of a local antecedent. Such an approach has been particularly developed in its consequences by Aoun *et al.* (1987), who actually propose that the two requirements of head and antecedent government apply in distinct components of grammar: PF and LF, respectively.[33]

The case discussed in this section provides a direct argument in favour of such independence of the head-government requirement. In fact, the trace left in the Spec of an NP has been shown to be sensitive precisely to the relationship it has with a head, namely the head governing the whole NP. Such a trace, hence extraction, is ungrammatical exactly in the cases in which we have some reason to suppose that it cannot be governed by the head in question. The ungrammaticality appears, then, to result from a typical violation of the head-government requirement. Now, as can be seen from our examples in this section, such a violation arises irrespectively of the presence of a local antecedent: in all the cases discussed, extraction moves the genitive phrase to the most local Spec of CP, hence without crossing any wh-island, a situation which satisfies any current definition of antecedent government (see Lasnik and Saito 1984; Chomsky 1986b; Longobardi forthcoming): yet, antecedent government does not save the structure, once the head-government requirement is not met.

The second theoretical conclusion concerns the way the head-government requirement and, hence, more generally, whatever principle it derives from, applies. The plausible suggestion was made in Lasnik and Saito (1984) and Chomsky (1986b) that traces not required by the Projection Principle can be deleted, probably along the way from S-structure to LF. The need for head government of the intermediate trace in Spec left by extraction from NP suggests that such a condition must be met independently of the possibility of dropping the trace in question, which is not one required by the Projection Principle. Thus, if this trace may truly delete at a certain point in the derivation, the head-government requirement must certainly be checked before such a point. If, for instance, the trace cannot delete before S-structure, the latter level is a very plausible candidate for the head-government requirement to apply to. So is the level of PF, as proposed by Aoun *et al.* in the reference cited, if trace deletion only takes place on the branch of grammar which leads from S-structure to LF.

The argument given in this section also favours our theory of extraction from NP over one like Zubizarreta's (1979) or Aoun's (1985):[34] the latter ones, in fact, acknowledge the crucial relevance of a relationship between Spec and the extracted genitive phrase but establish such a relationship via coindexing, without imposing the presence in Spec of a trace to be externally governed in every case.

Since NPs always require, for extraction, the presence of an intermediate trace in Spec but CPs, in simple cases, do not, another contrast predicted by our approach is the following:

(79)   a. ?*Di quale ragazzo la preoccupa una sorella?
           Of which boy worries her a sister?
        b. ?*Di quale ragazzo la deve conoscere una sorella?
           Of which boy must meet her a sister?
        c. Di quale ragazzo la preoccupa dover conoscere una sorella?
           Of which boy does it worry her to have to meet a sister?

In all three examples extraction takes place from an inverted subject of the relevant type. But ungrammaticality arises only when such a subject is an NP and direct government of a trace in Spec by the Verb would be required, thus as a head-government effect, not a CED one. Consider next that Belletti and Rizzi (1986) have argued that other postverbal NPs seem to have the status of non-internal arguments, i.e. experiencer objects of 'psychological' Verbs: our expectation, then, is that also the Spec of these NPs should not be accessible to external government and therefore that extraction should tend to be impossible. Although the data are slightly less sharp for some speakers, the conclusion appears to be essentially correct, as Belletti and Rizzi show:

(80)   a. ?*Mario di cui i recenti avvenimenti hanno spaventato una sorella
           Mario, of whom the recent events scared a sister
        b. ?*l'uomo politico di cui questa prospettiva preoccupa certi
           collaboratori
           the politician of whom this perspective worries certain aides

This case is of particular relevance with respect to *ne* extraction: in fact, the impossibility of *ne*-extraction from inverted subjects of unergative Verbs could be independently explained, following Burzio (1981), by lack of c-command between the clitic and its trace. This solution presupposes that at least one node (or one segment of a node) contains the clitic at S-structure without containing the trace, for example if clitics cliticize on V (see Kayne 1975), and external arguments must occur outside a node V' or adjoined to VP. Such a traditional explanation becomes, then, untenable if clitics cliticize on *I*, as proposed by Kayne more recently (class lectures, MIT, 1986).[35] In fact, it is precisely on the inflected verbal element that clitics normally appear, on the surface. However, now we may construct a direct empirical argument for the insufficiency of a c-command approach to the non-extractability of *ne* for non-internal arguments:[36] in fact experiencer objects of 'psychological' Verbs, being marked Accusative, can be cliticized as a whole, suggesting that their base position is c-commanded by the clitic landing-position and providing a crucial minimal contrast with *ne* extraction, whose ungrammaticality cannot, then, be imputed to lack of c-command:

(81)   a. La situazione lo turba
          The situation bothers him
      b. ?*La situazione ne turba un collaboratore
          The situation of-him bothers an aide

Example (81)b constitutes, then, a further argument for the obligatoriness of head government of a trace in the Spec of the NP.

Another largely correct prediction to which we are led, on the basis of our proposal and of the facts discussed in the preceding section, is that extraction from a preverbal subject NP should induce milder violations in simple cases, like (82), than the standard expected CED violation:

(82)   ?Maria, di cui una ex-segretaria ha sposato il marchese di Ripafratta
        Maria of whom a former secretary married the marquis of Ripafratta

The reason is that in (82) the trace in the Spec of the NP could be governed, across IP, and NP, by the head of CP coindexed with the antecedent, exactly as in the cases of section 5.

Accordingly, the following minimal contrasts are to be expected as well, on analogy with the examples of extraction from sentential subjects in (43) and (49) above:

(83)   a. ?Maria, di cui penso che una ex-segretaria abbia sposato il marchese di Ripafratta
          Maria of whom I think that a former secretary married the marquis of Ripafratta
      b. ?*Maria, di cui rimpiango/mi preoccupa che una ex-segretaria abbia sposato il marchese di Ripafratta
          Maria of whom I regret/it worries me that a former secretary married the marquis of Ripafratta
      c. *Maria, di cui non ricordo quando una ex-segretaria abbia sposato il marchese di Ripafratta
          Maria of whom I don't remember when a former secretary married the marquis of Ripafratta

A slightly weakened violation is also systematically attested in the non-inverted counterparts of examples like (66) above:

(84)   a. ??Gianni, di cui un amico mi ha ricattato
          Gianni, of whom a friend blackmailed me
      b. ??la nuova legge, di cui la semplice proposta ha movimentato l'attività parlamentare

the new law, of which the mere proposal has stirred up the
parliamentary activity
  c. ?Maria, di cui le parole finali mi hanno fatto riflettere
      Maria, of whom the final words made me reflect
  d. ??il nostro complice, di cui un interrogatorio mi ha danneggiato
      our accomplice, of whom an interrogation damaged me
  e. ??Di quale parlamentare certi collaboratori ti hanno presentato a
      Maria?
      Of which congressman have certain aides introduced you to
      Maria?[37]

Although all these examples are somewhat marginal, especially the last
two, they always represent an improvement with respect to (66). Notice
also the obviously increased unacceptability of an example like (84)b when
the Spec of the NP is already occupied by a possessive, which makes it
inaccessible to the trace of the extracted genitive:

(85) a. *la nuova legge, di cui la tua semplice proposta ha movimentato
          l'attività parlamentare
          The new law, of which your mere proposal has stirred up the
          parliamentary activity

These facts all support our hypothesis of the accessibility of the Spec of a
complement to government by the head selecting such a complement, in
this case by C selecting IP. It also follows straightforwardly that the
improvement manifested in (84) only concerns cases of wh-movement and
not of *ne* extraction, since *ne* does not land in pre-IP-position, so that it
may not index C, the relevant head.

However, the intermediate status of sentences like (84) or like (41)a and
b and (48) of the last section, still remains unexplained. In principle, such
marginality might be attributed to at least two factors: government across
two maximal projections; or the Spec–head coindexing rule in pre-IP
position. It is conceivable that both factors play a role, perhaps the latter
more than the former. In fact, there arise analogous situations where there
is government across two maximal projections by a lexical category,
actually a Verb, and the result, although usually less than perfect, is not
as marginal as in the cases in question:

(86) a. ?Ne ritengo un fratello colpevole
          Of-him I believe a brother guilty
      b. ?Gianni, di cui ritengo un fratello colpevole
          Gianni, of whom I believe a brother guilty
(87)   ?Gianni, di cui non ricordo quale amico ti volesse ricattare
          Gianni, of whom I do not remember which friend wanted to
          blackmail you

In (86) the two maximal projections crossed by government into the relevant Spec are small clause and NP; in (87), a kind of example discussed in Spanish by Torrego (1986), they are CP and NP.[38]

7 Scope ambiguities

A typical way of determining the extraction site of a moved phrase consists of identifying some peculiar formal property uniquely associated with such a position and showing that it is shared by the moved element in question. Analogous arguments can obviously be constructed considering interpretative properties. Our final arguments (except, perhaps, for the tentative one of n. 57) for the obligatoriness of movement to Spec as a prerequisite to extraction from an NP have, in fact, to do with quantificational ambiguity. We will show that genitive phrases extracted from NPs in Italian display the scopal behaviour predictable for the Spec position and not that of the postnominal position. Consider the following phrases:

(88)   la presentazione di cinque studenti a ogni nuovo professore
         The introduction of five students to every new professor

In (88) three options are available: the universal quantifier may take scope over the cardinal one, or vice versa, or, finally, the quantifiers may be read as independent of each other. The case relevant for our argument is the first one. Consider now, as an intermediate step, that, if a quantified genitive phrase is extracted out of an NP, 'reconstruction' of the scope relationship established before wh-movement is usually possible:

(89)   a. Penso che ogni professore potrà correggere i compiti di cinque
            studenti
            I think that every professor will be able to correct the assignments
            of five students
         b. Di quanti studenti pensi che ogni professore potrà correggere i
            compiti?
            Of how many students do you think that every professor will be
            able to correct the assignments?

Thus, (89)b tends to preserve the strongly favoured reading of (89)a, with *ogni* ('every') taking wide scope over the cardinal quantifier (*quanti* ('how many')), although it is clear that *di quanti studenti* is not contained within its scope at S-structure. This is because the scope of the universally quantified NP does not extend beyond the embedded clause of which it is the subject, a general property of this class of quantifiers, briefly discussed with respect to Italian in Longobardi (1986). The most reasonable conclusion is then that *quanti* is construed in the scope of *ogni* by virtue of the position occupied before wh-movement. For a discussion of partly similar cases, see also Cinque (1982).

However, if wh-movement applies to a phrase like (88), the scope possibilities tend to change:

(90)   Di quanti studenti consigli la presentazione ad ogni nuovo professore?
        Of how many students do you recommend the introduction to every new professor?

In (90) the wide-scope reading of *ogni* over *quanti*, albeit not totally impossible, becomes quite marginal. The contrast between (89) and (88)/(90) is, so far, unexpected. Notice, however, that exactly the same phenomenon arises with movement to Spec in English, a language where a quantified phrase may visibly land into such a position:

(91)   five students' introduction to every new professor

The phrase (91) contrasts in meaning with the gloss of (88): the latter has essentially the three scopal options of its Italian original; (91), instead, tends to disfavour the wide-scope reading of the universal quantifier, precisely as in (90), the Italian example with wh-movement. The phenomenon suggests a particular prominence of the prenominal position and shows that movement to Spec does not readily allow for scope reconstruction.

Whatever the quantification-theoretical implications of this fact may be (see for recent approaches to the problems of quantification in NPs, Delfitto 1987; Aoun and Li 1987), we are now in a position to explain the otherwise mysterious behaviour of (90) by crucially relying on the hypothesis of extraction through Spec. In fact, if NP internal movement to Spec always deletes the dependent reading of the genitive phrase appearing in configurations like (88) without the possibility of reconstructing it, then the interpretation of (90) follows as a direct consequence of the required movement to Spec of NP before wh-extraction. Thus the interpretative property of (90) directly supports our main hypothesis.

An argument in the same vein, but supported by much sharper evidence, concerns the contrast between the so-called naturally and inversely linked readings (see May 1977; Huang 1982). Notice, to start with, the ambiguity of a sentence like (92) in Italian:

(92)   E' difficile recensire i libri di molti autori
        It is difficult to review the books of many authors

Example (92) may mean either that many authors are such that the books of each of them are difficult to review (inversely linked reading, with wide scope of the genitive argument on the head) or that the books collectively written by many coauthors are difficult to review (naturally linked, with scope reversed). If we now wh-extract the quantified argument, the naturally linked reading totally disappears:

(93)   Di quanti autori è difficile recensire i libri?
        Of how many authors is it difficult to review the books?

Thus, (93) cannot ask for the number of coauthors such that it makes it difficult to review a book, say, because it becomes hard to single out and evaluate the contribution and the scientific orientation of each author. The extremely sharp contrast in interpretative possibilities between (92) and (93) is immediately reducible under the movement-through-Spec hypothesis if, again, we simply examine English. It is well known that the interpretative contrast between (92) and (93) neatly reappears in (94):

(94)   a. I know supporters of many politicians
        b. I know many politicians' supporters

The naturally linked reading, present as an option beside the inversely linked one in (94)a, disappears under movement to Spec in (94)b. A theoretical discussion of this phenomenon can be found particularly in Fiengo and Higginbotham (1981). The same considerations holding in the previous case apply here as well: movement to Spec deletes, without any chance of reconstruction, one of the readings, exactly as wh-extraction does in Italian, a similarity which is readily explained if indeed wh-movement necessarily results from previous movement to Spec.[39] Notice, finally, that the argument is made particularly strong, by the fact that the sharpness of the English judgements on (94)b is matched by the sharpness of Italian (93), and the relative weakness of the English phenomenon in (91) is again perfectly matched by the equally less sharp judgement concerning (90) in Italian.

8   Nouns and Verbs as governors

In this section we will explore a way to derive the proposed account of extraction from NP in a principled manner. Recall that the assumption we want to derive is that Nouns are appropriate governors just for empty categories whose antecedents are contained within their maximal projection NP, whereas Verbs are not subject to such a limitation.

A hypothesis of Kayne's (1983), embedded in the formulation of his Connectedness Condition (later adopted and slightly modified in Longobardi 1983, 1985a and b), may provide us with an adequate theoretical framework: he distinguishes between structural and non-structural governors and claims that only the former allow a trace they govern to have an antecedent outside their maximal projection. In Kayne (1983) there is no exhaustive analysis of the various heads from this viewpoint: Kayne only states that while Verbs are always structural governors, Prepositions, instead, are structural in English but not in Romance.

However, the assignment of each category to either of the two classes is by no means just a stipulation: some criteria for the distinction (i.e. for classifying together Verbs and English Prepositions as opposed to Romance Prepositions) were made explicit in Kayne (1981b): in essence, non-structural governors govern only categories that they subcategorize for (or that they s-select in Pesetsky's 1982 sense), structural ones govern independently of subcategorization, as e.g. Verbs in the cases of small clauses, raising, ECM. That English Prepositions are structural can be seen from the occurrence of *for* as an infinitival Complementizer, i.e. in the C position, governing and Case marking the subject of IP, to which it is semantically unrelated; none of the Prepositions arguably appearing in C in Romance govern the subject position, hence allowing PRO and blocking a lexical NP.

We will follow Kayne in tying together, as an empirical hypothesis, these two properties, i.e. the failure of a category to govern elements unrelated to its selectional frame and the failure to allow straight extraction outside the maximal projection, and we will try to explain the fact that Nouns exhibit the latter property by showing that they also display the former one. Consider, in fact, the following properties of Nouns, widely discussed in the literature (see Stowell 1981; Kayne 1981c), which distinguish them from Verbs and all concern the relationship between a head Noun and categories semantically unrelated to it:

(95)   a. Nouns never select a null complementizer ('I believe (that) John is
           intelligent' vs 'my belief *(that) John is intelligent' (see Stowell
           1981))[40]
        b. Nouns do not allow raising: ('Mary appears to have left' vs
           '*Mary's appearance to have left'; from Kayne (1984, p. 142))
        c. Nouns do not allow 'passivization' across sentence boundaries:
           ('The baby is estimated to weigh about 8 pounds by the doctor'
           vs. '*The baby's estimation to weigh 8 pounds by the doctor';
           from Kayne (1984, p. 143))

d. Nouns do not allow 'raising' or 'passivization' out of small clauses either ('Mary appears/is estimated intelligent' vs '*Mary's appearance/estimation intelligent')

These facts can be readily explained if the traces of NP-movement left behind in (95)b, c and d, and, as proposed by Stowell (1981), the empty Complementizer position which represents the head of Cmax in case (95)a need all be governed by a head and if Nouns, unlike Verbs, can never govern elements such as these, which are not part of their selectional frame.[41]

Notice that the case in (95)b, c and d may also be explained in terms of Case-theory, since they are independently excluded by Chomsky's (1986a) Uniformity Condition, which requires that Case-marking by inherent Case assigners like Nouns take place only (and obligatorily) as a consequence of θ-marking: since the raised NP in the cases in question is not θ-marked by the head Noun, it should be unable to receive Genitive Case from it. However, case (95)a is still likely to exemplify a difference between Verbs and Nouns which appears to point to the inability of the latter heads to govern (and not just to Case-mark) a category they do not select.

Notice, however, that our approach is already able to derive half of the Uniformity Condition for Nouns: consider, in fact, that the Uniformity Condition, as a biconditional, consists of two parts:[42]

(96)   If α (for α = inherent Case-marker) θ-marks β, then it Case-marks β and if α Case marks β, then it θ-marks β

Now, by their non-structural nature Nouns will only govern phrases that they select – we suggest – hence, in most relevant cases, that they θ-mark: if Case-marking always takes place under government, we can so derive the second part of the Uniformity Condition. As for the first part, it is essentially meant, in Chomsky (1986a), to capture, in conjunction with the claim that inherent Case-markers must both assign and realize their Case under government, the fact that arguments of N never undergo external NP movement, even in cases where it would not be blocked by binding considerations:

(97)   *John is likely that pictures *t* will be published

Under standard assumptions about A-chains, (97) is ruled out if Genitive is obligatorily assigned to *t* (for NP-internal A-chains see Chomsky 1986a and ch. 3, sect. 12 below). It is likely that this remaining part of the Uniformity Condition must itself make reference to our distinction between structural and non-structural governors. Consider, in fact, that such a part of the condition may be problematic if extended to Genitive assigned by Adjectives, at least if such pairs as those of note 29 above are related by movement. For, if Adjectives (which are structural governors: see directly below) allow NP-movement of their internal argument outside the maximal projection, like ergative Verbs and English Prepositions ('*This bed was slept in recently*'), the Uniformity Condition must be made sensitive to the distinction between types of governors. Then it could be so formulated as in (98):

(98)   If α (for α = non-structural governor) θ-marks β, then it Case-marks β

Another case which does not seem to be merely reducible to Case considerations is provided by the following paradigm:

(99)   a. It is certain that John will leave
        b. John is certain to leave
        c. It is a certainty that John will leave
        d. *John is a certainty to leave

With an Adjective, raising, hence government, of the embedded trace is perfectly possible, at least in English, but with the corresponding Noun it is impossible in every well-analysed language, even if the raised NP eventually receives Nominative, a structural Case, from I. Notice that the violation in (99)d is far more severe than any normal Complex Noun Phrase Constraint (CNPC) violation, something which is explained by reducing such a case (also) to an instance of lack of head government for the trace, due to the fact that Adjectives but not Nouns are structural governors. In fact, English Adjectives, in addition to raising, allow *that* deletion:

(100)   a. A person absolutely sure you are able to succeed is your friend John
        b. It was already clear Mary could win

Predictably, they allow extraction of their complements, a property which seems to hold crosslinguistically, even if there is no independent evidence of movement into their Spec; moreover, any type of complement of an A can be extracted, irrespective of the kind of Preposition introducing it (i.e. it need not be a genitive argument), and even two complements may undergo extraction at the same time, as in the Italian examples below:

(101)   a. il denaro, di cui non so proprio con chi lei sia generosa
        money, of which I really don't know with whom she is generous
    b. una caratteristica in cui le sono simile
        a feature in which I to-her am similar

On the contrary, the impossibility of a similar multiple extraction from NPs follows, according to our hypothesis, from the independent impossibility of multiple possessivization (particularly severe in the prehead Spec position: see ch. 3, sect. 6 on this point):

(102)   a. *Maria, di cui ignoro di quale collezionista abbiano messo in vendita un ritratto
        Maria, of whom I ignore of which collector they put on sale a portrait
(103)   *Il mio suo ritratto
        my her portrait

These differences crucially suggest, then, that movement through Spec for extraction from AP is at least unnecessary. We can thus plausibly conclude that Nouns are non-structural governors, so that the Connectedness Condition will force traces governed by them to have a local antecedent within NP. A trace in the Spec of an NP, while counting as a local antecedent for the more embedded trace of a Noun complement, is licensed, in the admissible cases of extraction, by government by a Verb, i.e. a structural governor which consequently allows for either clitic placement or wh-movement.[43] The fact that Verbs are structural governors is responsible, under this analysis, also for the crucial differences between extraction from VP and extraction from NP: extraction from VP is usually possible for any kind of argument of V (i.e. it is not restricted to a 'designated' argument, like the 'subject' in NPs), it does not display scope reversal phenomena of the type discussed in section 6, and, finally, it is possible for more than one argument at the same time, as in (104):

(104)   Maria, a cui non so di che cosa parlare *e e*
        Maria, to whom I do not know about what to speak

9   The Consistency Principle

Thus far, we have said nothing about the way arguments extracted out of NPs are assigned their Case. As we recalled before, the only arguments which can move out of an NP in Romance are of the form *di* (Spanish and

French *de*)+NP or of the corresponding pronominalized form, like *ne* (French *dont, en*). Following Chomsky (1986a) among others, we will suppose that these forms are all ways of realizing the abstract Genitive Case assigned by the Noun to its direct arguments. Given that such a realization through the insertion of a Preposition only takes place to the right of the head Noun, this fact may perhaps cast doubts on our hypothesis that all extractions out of NPs come from the prehead Spec position.

However, it is possible to assume that such phrases, extracted in two steps from the NP (first moving to Spec and, then, outside), are assigned Genitive Case in the original postnominal position and inherit it from the most embedded trace. It is not crucial for this analysis whether, following Chomsky (1986a), we must distinguish between assignment (at D-structure) and realization (at S-structure, or anyway after NP-movement) of Genitive. However, if this is the case, as we admit also on the grounds of the analysis presented in ch. 3, then the rules for assignment and realization of Genitive, when it is not further specified as [Poss], should be roughly the following:

(105)   NP → (+Gen) if governed by N[44]
(106)   NP (+Gen) → [$_{PP}$di+NP]

An extracted NP would be transmitted Genitive (with the specific information on its realization) by its trace, as for all other Cases, e.g. Accusative, under movement. Also, if realization took place before wh-movement, the two rules might stay unchanged and the only consequence would be that the extracted phrase should already move under the form of a PP. The proposed analysis faces, however, two non-trivial problems. The first has to do with the following question: if Genitive Case can be transmitted to an extracted NP through the intermediate trace in Spec or, alternatively, if the latter position can be moved into by a PP on its way out of the NP, why is it impossible for the same PP to appear as a realization of Genitive in Spec? In other words the question concerns the ungrammaticality of examples like (107)a which might have been derived from (107)b:

(107)   a. *Ho visto (il) di mio fratello libro
                I saw (the) of my brother book
             b. Ho visto il libro di mio fratello
                I saw the book of my brother

Our proposal is that the ungrammaticality of (107)a is a consequence of an independent surface constraint which we may try to formulate by developing some insights due to Emonds (1976) and Williams (1982; see also Levin and Rappaport, 1986). Consider in fact that in many consistently right-branching languages, in Romance and English for example, a constituent appearing on the prehead side of an NP cannot be expanded to the right of its head. Such is the case, for example, with the AP in (108):

(108)   a. una triste avventura
           a sad adventure
        b. una davvero/più/egualmente triste avventura
           a really/more/equally sad adventure
        c. *una triste per Mario avventura
           a sad for Mario adventure

A similar description seems to hold for adverbs in the prehead position of APs and PPs as well (see Emonds 1976):

(109)   a. Quell'uomo d'affari, ora sorprendentemente ricco, era partito
           dall'Italia in condizioni miserevoli
           That businessman, now surprisingly rich, had left Italy in miserable
           conditions
        b. Quell'uomo d'affari, ora tanto più sorprendentemente ricco in
           quanto era partito dell'Italia in condizioni miserevoli, è un tipo
           simpatico
           That businessman, now so much more surprisingly rich as he had
           left Italy in miserable conditions, is a nice fellow
        c. *Quell'uomo d'affari, ora sorprendentemente per noi ricco, era
           partito dall'Italia in condizioni miserevoli
           That businessman, now surprisingly for us rich, had left Italy in
           miserable conditions

Exactly the same results can be obtained by substituting $[_{P'}$ in buona forma] ('in good shape') or the participial $[_{V'}$ favorito dalla fortuna] ('favoured by fortune') for $[_{A'}$ ricco] ('rich').

   Notice also that, when it does not occur in the Spec of a lexical category, the adverb *sorprendentemente* may retain its complement, as in the following case:

(110)   Sorprendentemente per noi, Maria decise di sposarlo
        Surprisingly for us, Maria decided to marry him

It is clear, on the other hand, that non-lexical heads, i.e. I and C, may be preceded even by heavily right-branching constituents, like preverbal subjects and topicalized or wh-moved phrases (see Chomsky 1986b).

We will thus tentatively try to generalize the observation and derive the phenomenon from (111), conceived of as an S-structure (or surface structure) filter:

(111)   Consistency Principle:
         An XP immediately expanding a lexical category on the non-
         recursive side is directionally consistent in every projection.

(By 'recursive side' we mean that side of the head on which internal arguments or complements in the X'-theoretic sense occur, by 'non-recursive' side we refer to the opposite one.) Principle (111) is intended to mean that if the non-recursive side of a lexical category α is, say, the left one, then a phrase βmax immediately dominated by α^n in such a position, as well as its lower projections, can be further expanded only to the left of the head β. This formation captures the facts of (108) and (109), while making an additional prediction for languages which are cross-categorially inconsistent in the definition of the recursive side. In fact, in a language like German where Ns (along with Cs and most Ps) seem to occur with complements to the right but Vs (and perhaps Is) with their complement to the left, and As appear to have both options (Haider 1987), we expect to find grammatical phrases of the form (112) – actually a correct prediction, as noticed in the references mentioned above:[45]

(112)   a. ein seinen Freuden treuer Mann
            a to his friends faithful man
         b. die vielen in diese Frau verliebten Männer
            the many with this woman in love men

Exactly on the same grounds we are able to predict a curious phenomenon in Italian: at a certain stylistic level, many Adjectives and participles allow their complements to occur either to the right or to the left of the head, especially if such complements are pronominal, yielding on the surface a 'Head-last' order:

(113)   a. i servitori più fedeli a lui
            the servants most faithful to him
         b. i servitori a lui più fedeli
            the servants to him most faithful[46]

Now, when APs like the previous ones are moved to a prenominal position, i.e. on the non-recursive side of the head Noun, only the preadjectival complements may survive, as in German, although with an increased literary flavour:

(114)   a. *i più fedeli a lui servitori
         b. gli a lui più fedeli servitori

This appears to be another non-trivial consequence of the Consistency Principle and, if Giorgi and Longobardi (this vol., ch. 3) are right in arguing that the prenominal position of APs in Romance Noun Phrases is a derived one, (114) confirms that such a principle must hold after movement rather than just at D-structure.

According to the Consistency Principle we will interpret possessive constructions of the form NP + 's in English as Postpositional Phrases headed by 's. This is independently suggested by the rigidly phrase-final position of the 's morpheme and makes structures like (115) or like (40) of section 4 above compatible with (111):

(115)   The king of England's crown

A final prediction of our formulation of the Consistency Principle is that left-branching phrases should not occur on the right side of basically left-recursive XPs, like VPs in German or Dutch. One case in Dutch is likely to bear out this prediction: in fact, some motion Verbs take either prepositional or postpositional complements to their left:

(116)   a. …dat hij [$_{PP}$ op de berg] klom
            …that he climbed on the mountain
         b. …dat hij [$_{PP}$ de berg op] klom[47]

Like other PPs, this can be moved to the right of the Verb (the non-recursive side of Dutch VPs), but here only the prepositional form may surface:

(117)   a. …dat hij klom op de berg
         b. *…dat hij klom de berg op

Thus (117)b brings further support to (111). As H. van Riemsdijk (p.c.) pointed out, the conclusion can be reinforced by the observation that no such restriction arises on the right side of NPs, which seems to be the recursive one in Dutch as well, so that minimal contrasts like the following arise:

(118)   a. de reis de berg op
            the trip up the mountain
         b. *…dat hij reisde de berg op
            …that he travelled up the mountain

Going back now to the ungrammaticality of (107)a, and its equivalents, we notice that the realization of Genitive Case as PP of the form *di* + NP to the left of the head Noun yields a violation of the Consistency Principle. The grammaticality of wh- or clitic extraction, which in our analysis must leave an intermediate trace in Spec, suggests, then, either that what moves out is categorially still a Genitive NP, and not a PP, or that an intermediate PP trace need not be so internally structured as to count as a branching constituent for the Consistency Principle.

The other potential problem announced at the outset concerns the non-existence of exceptional Case-marked NPs occurring in the Spec of an NP or extracted through it.

Such a fact seems to break the assumed parallelism with other clearer cases of government into Spec. However, there are independent reasons for expecting the case in question not to arise. First, it is conceivable that a Verb governing an NP containing another NP in its Spec may only have one structural Case to assign, in such a way that just one of the two NPs could be so marked (thus necessarily the larger one, to escape the Case Filter). Second, Chomsky (1986a) has argued that Genitive Case is a so-called inherent Case, i.e. differently from Nominative and Accusative it is a θ-related Case, subject to the Uniformity Condition (see sect. 8). This means essentially that if a Noun assigns Genitive to an NP, it θ-marks it and, vice versa, that, if a Genitive Case-marker θ-marks an argument which takes Genitive, the assignment is obligatory, actually a direct consequence of θ-marking at D-structure. Now, if we assume that no position can be doubly Case-marked and that a chain may not contain more than one Case position, as argued in Chomsky (1986a), then, from the second part of the Uniformity Condition it follows that no argument of a head Noun may ever undergo exceptional Case-marking.

10   Uniqueness and minimality

The analysis of extraction from NP we have presented seems, thus, to work satisfactorily for the Romance languages. English, however, poses a potential problem.

English has lexical NPs occurring in the Spec of an NP and realizing Genitive Case through the possessive Postposition *'s*: now, such NPs, which could in principle provide the most visible case of extraction out of Spec, are instead rigidly unmovable. The problem is exemplified in (119):

(119)   a. *Whose did you see *e* mother
         b. *John's I read *e* new book

Notice, first of all, that it is not likely that the contrast in extractability between *NP's* and *di NP* has to do with different ways of realizing Genitive Case (more synthetic, with a Case ending, vs more analytical, with a PP). In fact, we have already noticed that the *'s* morpheme seems to be the head of a marked postpositional construction and not a real Case ending. We will rather focus on another difference between *NP's* and *di NP* phrases. Consider thus that *NP's* is the specific realization of Genitive Case on Noun Phrases appearing in the Spec of a nominal construction (i.e. a phrase headed by N or by a gerund). The plausible assumption is that such a Case realization takes place under government, precisely government by the nominal head, as suggested by Chomsky (1986a) for the realization of all inherent cases. We will obtain an explanation for the extraction facts if we force such an internal government to be the only one available, thus by excluding the external government by V which allows for relatively unbounded movement in Romance.

Let us propose, to this end, the following descriptive condition, most likely a theorem of a properly formulated Minimality Condition in the sense of Chomsky (1986b), whose definition will be formally elaborated in section 12:

(120)   Uniqueness Constraint on Government:
          If a position β is governed by a lexical head α, it has no other
          governors

To conform to this principle, a phrase in the Spec of a lexical head has to choose between being governed by the latter or by an external governor. The choice of restricting the Uniqueness Constraint, and the Minimality Condition, if the former is to be eventually built into the latter, to lexical governors is due to the fact that Specifiers of I and C appear to be available to external government, in cases like the following:

(121)   a. Who (do you think) *e* left?
          b. Why do you think *e* that he left?

At least in the first case we could expect I to govern the subject position, protecting it from external government, since it is normally supposed to Case-mark it. However, practically anyone's theory of wh-movement of nominative subjects assumes the Spec of I to be governed from Comp, hence externally to IP.[48] Mainly for this reason we will suppose the lexical/non-lexical distinction to play a role in the Spec accessibility to an external governor. Now, if the special realization of Genitive to the left in English NPs must really take place under government by the head (or by N'), it follows that an *XP's* phrase will have to refuse external government by a V. Phrases of the form $di + \text{NP}$ in Italian will instead succeed in receiving their inherent Genitive Case under government by the head to the right, and then, once moved to Spec, will be able to accept external government as required for extraction.

The discussion above leads us in turn to consider other cases in which extraction of phrases overtly appearing in the Spec of NP appears to be impossible. One case concerns the sharp impossibility of topicalizing, with or without the article, an expression of the adjectival sort (e.g. possessives, descriptive Adjectives) which may appear in the Spec of an NP in languages like Italian, agreeing with the head Noun:

(122)   a. He visto la tua nuova automobile
            I saw your new car
         b. *TUA ho visto la nuova automobile
         c. *LA TUA ho visto nuova automobile
            YOUR I saw new car

The other important case has to do with the contrast in extractability between the French QPs mentioned above and their counterparts in many other languages such as Italian, English or German:[49]

(123)   a. *Quanti hai incontrato ragazzi?
         b. *How many did you meet boys?
         c. *Wie viele hast du Jungen getroffen?
(124)   Combien as-tu rencontré de garçons?

Both cases just reviewed may fall together and be explained away if we consider that words like French *beaucoup* or *combien* do not undergo any agreement process with the head. Such agreement is, instead, overtly and obligatorily manifested with respect to the number feature in the English example, with respect to number and gender in the Italian ones. Finally, German and the other Case-inflected languages, like Latin, show that the agreement extends to Case. Let us hypothesize now that even in languages with no overt Case inflection this agreement process is necessary precisely in order to satisfy PF Case requirements on these elements and, then, that it may take place only under government of the Spec by the head.

To put the question in another way, we suppose that if a context of government of β by α goes along with Case-agreement between α and β, then such government will not be dispensable (e.g. for the sake of escaping the Uniqueness Constraint, i.e. Minimality effects).

It follows that (122) and (123) are ungrammatical for the same reason as (119), i.e. under the Uniqueness Constraint (120) the material in Spec cannot accept external government by the Verb and is thus unextractable.

Consider now the French case again: how do French QPs, if they do not undergo agreement, receive a Case? It is reasonable to conclude that they are Case-marked by their external governor, e.g. by the Verb which allows them to move out of the NP. The question must then be raised, in turn, of why such a possibility does not extend to the QPs of the other languages discussed.

In order to provide an answer, let us suppose that the Case which is assigned to an NP in order to satisfy Chomsky's (1986b) Visibility Condition for θ-assignment in LF may be realized in two ways: either it percolates down to the head or is realized on the Spec, but not both: suppose now the Case percolated to the head is transmissible to categories needing it (articles, APs, QPs) in Spec or elsewhere through agreement, but not the opposite. Suppose also that, in addition to LF visibility requirements, a head Noun, like articles and Adjectives, always needs a Case for its morphological realization (PF visibility); it follows that direct Case-percolation to the Spec is allowed only in languages and constructions exhibiting another way of Case-marking the head. French does have such a means of Case-marking the head Noun through the genitivization rule which inserts *de* between the QP and the rest of the NP.[50] The other languages considered lack this possibility, hence their QPs cannot but agree with the head, under government by the latter, and are thus unavailable for external government and extraction.

Consider now another possible consequence of the proposed analysis: if the Case requirements for QPs in the Spec of NPs are only of a morphological nature and not of an interpretative one (i.e. if they have nothing to do with the LF visibility condition of Chomsky 1986a, imposing the presence of Case on thematic NPs), we can expect such requirements to be suspended in the case of a Spec with null morphology, i.e. of a phonetically empty QP. Of course, the empty QP will be exempt from the Case requirements only if it does not have to transmit Case to a non-empty antecedent: e.g. the traces of the QPs in (123) must agree with the head Noun in order to get a Case to be transmitted through an A'-chain (see Cinque 1982) to the fronted wh-QP. In constructions allowing this wh-QP to be phonetically unrealized (or, in a more traditional terminological setting, 'deleted in Comp'), however, we expect the morphological case requirements to be irrelevant, and this agreement to be dispensable: the consequence should be that extraction by means of external government ought to be possible. A case in point is, in fact, represented by the so-called 'Comparative Subdeletion' rule (see Bresnan

1976; Chomsky 1977). While French and English differ sharply with respect to sentences like (123) and (124) they are quite the same with respect to (125) and (126) and other similar examples:[51]

(125)   a. J'ai autant de frères que Marie (a) de sœurs[52]
         b. I have as many brothers as Mary (has) sisters
(126)   a. Jean a plus d'argent que Marie n'a d'amis (from Kayne 1984, p. 68)
         b. John has more money than Mary has friends

It is arguable that in these sentences, as in other comparative constructions, wh-movement of an empty (or later deleted) QP has taken place from the Specifier of the embedded object NPs. If this is really the case, the disappearing of the contrast in extractability between French and English exactly when the A′-chain ending in the QP trace is headed by a phonetically empty antecedent is expected under our general approach. In (127), instead,

(127)   *It is many that I met friends

even if we do not want to assume that *many* has been itself moved (see Chomsky 1977) from the QP trace position, we can suppose that it must actually head the A′ chain of such a trace, perhaps involving an empty QP in the Spec of Comp (see Cinque 1982), and that this is the only way it may receive its Case; given our general hypotheses, the *e* should be governed by *friends* and this fact rules out the sentence.

It is also noteworthy that our generalization about extraction of QPs is confirmed by Italian, which never allows an empty wh-QP in comparative sentences without V-gapping and predictably does not have, in these cases, any 'Subdeletion' construction:[53]

(128)   a. *Ho più amici che ne hai tu
            I have more friends than you of-them have
         b. Ho più amici di quanti ne hai tu
            I have more friends than how-many you of-them have
         c. *Ho più fratelli che tu hai sorelle
            I have more brothers than you have sisters
         d. *Ho più fratelli di quante tu hai sorelle
            I have more brothers than how-many you have sisters

It is interesting to notice, however, that when a constituent roughly corresponding to a verbal projection is gapped, Italian appears to admit of comparative null operators:

(129) a. *Ho più libri io a Roma che tu ne hai a Milano
   I have more books in Rome than you have in Milan
  b. Ho più libri io a Roma che tu a Milano
   I have more books in Rome than you in Milan

Exactly in this case we must thus expect Comparative Subdeletion to be possible also in Italian:

(130) Ho più libri io a Roma che tu dischi a Milano
    I have more books in Rome than you records in Milan

Example (130) shows that our prediction is confirmed.

11 Specifiers and extraction in APs

Discussing the French genitivization rule and the pattern of Comparative Subdeletion immediately suggests an extension of our analysis of Minimality phenomena to APs. The similarity of behaviour of NPs and APs with respect to such constructions is, in fact, striking. Consider the first one: Rumanian APs introduced by the QP specifier *cît* ('how') undergo a process of prepositional insertion similar to French genitivization; in these cases *cît* may be extracted alone, as noticed by Grosu (1974) and Taraldsen (1984):

(131) a. Cît de frumosasă e Maria!
   How of beautiful is Maria!
  b. Cît e Maria de frumoasă!
   How is Maria of beautiful! (from Grosu 1974)[54]

But when *cît* introduces NPs, with the meaning 'how much' and no chance of *de* insertion, it can never be extracted, exactly as in Italian or English:

(132) a. Cît vin ai băut?
   How much wine have you drunk?
  b. *Cît ai băut vin?
   How much have you drunk wine?

Obenauer (1976) and Taraldsen (1984) explicitly suggested that the difference between (131)b and (132)b is due to the unavailability of *de* insertion in Rumanian NPs. Grosu reports also the occurrence of another QP in the Spec of Rumanian APs, namely *ce* ('how'), which does not induce *de* insertion and, in fact, cannot be extracted alone:

(133) a. Ce frumoasă e Maria!
   How beautiful is Maria!
  b. *Ce e frumoasă Maria!
   How is beautiful Maria!

Consider now Comparative Subdeletion, exemplified with English:

(134)   a. How long do you think the bridge is?
         b. *How do you think the bridge is long?
         c. The bridge is as long as the mountain is high

Again Comparative Subdeletion, i.e. a chain headed by a null QP, allows gapping of a Spec in languages and constructions where this is otherwise impossible.

The whole pattern suggests that the two following properties hold of As as well as of Ns: (1) they are not sufficient governors for extraction of their modifiers in Spec (so that Spec accessibility to an external governor is required); (2) they are usually able to protect their Spec from an external governor but lose this possibility exactly in the same cases as Nouns do, i.e. under genitivization and in the case of traces with null antecedents (Comparative Subdeletion). While the first property is expected for Nouns, in our framework, since they are anyway non-structural governors, it is less so for Adjectives, which behave as structural governors, as we have argued above. We may try to account for the first property adopting Kayne's (1983) notion of 'canonical government' and proposing it as a necessary ingredient of proper government: the latter will be defined as follows, minimally developing the notion elaborated in Longobardi (1985b; see n. 3 above):

(135) α properly governs β iff
         α canonically governs β and
         α selects γ which dominates β
         (where γ and β may coincide, under a reflexive interpretation of the notion 'dominance')

'Canonically governed' will be understood, *à la* Kayne (1983), as 'governed in the same direction as internal arguments of V' or even relativized to the direction of internal arguments for each different head (the crucial predictions have to do with crosscategorically inconsistent languages, which we will not analyse here).

An argument in favour of this directional formulation comes from the comparison of English and Italian. In Italian measure modifiers of APs occur on the right of the head A much more easily than in English:

(136)   a. Mario è intelligente più di te
         b. Il ponte è lungo 3 km
         c. Gianni è intelligente tanto quanto Maria
(137)   a. *Bill is intelligent more than you
         b. *The bridge is long 3 km
         c. *John is intelligent as much as Mary

Using a suggestion originally formulated by G. Cinque (p.c.), we may attribute to this basic difference the responsibility for another striking contrast between English and Italian; in Italian it is, in fact, perfectly possible to extract such measure phrases:[55]

(138) a. Quanto è intelligente Mario?
           How is Mario intelligent?
       b. 330 km, quanto, più o meno, Pisa è distante da Roma, sono un
           lungo percorso
           330 km, how, more or less, Pisa is far from Rome, are a long
           distance

Let us assume that the relationship between A and these measure XPs is universal by one of selection in the sense relevant for proper government; now the difference in extractability follows, under canonical government, from the hypothesis that the trace in D-structure is on the right of the head in Italian, but on the left in English, an idea independently suggested by (136) and (137) above.[56]

Let us now analyse the second property, that concerning Spec protection on the part of a head A: the simplest way to account for it in the framework previously developed and to capture the similarity between APs and NPs is that of hypothesizing that AP modifiers of the sort in question need to be assigned some formal licensing feature (formal in the sense of not being required other than in PF, hence not by null antecedents), playing the same role as Case in our explanations of section 10. Such a feature should, thus, be transmitted by the head A in normal cases, but could also be assigned by a higher Verb when the adjective undergoes a process of P insertion as in (131). There is some evidence that at least in some cases the feature in question may precisely be Case, the most desirable conclusion, since it completely assimilates the phenomena of this section to those discussed in the previous one about NPs.

In fact, in a morphologically Case-inflected language, like Latin, measure phrases are always marked for Case (generally Accusative in Latin, sometimes Ablative; cf. Ernout-Thomas 1972, pp. 30, 95 and 111). The same can be said for QPs corresponding to *very* or *much*, to *how* or *how much*, which display an Accusative/Ablative alternation (*multum, multo, quantum, quanto*) that appears to be governed mostly by the positive/comparative nature of the adjectival head: Ablative is selected by the comparative morpheme of the Adjective, rather in the way it selects *much* or *viel* instead of *very* and *sehr* in modern English and German.

Generalizing these observations, we will then suppose that, as in NPs, QP-specifiers and measure phrases of APs need to receive a Case for morphological realization, which is normally transmitted by the head A, but can be assigned from outside (by a higher copular Verb selecting the AP) when the adjectival head satisfies Case-requirements by other means, as we assume to be the case in the Rumanian examples above. Only in the latter case can an overt phrase in Spec of AP be governed from outside (it is not protected by Uniqueness or Minimality) and be extracted. Traces in the Spec of an AP which are in a chain headed by a null operator do not have to satisfy morphological Case requirements of any sort, and, as such, are never protected from external government by a relation with the head A: hence, again, the peculiarity of Comparative Subdeletion.

12   The definition of government

Let us try now to rework the definition of head government according to the conclusions we have reached throughout the chapter. A possible formulation is the following, which distinguishes conditions on the two elements involved, (139)a, and conditions on the configuration, (139)b and c:

(139)   a. a head α governs β iff
         (a) i. α is intrinsically a structural governor ($[+V]$ universally, also P in English)
             or
         ii. α s-selects β
             or
         iii. α and β are coindexed
             and
         (b) α m-commands β
             and
         (c) (Minimality Condition)
             $\exists$ no γ, γ including β and excluding α, such that
             i. γ is a non-internal argument of α
                or
             ii. β is canonically contained or lexically C-marked in γ

In (139)a we aim essentially to capture the behaviour of non-structural governors like Nouns, which play a crucial role in our analysis of extraction from NP. Consider now the Minimality Condition: by 'canonically contained' we refer to containment on the recursive side (to the right of the head of γ in English or Italian), freeing access of external governors just to Specs and heads, and by 'lexically C-marked' we mean 'marked with some formal feature, typically Case, by a lexical category', so as to achieve the relevant effects of the Uniqueness Constraint on

Government (120).[57] Finally (139)c (i) is meant to state the barrierhood of non-internal arguments, like inverted subjects, to government of their Spec from outside. Proper government remains as in (135) above.

In (139)a structural government is represented by cases (i) and (iii). That (iii) must count as structural government is natural, since it does not depend on inherent lexical properties of the governor. In addition to this consideration, notice that if I, being excluded from the lexical $[\pm N, \pm V]$ classification, must also be excluded from the class of intrinsic structural governors it must be considered to properly govern VP under coindexing with its head, a possibility suggested in Longobardi (1985a, b): now, it is clear that this government is structural, because it allows for unbounded movement of the governee under VP fronting, obviously without successive cyclicity through the Spec of IP:

(140)   Parlato di Gianni, credo proprio che Maria non abbia
          Spoken of Gianni, I really believe that Maria has not

Crucial use of the structural nature of government under coindexing will be made directly. Consider, in fact, that the definitions in (139), combined with a constraint on non-structurally governed traces of the kind examined in section 8, make the following crosslinguistic prediction: extraction of an argument of an NP will only be possible (apart from extraposition cases) in languages and constructions where such an argument is governed (hence θ-marked and Case-marked) by the Noun in a certain position and then moved to another position on the non-recursive side of the head, so as to become accessible to external structural government.[58]

A possible case which bears out this prediction is that of Modern Hebrew as described in Borer (1984; see also Aoun 1985 and, with a different phrase structure, Ritter 1986; Shlonsky 1988): superficially, NPs in such a language appear to be rigidly head-first with respect to all arguments; they look in this respect like Romance NPs, as studied in chapter 3, with the difference that there is no rule, like possessivization, licensing movement of one argument to the prehead non-recursive position. Accordingly, the situation appears to be that, in normal cases, no extraction takes place out of an NP, as we predict.[59] There is, however, one important exception to this generalization: an argument of NP can be extracted when it is 'doubled' by a clitic-like affix occurring on the head Noun. This fact is also interpretable, and actually expected, in the framework we have developed. Consider, first of all, that the disjunctions in (139)a lead us to the expectation that although Nouns, as non-structural governors, cannot normally govern outside their s-selectional frame, they will be able to do so under coindexing. This conclusion is supported by the fact that English *that* deletion, impossible in Noun–Complement structures, is grammatical in relative clauses:

(141)   A woman (that) I liked suddenly arrived

In fact in (141) the N projection heading the relative construction is likely to be coindexed with a null operator in the Spec of the relative CP and the latter, via Spec–head agreement (see Chomsky 1986b), may be coindexed with the empty C. By transitivity of coindexing, such an empty slot will be governed by the head Noun under (139)a.[60] Notice that the existence of a requirement of head government for the empty C is confirmed by (142), whose contrast with (141) also reinforces our previous suggestion that this relation obtains directly at S-structure or in PF (anyway independently of the possibility of reconstructing the extraposed relative), e.g. along lines discussed in Aoun *et al.* (1987):

(142)   A woman suddenly arrived *(that) I liked

Under coindexing, thus, Nouns behave like structural governors. Suppose now that the Hebrew affixation in question is a way of coindexing the head Noun with one of its arguments: it follows that the latter will be governed by the Noun through coindexing, over and beyond their selectional relationship: namely, the Noun will act with respect to that argument as a structural governor and, thus, extraction will be allowed even without previous movement to Spec.

Appendix: On some apparent violations of Cinque's generalization

The behaviour of head Nouns like *need* (Italian *bisogno, neccessità*) may seem at first sight to provide an exception to what was referred to as 'Cinque's generalization', i.e. the fact that extraction of an argument of N is possible only if possessivization of the same argument is possible.

It is actually true that (143) in the relevant sense is widely impossible in Italian, whereas the examples of (144) are perfect:

(143)   il suo bisogno
         its need (* = the need for it)

(144)   a. Ne ho bisogno
            I of-it have need
         b. Di che cosa hai bisogno?
            Of what do you have need?

However, the grammaticality of (144) is a relatively isolated fact, dependent on the lexical choice of the expression *aver bisogno*: with most Verbs extraction becomes clearly impossible:

(145) *Ne sostengo/ricordo/disapprovo il bisogno (in the relevant reading, i.e. when *ne* is the object)
I of-it assert/remember/disapprove the need

(146) *Di che cosa sostieni/ricordi/disapprovi il bisogno?
Of what do you assert/remember/disapprove the need?

Examples (145) and (146) show, thus, that no violation of Cinque's generalization arises, apart from the case in (144) and a few others. An appropriate theory must then block (145) and (146) and allow (144) in some marked way. A solution for (144) is, in fact, straightforward: consider that *aver bisogno* is the only case where *bisogno* may occur in the singular without any Determiner. This may already suggest that *aver bisogno* has peculiar compositional properties which make it into a single Verb taking a genitive complement. This is confirmed by the following properties:

1. Adverbs construed with the matrix Inflection can be freely interpolated between *aver bisogno* and its complement, but not with other Verbs:

(147) a. Avrò bisogno, domani, di tutti voi
I will have need, tomorrow, of you all
  b. ?*Sosterrò il bisogno, domani, di tutti voi
I will assert the need, tomorrow, of you all

2. The CNPC can be freely violated, even by non-subcategorized PPs:

(148) a. In che modo hai bisogno che io ripari la macchina *t*?
In which way do you have need that I fix the car?
  b. *In che modo sostieni il bisogno che io ripari la macchina *t*?
In which way do you assert the need that I fix the car?

3. *Aver bisogno* moves along as a single unit, leaving the genitive phrase behind, in causative constructions:

(149) a. Farò aver bisogno a Mario del mio aiuto
I will make have need to Mario of my help
  b. ?*Farò sostenere il bisogno a Mario del mio aiuto
I will make assert the need to Mario of my help
  c. Farò sostenere a Mario il bisogno del mio aiuto
I will make assert to Mario the need of my help

Notice that for some speakers in (149)a it is even possible to drop *a* before the subject, i.e. *aver bisogno* may assume the behaviour of intransitive Verbs:

(150) a. (?)Farò aver bisogno Mario del mio aiuto
I will make have need Mario of my help
  b. **Farò sostenere il bisogno Mario del mio aiuto
I will make assert the need Mario of my help

4. *Aver bisogno* gaps as a unit in comparative V-gapping, leaving out the

complement, whereas normal V + N strings do not:
(151)   a. Ho avuto bisogno di Maria più spesso che di Gianni
             I had need of Maria more often than of Gianni
         b. ??Ho sostenuto il bisogno di Maria più spesso che di Gianni
             I asserted the need of Maria more often than of Gianni

Other arguments point to the same conclusion: *aver bisogno* can be analysed as a compound Verb with a genitive (or sentential) complement. Semantically, such an expression has the property that the understood subject of *bisogno* is obligatorily controlled by the subject of *avere*. This property also holds of some essentially synonymous expressions involving another Verb, *provare* ('experience'), where *bisogno* cooccurs with an article, like *provare il bisogno* ('experience the need') and of cases in which it may even take modifiers, like *provare (avere) un gran bisogno* ('experience (have) a great need'): these expressions share with *aver bisogno* also all the properties which seem to motivate an idiomatic reanalysis (with the exception of that exemplified in (150)a). This might be taken to suggest that the obligatory control of the subject of *bisogno* is a prerequisite to the idiomatic interpretation. Exactly the same facts and conclusions can be reproduced for other apparent exceptions to Cinque's generalization like *avere* (or *provare*) *paura*, *vergogna* ('fear, shame'), and for Spanish *tener necesidad* ('to have need'), mentioned to Torrego (1986) as a potential problem for what we called Cinque's generalization.

Recall further that, unlike their English counterparts, many 'unaffected' objects in Anderson's (1979) sense can be possessivized in Italian, as noticed by Cinque (1980), a generalization to some extent confirmed for French, Spanish and Catalan as well and theoretically explored in chapter 3 below. One consequence is that there may be complements of N extracted in Romance without violating Cinque's generalization, just because they can also be possessivized in such languages, although this may be unexpected from the viewpoint of their behaviour in English. A typical example is that of *conoscenza* ('knowledge'), whose object can often be possessivized, and hence extracted, in Romance, even if it falls into Anderson's 'unaffected' class in English:
(152)   a. l'argomento di cui è richiesta la conoscenza
             the subject of which knowledge is required
         b. A proposito dell'algebra, è richiesta la sua conoscenza
             Speaking of algebra, its knowledge is required

It seems, in conclusion, that no real violation of Cinque's descriptive constraint is actually possible. For other evidence against apparent counter-examples see also Cinque's (1980) discussion.

3* NP parametrization: the Head–Subject hypothesis

A. GIORGI AND G. LONGOBARDI

Introduction

The first attempt to capture word-order restrictions in the framework of generative syntax was made by means of explicitly stating order in the format of phrase-structure rewriting rules: thus, in an 'Aspects' model, (1) was the typical rule expanding the VP of a transitive Verb for languages like English or Italian, and (2) the rule for the same purpose in so-called OV languages such as Turkish or Japanese:

(1)   VP→V NP
(2)   VP→NP V

With the development of X-bar theory in Chomsky (1970) and Jackendoff (1977), it became possible to formally express a number of generalizations concerning the identity of subcategorization and selection for lexically related words belonging to different syntactic categories (like *belief* and *believe*, *proud* and *pride*); but, as noticed by several researchers (Lightfoot 1979; Graffi 1980; Hawkins 1982, 1983), it also became finally possible to capture in a formal way one typological generalization emerging from J. Greenberg's (1966) pioneering work on implicational universals: i.e. the fact that in most languages in which the direct object follows the Verb, the complements of a Preposition and of a Noun do the same, and vice versa.[1] In fact, rules like (3) and (4), with X freely ranging over the various lexical categories, should represent the unmarked case, according to Greenberg's results, and, at the same time, are formally simpler than a set of separate rules stipulating a specific word order for each major phrase:

(3)   X'→X XP
(4)   X'→XP X

Later on, Stowell's (1981) dissertation suggested that the very notion of 'rewriting rule' could be eliminated, thereby avoiding some redundancy existing in the 'Aspects' system between the categorial component and the

113

information stored in the lexicon. It has become current, now, to think of base structures as directly projected out of the subcategorization properties of lexical items under the constraints imposed by X-bar theory (which also licenses the generation of some lexically unselected material, e.g. Spec positions). The informational content of general rules like (3) and (4) is now expressed through a word-order parameter, formulated, according to Chomsky (1986a) and abstracting away from the position of Spec, in the terms 'head first' vs 'head last'. An empirically more refined proposal has been made by Koopman (1984) and Travis (1984) suggesting that such a parameter has to be split into two parts, one concerning the direction of θ-role assignment and the other that of Case-marking, whose settings coincide in all the unmarked cases, but may occasionally diverge.

In this chapter, by comparing the internal structure of Romance and Germanic NPs, we will propose a further analysis of the 'head-first/-last' parameter or of equivalent notions into two parameters: one specifying the order, with respect to the head, of internal arguments (i.e. the direction of assignment of internal θ-roles), the other determining the order of the argument being assigned the external θ-role and of other phrases, among which APs, whose semantic function can be assimilated to the latter by some criteria.[2] The two parameters, termed Head–Complement and Head–Subject parameter, respectively, will be shown to be set in the same direction in Romance but to diverge in Germanic, with a number of far-reaching consequences for the internal structure of NPs and, probably, of other lexical phrases. In the traditional terminology of syntactic typology our claim is that the positional occurrences of subjects and objects must be kept distinct for Verbs as well as for Nouns, and that from this viewpoint Germanic languages tend to be basically SNO, whereas the Romance ones are basically NOS. The distinction we make between the ordering of subjects and complements with respect to the head will also be shown to regularize so far unexplained exceptions noticed by Greenberg for one of his universal correlations.

The chapter is organized as follows: sections 1–5 are devoted to showing how the differences in the occurrence of genitive arguments, in the distribution and meaning of the two main classes of Adjectives, and in the structure of nominal compounds arising between, say, English and Italian, all follow, in interaction with independently known principles of grammar, from a different setting of the Head–Subject parameter. Here too, we show that the proposed hypothesis comes close to deriving another of Greenberg's universal generalizations, induced on the basis of thirty languages out of which only two belonged to the Germanic–Romance domain, i.e. were part of the data we started with. In sections 6–9, we analyse some further and subtler differences between English and Italian, which, unlike the previous ones, would be impossible to learn on the basis of positive evidence, if they were not related by UG to the previous, more visible, properties of the parameter. The tying together of the two types of properties will thus represent an instance of the successful integration of detailed typological analysis and acquisition (poverty of stimulus) considerations which has so much furthered the study of comparative syntax. In section 10, we address the problem of some potential doubts cast on the unity of the proposed parameter by the behaviour of German and Dutch NPs. The exception will be shown to be only apparent, if an elaborated version of Travis's idea that in marked cases the direction of θ- and Case-marking may diverge is assumed. Finally, in sections 11 and 12, we analyse the categorial status of so-called possessive elements in several languages and some intricate consequences arising from their distributional and interpretative properties for the theories of landing sites and of empty categories: in particular, it is argued there that the possible targets of syntactic movement cannot be limited to the positions termed Spec, but must include in Romance other positions not strictly subcategorized as complements of a head.

Considering the major syntactic parameters, there is some reason to believe that the setting of the Head–Subject one is among the most deeply rooted typological characteristics in the structure of a language: for instance, the unity of *Romania* appears to be very substantial with respect to the value of this parametric choice, exactly as for the Head–Complement parameter, while it is broken, most notably by French, with respect to other parameters: e.g. the null subject one or those which govern the categorial status of possessives. On the other hand, the study of the Head–Subject parameter displays some affinity with that of null-subject phenomena in that, in addition to revealing several intricate typological consequences, it appears to constitute a useful tool to probe the most abstract 'cores' of current syntactic theories, in particular the theory of empty categories: in fact, in the course of the discussion it will be shown that two important generalizations about the distribution and interpretation of certain Adjectives and the patterning of understood subjects of NPs can hardly be captured in a theory not including syntactically realized empty categories of a − and + pronominal nature, respectively. The phenomena bearing on the Head–Subject parameter support, thus, in the strongest way, the existence of categories such as trace and PRO in the correct theory of UG.

We would also like to stress, however, that we regard our work in this chapter as a methodological experiment, namely as a partial and limited attempt toward bridging the gap between a study of UG based on the in-depth syntactic analysis of one or few languages (jointly with consider-ations of abstract learnability: poverty of stimulus and related innateness issues) and one based on more superficial descriptions of a larger number of languages. In pursuing this research strategy, advocated among others by Hawkins (1985) and leading ultimately to an approach which might be termed generative typology, we have tried to follow R. Kayne's original insight that the study of comparative syntax should best start with the comparison of closely related languages, later extending the typological coverage in a stepwise fashion. It is in this sense that we hope that the comparative analysis of Romance and Germanic Noun Phrases may contribute models and hypotheses exploitable in a progressively enlarged domain of empirical inquiry.

1   The definition of the directionality parameter

As we have said, the main parametric variation we are going to analyse concerns, roughly, the directionality of the external θ-role assignment within a lexical category in Romance on the one hand and in Germanic on the other. We will especially consider data from English and from Italian, but most of our observations can be extended to French, Rumanian, Spanish, Catalan and other Romance languages, as well as to Norwegian, Swedish, and other Germanic languages. To be more precise, among the phrases licensed by a lexical head, we make a crucial distinction between subcategorized arguments (i.e. internal arguments, required by the Projection Principle) and elements bearing to the head a semantic relation which may be termed *external* (not required by the Projection Principle: subjects and, in nominals, possessors and elements predicated of the head). This distinction seems to be a natural one, as noted by Chomsky (1986b, p. 46; see also Jaeggli 1986, p. 590). Within NPs all such elements are realized inside the maximal projection and the distinction in question can be in part shown to correlate with different levels of structural attachment, as suggested by the results of the preceding chapters. In chapter 1, some structural differences were proposed, mainly on the grounds of binding evidence, between the internal θ-roles of N and the external one. We will not discuss the relevant data again here, but we will simply assume that Nouns assign internal θ-relations inside a non-maximal projection, call it N′, and the external one under a higher projection. We assume the external θ-role to be identifiable as such in the θ-grid contained in the lexicon. Moreover, in chapter 2 it has been shown that the level of attachment of possessors, i.e. of all those genitive elements semantically connected with the head in a looser way than through a specific θ-role (Higginbotham's (1983) R-relation), is still higher than that of arguments expressing the external θ-role (if present). In fact, a possessor can bind elements within an argument bearing an external θ-role, for instance an agent, but not vice versa. This fact suggests that even structurally the possessor is certainly not an internal argument, since it seems not to be c-commanded by the external one. Therefore the structure of an NP is likely to have at least the following layers, abstracting away for the moment from the occurrence of the Spec position:[3]

(5)

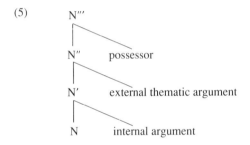

N′ is thus the domain of strictly subcategorized arguments, excluding both agents and possessors: we may slightly generalize the result by supposing that all other semantic functions licensed by the head are defined outside N′.[4] We can assume, thus, that it is not only possessors and agents which are defined outside N′, but that all the non-thematic elements somehow selected by the head (i.e. except adverbials), such as APs licensed as predicative modifiers of the Noun, are projected as external functions as well, since their presence is not required by subcategorization. Our parameter can be stated as follows: while internal arguments (β) are projected to the right of the head both in Romance and in Germanic, external semantic functions (α) are licensed at D-structure on the right in Romance but on the left in Germanic: if our structural hypotheses are correct, the effects of the parameter can be presented as in (6), where we simplify the hierarchical structure, for expository reasons:

(6) Romance:

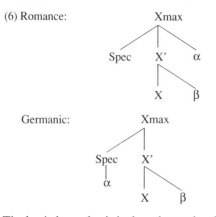

Germanic:

The basic hypothesis is thus that a simple parameter like 'head first'/'head last' is still insufficient to capture the phrase-internal word-order generalizations which, before Stowell (1981), used to be expressed in a less principled way by means of phrase-structure rules. We claim that two such parameters are required: slightly generalizing the meaning of 'subject' to cover all the cases referred to above, they will be termed 'Head–Complement' and 'Head–Subject' parameter. As a consequence of their opposed settings in languages like the Germanic ones, in fact, the head of NP would basically occur between its main arguments.[5] The idea represents, therefore, a further step in the direction pointed out by Koopman (1984) and Travis (1984), who proposed to subsume linear-order generalizations along with many of Greenberg's (1966) typological observations under parameters concerning the direction of θ- and Case-assignment and their interaction: our proposal, in fact, essentially amounts to relativizing the direction of θ-assignment to the distinction between internal and external θ-roles. The approach here advocated for the Germanic languages will also solve a problem of typological inconsistency noted by Greenberg (1966): in fact, he remarked about two Germanic languages, namely English and Norwegian, that they represented exceptions to two of his major correlations: those holding between the existence of Prepositions (as opposed to Postpositions), on one hand, and the postnominal position of Genitive and Adjectives, on the other. However, in the more detailed theoretical framework independently proposed here, these are no longer exceptions, but predictable results. In fact, objects of Prepositions are complements, hence they are ordered in accordance to the Head–Complement parameter, which is set to the right in English and Norwegian for all lexical heads: some genitive phrases and the Adjectives, instead, are basically ordered, as we shall see, by the Head–Subject parameter, which is set to the left in Germanic.

This result provides, then, a good example of how more abstractly founded hypotheses may sometimes not only subsume the main achievements of inductive typology, but even attain better empirical adequacy.

2   Prenominal and postnominal Genitives

A first consequence of the Head-Subject parameter concerns the existence of prenominal Genitive in Germanic but not in Romance:[6]

(7)   a. John's book
        b. *il Gianni + GEN libro
           the Gianni + GEN book

The possibility of having such a realization of Genitive only in Germanic follows from our directionality parameter in conjunction with Koopman's (1984) and Travis's (1984) theory on the interaction of θ- and Case-marking. They argue that, in the unmarked situation, θ-role and Case are consistently assigned in the same direction. Supposing for the moment that all Romance and Germanic languages are unmarked cases (but for German and Dutch see sec. 10 below), θ-assignment and Case-marking should be consistent. Let us assume, in fact, that Koopman's and Travis's principle holds for Case realization at S-structure (in the sense of Chomsky's 1986a discussion of the Uniformity Condition): if Germanic Ns are able to θ-mark on both sides, we must expect them to be able to trigger Case realization bidirectionally as well, whereas Romance Ns, which only θ-mark to their right, are expected to allow Case realization just in that direction. What follows from this idea is that at the surface level we will be able to find Genitive-marked elements only on the right of N in the Romance languages, but on both sides in the Germanic ones, an apparently correct prediction throughout the whole range of languages considered.[7]

It is true that pronominal and anaphoric arguments can appear to the left of N also in Romance as possessives, preceded or not by a Determiner (see sect. 11):

(8)   a. il suo libro

    b. son livre
      his/her/its book

These elements, however, do not show in their surface realization any normal mark of Genitive and their ending agrees with the head Noun in gender and number, as Adjectives and Determiners usually do; this property, in Indo-European languages with overt Case inflections, like Latin or German, to mention just two, systematically goes along also with Case agreement. We will then assume, following the proposal in chapter 2, that possessives realize a Case by inheriting it through agreement with the head, exactly like regular Adjectives and Determiners. The categorial status of possessives will be discussed in detail in section 11.

Since the base-generated θ-position is always on the right in Romance, whenever a prenominal argument appears it must have been derived via movement from a postnominal position. The only elements which can move, however, are those which can be Case-marked through agreement, since no direct Genitive realization in prenominal position is possible in Romance.

A second consequence of our parameter concerns postnominal occurrences of Genitive-marked elements. From our proposal it follows that in the Germanic languages the postnominal position of external arguments must always be derived via movement from the thematic Spec position, whereas in Romance it is the regular θ-position directly projected at D-structure.

Consider, however, that the movement in question is not an instance of the 'core' cases of movement discussed in Chomsky (1986b), i.e. it is not substitution into Spec. Rather, it is a rightward movement rule, most likely an adjunction to some projection of the head Noun. Rightward movement rules are known to be typologically quite marked (wh-movement, for example, seems to be leftward in most languages where it occurs[8]) and, when they appear, they are often subject to peculiar conditions with a 'stylistic' or 'functional' flavour which never seem to affect 'core' leftward rules. At least, this appears to be the case in the kind of languages we are considering here: the most typical rightward rules of English, i.e. extraposition and Heavy NP Shift, provide good examples.

Given our parametric analysis of Noun Phrase structure, we are thus led to the expectation that at least in some Germanic languages conditions of the sort just mentioned may appear to constrain the postnominal surfacing of external arguments, though not of internal ones, and, further, that this will never be the case in any Romance language. Consider, in fact, the following structures with the genitive NPs understood as possessor phrases:

(9)   a. il libro di Gianni
           the book of Gianni
        b. *the *e* book of John
        c. the *e* book of the man I met yesterday
        d. ?the book of John Smith
        e. ?the book of that man
        f. the legs of the table

In English, (9)b, whose contrast with Italian (9)a has not been paid much attention in the recent literature, is ungrammatical, but (9)c is considered much more acceptable. We attribute the difference to the fact that, under the suggested analysis, in (9)c the rightward movement is an instantiation of Heavy NP Shift with its familiar conditions. Examples (9)d and e suggest that an NP may count as 'heavy' with respect to such a rule in a slightly extended way, presumably if it already branches and if the Determiner is stronger than just an article; in (9)f the licensing condition for rightward movement might also involve inanimacy.[9] Essentially the same paradigm holds concerning arguments bearing real external θ-roles, as, e.g., in the 'agent' reading of the genitive phrase of (9)a-e (i.e. as the author).[10]

As can be seen, not all the conditions licensing the postnominal occurrence of a genitive external argument in English are reducible to heaviness, although the notion seems to play the most crucial role.[11] Whatever their theoretical status, what is relevant about these conditions is that while they are partially shared by most other rightward movement rules and by no leftward movement to Spec, they are totally unprecedented as conditions on base-generation of arguments: this fact strongly suggests the correctness of our movement hypothesis. Internal arguments, such as genitive NPs θ-marked as themes by the head N, are, instead, base-generated to the right also in English, as a consequence of the identical setting of the Head–Complement parameter in Romance and Germanic; their surfacing in that position is, expectedly, unconstrained:

(10)   a. The description of Mary was inaccurate
        b. The destruction of Rome was impossible
        c. The fear of Mary was great

We may notice, as a corollary, that (10)a and c are unambiguous in English since *Mary*, not being 'heavy', cannot be understood as an external argument, but their literal versions (11) are perfectly ambiguous in Italian, where Maria may be either the agent or the theme of the description and the experiencer or the theme of the fear:

(11)   a. La descrizione di Maria non era accurata (= 10a)
        b. La paura di Maria era grande (= 10c)

In fact, the other prediction of our hypothesis is that English and probably other Germanic languages should, in this respect, contrast with Romance, where the corresponding constructions with postnominal external arguments are, we claim, base-generated: thus, in no Romance language is there any constraint on postnominal Genitive singling out external vs internal arguments, and structures like (9)a are grammatical throughout the whole of *Romania*.

Let us finally recall that it has been argued by Giorgi (1986 and ch. 1) that some Nouns can be 'ergative' (in Burzio's (1981, 1986) sense) exactly as the corresponding Verbs: their unique genitive argument has thus been shown to be an internal one even on structural grounds, i.e. to hang from N' and not from higher projections. Consider in this light the following examples:

(12)   a. The appearance of Mary was sudden
        b. The entrance of Mary into the room was sudden

Examples (12)a and b are Nouns related to ergative Verbs, which maintain the properties of ergativity; therefore, as predicted by our hypothesis, their argument, which will be an internal one, can always appear in postnominal position even in English.

3   The distribution of predicative Adjectives

A property which sharply distinguishes Germanic and Romance concerns the position of predicative Adjectives with respect to the head N. By the term 'predicative Adjective', we refer to all those adjectival modifiers which predicate a quality of the head N without denoting an object in the world and functioning as an argument of the head.[12]

To clarify, consider, for instance, the following cases:

(13)   a. il vestito elegante
           the elegant dress
        b. l'invasione tedesca
           the German invasion
        c. *la nostra invasione tedesca della Grecia
           our German invasion of Greece

Elegante ('elegant') does not refer to an entity of the world, it is only a property which can be predicated of something, whereas *tedesco* ('German') can also 'refer'; in this case, in fact, the phrase is equivalent to *l'invasione dei tedeschi* ('the invasion by Germans') in which *tedeschi* is a clearly referential term functioning as an argument. *Tedeschi* and *tedesco* in these examples denote the same class of objects, so that *tedesco* can be claimed to have referential properties, in spite of the fact that it is an Adjective. As a consequence, in the unmarked reading, (13)c is ruled out by the θ-criterion.

Consider now the following examples:

(14)   a. una simpatica ragazza *e*
           b. a nice girl
           c. una ragazza simpatica
           d. *a *e* girl nice

Simpatica ('nice') is a typically predicative Adjective: in Italian, and in Romance in general, a non-complemented predicative Adjective can either precede or follow the head N, whereas, as shown by (14)b and d, in English, as in all the Germanic languages, only the prenominal position is admitted.

Notice that in Romance the two positions actually differ with respect to the information content they convey; in fact the prenominal position only has an appositive interpretation, whereas the postnominal one can either be restrictive or appositive.[13] Obviously, even in English a predicative Adjective can carry both meanings; nevertheless in English it can only precede.

This distributional difference can follow from the Head–Subject parameter if we consider that NP-internal APs can only be interpreted as external semantic functions, in the sense defined above, i.e. that they do not belong to the subcategorization frame of the N. Since external semantic functions are parametrized in the way we have discussed, it follows that in Italian the AP is base-generated in postnominal position, as in (14)c. In English, on the other hand, it is generated prenominally, as in (14)b; in Italian a structure like (14)a can be easily derived, since it is simply an instantiation of movement to Spec, a core case of movement, usually permitted without special assumptions. By contrast, the movement of the Adjective to a postnominal position in English, being a case of rightward movement, is not admitted unless some specific conditions hold.[14] The asymmetry is essentially the same as we found with free movement to Spec of possessives in Italian vs stylistically or functionally constrained rightward movement of genitive external arguments in English. Here, too, we may expect APs surfacing on the right to be licensed in English under special conditions, analogous to those governing rightward movement, if our general hypothesis is correct. Consider, in fact, the following example:

(15)   a *e* girl proud of her behaviour

In this case we find at work the same condition of heaviness which holds in (9)c. Notice, however, that, in the case of genitive NPs, a heavy one can still appear in prenominal position, while this is impossible with APs:

(16)   a. the man I met yesterday's book
        b. *a proud of her behaviour girl

The ungrammaticality of (16)b, however, is due to independent reasons discussed by Williams (1982) and reduced by Longobardi in chapter 2, on the grounds of previous work by Emonds (1976), under his Consistency Principle.[15] As a conclusion, then, we can say that roughly the same conditions which license the postnominal position of external arguments also license the postnominal position of APs.

Actually, the generalization that we have achieved through our parameter with respect to the linear position of simple Adjectives is likely to extend its empirical scope well beyond the limits of Germanic and Romance. In fact Greenberg has noted the regularity of the distribution of Adjectives, as is stated in his universal 19 (Greenberg, 1966, p. 87):

(17)   When the general rule is that the descriptive Adjective follows,
            there may be a minority of Adjectives which usually precede, but
            when the general rule is that descriptive Adjectives precede, there
            are no exceptions.

Greenberg analysed a sample of thirty languages among which just one Germanic language was included, namely Norwegian, and a single Romance one, namely Italian. Of course in order to reduce universal 19 with its extensive typological coverage under our Head–Subject parameter a further premise is required, namely that the Spec of NPs (i.e. the target of core cases of movement) be universally on the left of the head or that movement (e.g. of an AP) to Spec may instantiate a core case only under the additional condition of being leftward. Especially the latter version of the principle looks quite plausible: most well-studied cases of substitution into Spec or head are leftward rules, independently of the basic word-order facts of the various languages. Typical is the above mentioned example of wh-movement, which, when existing at all in the syntax of a language, seems normally to be leftward. Most likely, analogous considerations can be made for clitic-placement, and also for many V-movement rules in several European and African languages, discussed by Koopman (1984) and Travis (1984) among others.[16]

If some version of such principles is tenable the process of reduction of typological generalizations like Greenberg's to more abstract constructs developed within the generative framework will probably extend to cover universal 19, greatly increasing the predictive power and the factual support of our hypothesis.

4   The distribution of referential Adjectives

Greenberg's (1966) formulation of universal 19 already suggests that the class of Adjectives occurring in prenominal position in languages like the Romance ones is less than the totality. In this section we will provide a partial theoretical account for this correct observation, analysing the behaviour of what we have called before 'referential' Adjectives.

Let us first consider a paradigm of the kind analysed by Kayne (1981a):

(18)   a. the Italian invasion of Albania
        b. *the Albanian invasion by Italy
        c. Italy's invasion of Albania
        d. Albania's invasion by Italy

Kayne pointed out that an Adjective can express a θ-role, but, unlike essentially synonymous genitive phrases, never expresses an internal one.[17] The explanation he provides amounts to saying that an AP cannot get its thematic interpretation via a chain, in that it would not be able to bind a trace in argument NP position. Kayne already noticed the potential significance of the similarity between the ungrammaticality of (18)b and the fact that referential Adjectives expressing a thematic function of the head cannot bind an anaphor either:

(19)   a. *the Albanian destruction of itself/themselves
        b. Albania's destruction of itself
        c. the Albanians' destruction of themselves

Whatever the reason for the ungrammaticality of (18)b, it is likely that the same explanation should also extend to a phrase like (19)a. The basic generalization can, in fact, be formulated, as a first and very rough approximation, in the following terms: a referential Adjective may discharge a θ-role of the head (in Higginbotham's 1985 sense), but is insufficient as the antecedent for an anaphoric expression. This fact is also confirmed by several types of Italian anaphors:

(20)   a. *le opinioni americane$_i$ su se stessi$_i$
          the American opinion about themselves
        b. *le opinioni americane$_i$ su di sé$_i$
          the American$_i$ opinions about self$_i$ (third person reflexive
          unmarked for gender and number)
        c. *le opinioni russe e americane gli uni sugli altri
          the Russian and American opinions about each other

Although the statement of the generalization, which has an interest of its own, is incomplete and rather unprincipled, it seems to suffice to relate (18)b and (19)a. Suppose, in fact, that a θ-role were transmitted to a referential AP by a trace and could then percolate down to the argument: such a trace would probably be projected as an NP (the Canonical Structural Realization of direct arguments under the Projection Principle) and this empty NP, not being a variable (the trace of wh-movement), would be anaphoric, hence subject to an unsatisfiable binding requirement.[18] Notice that no theoretical framework dispensing with traces could capture such a generalization, so that the proposed analysis, and the extension of it we are going to present in this section, constitute one of the strongest arguments supporting the existence of traces, not only within NPs, but more generally in the theory of syntax.

Whether or not this account is ultimately correct, it is remarkable that the paradigm (18) is also found in Romance (and other languages), where the AP occurs postnominally:

(21)   a. l'invasione italiana dell'Albania
          lit.: the invasion Italian of Albania
        b. *l'invasione albanese da parte dell'Italia
          lit.: the invasion Albanian by Italy
        c. la sua invasione dell'Albania
          its invasion of Albania
        d. la sua invasione da parte dell'Italia
          its invasion by Italy

In spite of the fact that both the 'active' and the 'passive' version of the NP, (21)c and (21)d, respectively, are possible with a possessive, (21)b is ungrammatical. Since in Romance the AP surfaces to the right of the head the existence of a 'move α' relationship with a trace is not immediately obvious. In order to establish it and to create the conditions to generalize

Kayne's original account of (18)b to Romance, we must rely on the following assumption: even if an AP originated under N′, it would have to move under Nmax, to receive and realize agreement, under the independently plausible hypothesis that agreement with a head X can only be realized under Xmax.[19] In order to be interpreted, therefore, the AP in (21)b should bind a thematic trace. Given that this kind of binding is impossible, the structure is ruled out. Consider now that the generalization arrived at by Kayne (that thematic APs cannot bind a trace) in conjunction with our Head–Subject hypothesis makes an important prediction, namely that referential Adjectives, unlike predicative ones, will never surface prenominally in Romance, since in that case they should bind a trace in the postnominal θ-position; the prediction is straight-forwardly correct in all the Romance languages, as exemplified in (22):

(22)   a. l'invasione italiana dell'Albania
           lit.: the invasion Italian of Albania
      b. *l'italiana invasione dell'Albania
           lit.: the Italian invasion of Albania

Here, too, Germanic and Romance systematically contrast, since in Germanic a prenominal AP is in its base position and does not have to bind any trace to be interpreted. The difference within Romance between referential and predicative Adjectives, which we have shown in the previous section to be able to move to the prenominal position, is due to the fact that the latter do not have to bind an argument trace, but a truly adjectival one.

Furthermore, if our hypotheses are correct, we also expect other external semantic functions expressible by means of a referential Adjective to be governed by these restrictions. This prediction is actually borne out, since also those Adjectives which do not directly express an agent θ-role of the head, but a possessor, or an even looser relation (R-relation in Higginbotham's 1983 sense) are unable to appear prenominally in Romance:

(23)   a. un'automobile italiana
           lit.: a car Italian
      b. *un'italiana automobile
           an Italian car

This behaviour extends to all those Adjectives which can be identified as 'referential'; we have said above that this function may be distinguished from that of predicating a quality of the head. A clear, although not exhaustive, way of distinguishing predicative from referential Adjectives is considering that the latter cannot normally occur under modification of any sort:

(24)   a. un'invasione molto rapida/*italiana dell'Albania
           a very quick/Italian invasion of Austria
        b. un'invasione più rapida/*italiana della precedente
           an invasion more quick/Italian than the previous one

However, it is not the case that modified ethnic Adjectives like 'Italian' or 'German' are straightforwardly ungrammatical, or at least it is not always so. They can often be accepted if interpreted non-referentially, i.e. as predicative ones. This fact provides us with the opportunity of clarifying what being referential really means for an Adjective. Consider the following pair:

(25)   a. Il comportamento tedesco nel 1914 fu irrazionale
           The German behaviour in 1914 was irrational
        b. Questo è un tipico comportamento tedesco
           This is a typical German behaviour

The semantic implications of the two sentences differ: in (25)a the behaviour in question *has* to be that of Germany or Germans; in (25)b the person(s) or the country behaving *need not* necessarily be German, for the statement to be true, as first pointed out to us by T. Stowell (p.c.), but just to behave in a German-like way. We can conclude that in (25)a *tedesco* is referential, in the most general sense of this notion, i.e. has to denote an object in the world (Germany or Germans); which is not the case in (25)b. With the predicative meaning of (25)b, it is thus regularly possible to modify the Adjective:

(26)   a. un comportamento italianissimo
           a very Italian behaviour
        b. un comportamento più italiano di quanto mi aspettassi
           a behaviour more Italian than I expected

Especially when the predicative nature of these Adjectives is forced by modification, and by cooccurrence with an overt agent, it is even possible for them to appear in prenominal position in Italian, another subtle prediction of the framework of hypotheses that we have presented:

(27)   quel suo tedeschissimo comportamento
        that very German behaviour of his

On the grounds of the test of modification we can recognize as members of the referential class, bearing an R-relation to the head Noun, the

Adjectives in the following phrases and many others, thus correctly predicting their non-occurrence in prenominal position in Romance:[20]

(28)   a. *una corrente estremamente elettrica/più elettrica/elettricissima
            a current extremely/more/very electric
        b. corrente elettrica
            lit.: current electric
        c. *elettrica corrente
            electric current
(29)   a. *l'energia molto nucleare/relativamente nucleare/nuclearissima
            the energy very/relatively/very nuclear
        b. energia nucleare
            lit.: energy nuclear
        c. *nucleare energia
            nuclear energy[21]

Here, too, it is possible to have the prenominal position in the non-referential reading:

(30)   Un'elettrica Lollobrigida ha presentato il festival di ieri sera
         An electric (= brilliant) Lollobrigida introduced last night's festival

Consider finally example (31): in Italian there are Adjectives, like e.g. *popolare*, which can either have a predicative function, meaning 'famous', or a referential one, meaning 'related to the people, folk':[22]

(31)   a. una canzone popolare
            lit.: a song folk/popular
        b. una popolare canzone
            lit.: a popular song

In postnominal position both the R-related and the predicative meaning are available; in prenominal position the only possible meaning is the predicative one. Once again, this fact follows from our hypothesis.[23,24]

5   Directionality in Noun compounds

Intuitively related in an obvious sense to the Head–Subject parameter is the fact that Romance and Germanic languages also differ systematically with respect to the linear structure of Noun compounds: in all the Germanic languages since the earliest stages (see also Ramat 1986), the head of the compound is the rightmost element, whereas in Romance it is the leftmost one, a property which arises in simple binary compounds, but also in cases of recursive formation:[25]

(32)   a. il capo settore vendite
        b. *the head department sales
        c. *il vendite settore capo
        d. the sales department head

In Italian (32)a is grammatical; but its literal English translation, (32)b is not. The opposite holds for the English compound: (32)d is grammatical, but the Italian one, (32)c, is not.

The obvious way to subsume the contrasts in nominal composition under the Head–Subject parameter is assuming that the relationship between the head of the compound and the modifier is an external one, i.e. can be assimilated to that of 'subjects'. Notice that in this specific case there is little sense in the notion 'external' understood as a structural concept, namely as 'external to N'. In fact, Noun compounds syntactically behave rather like simple head Nouns and not like phrases – a fact noticed in the now vast literature on the topic (see, among others, Roeper and Siegel 1978; Lieber 1983) – and seem, thus, to result from a process of morphological incorporation. It is, however, possible to argue that, semantically, the modifier in a *tatpurusa* Noun compound never corresponds to an internal argument projected out of the subcategorization properties of the head. In many cases of nominal compounds the meaning of the modifier is already just that of a loosely R-related phrase, so that its prenominal position in Germanic should be straightforwardly expected:

(33)   a. sales department
        b. bird cage
        c. dog barber shop[26]

The apparent problem arises when we consider Germanic compounds whose modifier seems to be a real internal argument of the head, although obviously it still appears to the left of the head:

(34)   a. spaghetti eater
        b. bartender
        c. city destroyer

A closer look at the properties of such modifiers suggests, though, that we are not dealing with real referential expressions in argument position; therefore, they will not be licensed as internal arguments under the Projection Principle, hence to the right of the head as a consequence of the directionality of internal θ-marking. Consider, first of all, that these modifiers do not seem to occupy or bind any A-position comparable to that of regular internal arguments, as shown by the following contrasts in binding possibilities:

(35) a. The entrusting of a child to himself is a psychologically very
          delicate moment
      b. A child's entrusting to himself...
      c. *Child entrusting to himself...
(36) a. the informers of a person about himself
      b. a person's informers about himself
      c. *person informers about himself

Second, notice that in some of these cases the object of the head Noun can apparently be doubled:

(37) a. the bartender of Bill's bar (due to E. Williams, p.c.)
      b. his bird-watching of the nightingale
      c. the department head of the linguistic department
      d. the message transmission of such a document (J. Higginbotham,
          p.c.)

Analogous examples can sometimes be reproduced in Romance, as in the following Italian case:

(38)   il capostazione della stazione Termini
          the station master of the Termini station

Now, if the genitive phrase discharges (in the sense of Higginbotham 1985) the internal θ-role of the head, as seems reasonable, it follows from the θ-criterion that the modifier of the compound is not licensed through such a θ-assignment. Finally, consider that, as noticed by E. Williams in unpublished work, the modifier of a compound does not induce the same truth-value assignments normally triggered by a referential NP in object position:

(39) a. John is a Nixon hater, but he does not hate Nixon
      b. John is a hater of Nixon, but he does not hate Nixon

According to Williams's judgement, the latter sentence is a contradictory statement, but the former is not; we may thus argue that in (39)a the first instance of *Nixon* does not denote as a referential expression as the second one does. The facts now discussed can be plausibly taken to establish that compound modifiers, though licensed through an obvious semantic relationship with the head, have, however, the following properties:

(40)   a. They are licensed in their surface position and not via binding of a trace
        b. They do not discharge a θ-role of the head
        c. They are likely not to be referential arguments in the usual sense

Now, we may take the directionality of our Head–Subject parameter to affect all expressions licensed by a relation to the head different from internal θ-role assignment: then, whatever the precise interpretation assigned by the head to the various sorts of compound modifiers, the interpretative mechanism would be unavailable on the right in Germanic and on the left in Romance. This way, we can reduce the linear properties of Noun compounding in Romance and Germanic to the proposed difference in the value of the Head–Subject parameter.

6   Uniqueness of the argument in Spec

An important topic which we have only marginally considered so far concerns the structure of Spec: i.e. linear order and hierarchical relations of Adjectives, Determiners, possessives and quantifiers in prenominal position (see nn. 1 and 13 for some sketchy remarks and ch. 4 for more extensive discussion). In this section, we will discuss one aspect of this problem which interacts with our main concern, i.e. argument structure, and most likely with the Head–Subject parameter. It is possible, in fact, to observe an interesting pattern in English which finds no correspondence in Italian. Consider the following examples:

(41)   a. *his/*John's books of my favourite writer
        b. his/John's books by my favourite writer
(42)   a. ?*the books of John Smith of my favourite writer
        b. the books of John Smith by my favourite writer
(43)   a. i libri di Gianni del mio autore preferito
           the books of Gianni of my favourite writer
        b. i suoi libri del mio autore preferito
           his books of my favourite writer

In English NPs it is impossible to express at the same time the agent and the possessor, unless the agent is expressed by means of a *by*-phrase. In Italian, on the contrary, this structure is perfectly acceptable, i.e. both the agent and the possessor can be expressed in the genitive form at the same time. Italian allows both the structure with the prenominal possessive and that with two postnominal NPs, introduced by *di* ('of'); conversely, in English these structures are both ungrammatical. The pattern of Italian also extends to the other Romance languages, suggesting the usual typological distribution of the phenomenon (with the exceptions which we will discuss in sect. 10). Consider, in fact, the following examples from French, Spanish and Catalan:

(44)   a. les livres de Jean de mon auteur préféré
        b. ses livres de mon auteur préféré
(45)   a. los libros de Juan de mi autor preferido
        b. sus libros de mi autor preferido
(46)   a. els llibres d'en Joan del meu autor preferit
        b. els seus llibres del meu autor preferit

Notice that these restrictions are found in English only on the cooccurrence of the agent and the possessor; as already known, agent and theme can be both present, receiving Genitive Case, and even possessor and theme can coexist:

(47)   John's (A) description of Mary (T)
(48)   John's (P) picture of Mary (T)

It seems, therefore, that the presence of an internal argument does not interfere with that of an external one, either a possessor or an agent, whereas the latter two cannot coexist. Given its typological distribution and the fact that it concerns external arguments, as opposed to internal ones, it is most plausible that the constraint is related to our directionality parameter. Let us assume, in fact, that Spec, i.e. the pre-head position, is subject to a uniqueness filter for arguments, as a universal property of X-bar theory, holding then both in Romance and in Germanic and perhaps across all syntactic categories (see the so-called Doubly Filled Comp Filter). Since the external arguments, either possessors or agents, are generated on the left of the head, i.e. in the Spec position, in Germanic, it follows that only one such argument can be generated there, determining the impossibility for the agent and the possessor to cooccur. In other words, our proposal is that X-bar theory imposes, in the Spec position, the following universal filter on the syntactic representations derivable from the lexicon and potentially interpretable:

(49)   Argument Uniqueness of Spec:
        Only one argument may occur in each Spec position

Under this approach, (41)a is ungrammatical because the same argument slot should be occupied both by *John's* and by the trace of the shifted phrase *of my favourite writer*; (42)a is ungrammatical because two traces at the same time should occupy the prenominal slot. The fact that the restriction does not affect internal arguments follows now from the independently established principle that also in Germanic languages the latter are generated on the right. In Romance, on the other hand, the external arguments are also generated on the right and, therefore, the coexistence of the agent and the possessor does not interact with the requirement that Spec contain only one argument. It is possible that the effects of the hypothesis that also in Romance, as we have just said, Spec must be mono-argumental are manifested in Italian by the total ungrammaticality of the following example:

(50)   **i miei suoi quadri
        my his pictures

If one of the two arguments is expressed postnominally the acceptability of the structure substantially improves, as noticed e.g. by Cinque (1981a), even if it still does not attain full grammaticality:

(51)   ??i miei quadri suoi
        my pictures his

The non-complete acceptability of (51) must be related to the violation of an independent uniqueness requirement concerning possessivization (see ch. 2).[27]

The Argument Uniqueness Requirement for Spec will now be shown to play a crucial role in our analysis of further properties of NPs, especially in the account we will propose for some contrasts arising with control and binding phenomena and in a partial reinterpretation of Anderson's (1979) Affectedness Constraint.[28]

7   **Control**

We are now in a position to consider the most abstract consequences following from our parametric hypothesis. So far, we have examined a number of properties of Germanic and Romance which cluster together in a typologically interesting and revealing way. In principle, however, none of these properties seems to raise, in isolation, a totally insurmountable problem for acquisition from limited and positive evidence only. It is conceivable that any child endowed with a number of open parameters, each corresponding to one of the properties considered, could easily learn to set their values singularly by direct exposure to a sample of relatively few input sentences, exemplifying, for instance, the position of genitive phrases, that of Adjectives, the structure of compounds, the number of postnominal arguments in Romance. The next differences between Romance and Germanic that we are going to analyse would, by contrast, be completely unlearnable under normal conditions (they would require access to subtle intuitions, sometimes almost non-occurring sentence types and probably to direct negative evidence), were they not deducible from the independently motivated setting of the Head–Subject parameter. Roeper (1984) has shown that the unexpressed agent of an NP can satisfy the obligatory control requirements of (the PRO subject of) a purpose clause as well as an overt one, but that this is no longer the case if a direct object is raised to the Spec position:

(52)   a. I disapprove of the/their destruction of the ship to collect the insurance
       b. *its/*the ship's destruction to collect the insurance

Even if the strength of the contrast in English varies among speakers, it is surprising to remark that in Romance for no speaker is there a real contrast between the equivalents of (52)a and (52)b:

(53)   a. Disapprovo la (loro) distruzione della nave per PRO riscuotere l'assicurazione
       I disapprove of the (their) destruction of the ship to collect the insurance
       b. A proposito di questa nave, disapprovo la sua distruzione per PRO riscuotere l'assicurazione
       Concerning this ship, I disapprove of its destruction to collect the insurance

The following cases appear to be similar:

(54)   a. A proposito del prigioniero, considero immorale la sua detenzione dopo avergli promesso l'impunità
       Speaking of the prisoner, I consider immoral his detention after promising him impunity
       b. A proposito dei prezzi, la loro fissazione anticipata per scoraggiare gli speculatori mi sembra improbabile
       Speaking of prices, their anticipated fixing to discourage speculators seems to me unlikely

It is quite clear that both the subtle contrast of (52) in English and the corresponding lack of contrast of (53) in Italian cannot be learned: it is unlikely that the relevant evidence may ever be available in the primary data to any language learner. It is, thus, necessary to try to relate them to other well-manifested properties distinguishing the two languages.

We can show that our hypothesis about the values of the Head–Subject parameter already accounts without any addition or modification for the lack of contrast in Romance. Recall first that Roeper (1984) and Chomsky (1986a) have proposed to explain the English facts by suggesting that, in English, 'passivization' of an NP, i.e. movement of an internal argument to the Spec position, blocks control of PRO by the agent, because it obliterates an empty category, most likely another PRO, in the external θ-position: the latter therefore ceases to be available to satisfy the requirements of obligatory control, determining ungrammaticality.[29] This approach thus implicitly presupposes the uniqueness of a prenominal position for arguments which we have empirically argued for in the preceding section.

In Italian, on the other hand, passivization does not affect the control possibilities, since movement to Spec does not involve the position of the external argument, which is generated to the right of the head: thus that control is still possible even if the internal argument has been raised to Spec.[30] As we have suggested, the phenomenon extends to other Romance languages, e.g. French and Spanish, whose possessives display different distributional properties from the Italian ones (see sect. 11 for discussion):

(55)   a. A propos des prix, leur fixation pour décourager les spéculateurs me semble improbable
Speaking of prices, their fixing in order to discourage speculators seems to me unlikely

b. Por lo que respecta a esta nave, desapruebo su destrucción para cobrar el seguro
For what concerns this ship, I disapprove its destruction to collect the insurance

Other Germanic languages, by contrast, display the same behaviour as English, as shown, for instance, in these Norwegian and Swedish sentences.

(56)   a. ?Ødeleggelsen av skipet for å heve forsikringen er uhørt
The destruction of the ship to collect the insurance is outrageous
b. *Skipets ødeleggelse for å heve forsikringen er uhørt
The ship's destruction...
(57)   a. sänkningen av båten för att kamma in försäkringspengarna
the sinking of the boat to collect the insurance money
b. *Båtens sänkning för att kamma in försäkringspengarna...
The boat's sinking...

The relevant structural difference after movement to Spec can be represented as follows:

(58) a. Germanic: *$[_{NP}$ Poss$_j$N′[...PRO$_i$...]]
      b. Romance: $[_{NP}$Poss$_j$N′$[_{NP}e]_i$[...PRO$_i$...]]

Examples (58)a and b are the structures resulting from passivization; in Germanic, therefore, the empty subject position has been obliterated with the consequence that the PRO within the adverbial remains uncontrolled. In Romance, however, there is still a syntactic position, $[_{NP}e]$ (most likely another PRO-like category; see ch. 4 below), which can bind the embedded PRO, and the resulting structure is grammatical.[31]

It is clear that the Romance facts and their analysis that we have just provided represent the strongest argument in favour of the presence of a syntactically realized empty category of a pronominal kind in the subject position of certain NPs and of its obligatoriness for control. In fact, alternative conclusions to Roeper's and Chomsky's have been advanced, most notably by Williams (1986), essentially claiming that implicit arguments of head Nouns, understood as lexical properties of their entry but syntactically unrealized, can function as controllers.[32] However, if it is still conceivable that such implicit arguments may disappear, at least as controllers, when the NP undergoes a passivization process, it would be highly unnatural for this phenomenon to be sensitive to differences across languages, especially to differences concerning the linear order of syntactic categories. Therefore this alternative approach can offer no principled account for the contrast between Germanic and Romance, whereas the observed facts are totally expected in the framework that we have independently proposed; since the latter makes crucial use of the idea that NPs are configurational, like sentences, i.e. contain well-defined thematic and syntactic positions, in which visible and empty categories interact, the explanatory results achieved through it in this section directly support such an idea. They also confirm in one of the strongest possible ways the existence of (pronominal) empty categories both within NPs and in general.

8   Binding

If the presence of an actual empty category in the subject position of NPs is detected by its being active with respect to a syntactic phenomenon like control, we must expect analogous contrasts to arise with other phenomena which often function as tests for syntactic activity of unexpressed arguments: the clearest one is anaphoric binding.[33]

In fact, the contrasts we have found for control can be reproduced with anaphors. Consider, for instance, the following examples:

(59)   a. L'acquisto di questa droga solo per se stessi/per sé/per la propria famiglia non è un reato
        The purchase of this drug only for oneself/for self/for self's family is not a crime

        b. A proposito di questa droga, il suo acquisto solo per se stessi/per sé/per la propria famiglia non è un reato
        Concerning this drug, its purchase only for oneself/for self/for self's family is not a crime

(60)   a. La sperimentazione di un nuovo farmaco su se stessi/su di sé/sulla propria famiglia è sempre rischiosa
        lit.: The testing of a new drug on oneself/on self/on self's family is always risky

        b. La sua sperimentazione su se stessi/su di sé/sulla propria famiglia è sempre rischiosa
        lit.: Its testing on oneself/on self/on self's family is always risky

The anaphors *se stessi*, *sé* or *propria* are here understood as arbitrary in reference and coreferential with the equally arbitrary understood agents of the Nouns *acquisto* ('purchase'), or *sperimentazione* ('testing'), which thus satisfy their binding requirements. This happens independently of the position of the object phrase.

In Italian, therefore, there appears to be no contrast between the active and the passive form, whereas such a contrast arises in the roughly corresponding English examples:

(61)   a. The purchase of these drugs is not prohibited in this state
        b. Their purchase is not prohibited in this state
        c. The purchase of these drugs for oneself is not prohibited in this state
        d. *Their purchase for oneself is not prohibited in this state
        e. Drug-purchase for oneself is not prohibited in this state

In English, raising of the object to Spec does, in fact, obliterate the arbitrary empty category in subject position, as it did in (52) above. Notice that (d) and (e) minimally contrast in an interesting way, namely in (d) the subject position has been really obliterated by passivization; in (61)e, an example pointed out to us by T. Roeper, however, *drug* does not appear in Spec, as does *their* in (61)d, since it is the incorporated modifier in a Noun compound; it follows correctly, therefore, that an arbitrary $[_{NP}e]$ in the subject position is still available to bind the anaphor. Notice that the existence of a contrast between Italian and English provides an argument in favour of the claim that even arbitrary anaphors at least in complement position need an antecedent: in fact, if they were able to get their arbitrary reference independently of the presence of an antecedent with this interpretation in subject position, we would expect the sentences to be grammatical in every case. Consider, moreover, that it is possible to reproduce the same contrasts even with non-arbitrary anaphors; let us now examine this class of cases:

(62)   La sperimentazione di tali farmaci sulla propria$_i$ famiglia/su di
        sé/su se stesso fece di Mario$_i$ un complice del piano criminale
        The testing of these drugs on self's family/on self/on himself
        turned Mario into an accomplice of the criminal plan

In the interpretation of (62), the understood antecedent of the anaphor and the understood agent of the experimentation must both be *Mario*; this suggests that *Mario* controls the agent of the NP, which actually binds the anaphor, *propria* or *sé*. Notice in fact that the antecedence relation between *Mario* and the anaphor cannot be direct for lack of c-command (and of P-command in Giorgi's 1983 sense) and always needs to be mediated by the subject of the NP; if this does not refer to *Mario*, the sentence becomes ungrammatical:[34]

(63)   *La mia sperimentazione di tali farmaci sulla propria famiglia/su
        di sé/su se stesso fece di Mario un complice del piano criminale
        My testing of these drugs on self's family/on self/on himself
        turned Mario into an accomplice of the criminal plan

In (63) the agent of the experimentation is expressed by *mia* ('my'), which due to mismatch of features cannot bind the third person anaphors *propria*, *se stesso* or *sé*. The ungrammaticality of the sentence therefore shows that *Mario* is not able to bind them directly.[35]

Consider now that, as predicted, we do not find a contrast with the passivized NP:

(64)   A proposito di tali farmaci, la loro sperimentazione sulla propria$_i$
        famiglia/su di sé$_i$/su se stesso$_i$ fece di Mario$_i$ un complice del
        piano criminale
        Concerning such drugs, their testing on self's family/on self/on
        himself turned Mario into an accomplice of the criminal plan

In (64) *loro* ('their') resumes *tali farmaci* ('such drugs'), confirming that even if the possessive expresses an internal argument, the agent is still syntactically present and thus available for binding in Italian. Again, this is not the case in English, where sentences of a comparable type do contrast:

(65)   a. The delivery of those packages to each other$_j$ took [John and Mary]$_j$ five hours
      b. ?*Their$_i$ delivery to each other$_j$ took [John and Mary]$_j$ five hours

In (65)a *John and Mary* is understood as coreferential with the anaphor and with the unexpressed subject of the delivery; in (65)b, if *their* stands for *those packages*, the structure becomes ungrammatical, since the anaphor, we may conclude, remains unbound. We are led to the same conclusions, as expected, by the Scandinavian (Swedish) examples below:

(66)   a. Försäljning av droger till sin bror/varandra är oetiskt
        (The) sale of drugs to self's brother/each other is immoral
      b. Drogernes försäljning till *sin bror/ens bror/*varandra är oetiskt
        Drugs' sale to self's brother/one's brother/each other is immoral

The anaphors *sin* and *varandra* remain unbound in (66)b, while they are understood as coreferential with an arbitrary subject of *försäljning* in (66)a. Notice that, as predictable, *ens*, the non-anaphoric arbitrary expression corresponding to English *one's*, does not cause ungrammaticality, although unbound, in (66)b.

Consider also the following case:

(67)   a. John's placement of me next to him/himself
      b. The placement of me next to him/himself was John's main concern
      c. My placement next to him/*himself was John's main concern

In (67)a and b both the anaphor and the pronoun are considered acceptable, even if for some speakers there can be a preferred option. Again, in (67)b, with the anaphor, *John* must also be understood as the agent of the placement, in order to provide a c-commanding antecedent for *himself*. Accordingly, in (67)c the only possible alternative is the one with the pronoun, whereas the anaphor is not acceptable. This, once more, points to the conclusion that the anaphor cannot be bound if the NP has undergone passivization, since the agent position is no longer available.

9   The Affectedness Constraint

Let us consider now another phenomenon which appears to be connected to our parameter. It is well known (see Anderson 1979) that in English a certain class of Ns does not admit the 'passive' construction, i.e. the realization of an object in the possessive form. Anderson (1979) defines such objects as 'unaffected' in the traditional thematic sense and proposes the generalization that if the head Noun does not express an action which 'affects', i.e. modifies, the state of the object, the latter cannot be possessivized; we will discuss shortly her exact formulation of the relevant constraint. On the other hand, Cinque (1980, p. 51) observed, without attempting an explanation, that in Italian the class in question is bipartite: some of these NPs can be passivized, whereas others still cannot, thus making Anderson's generalization at least questionable. Again, the difference raises an acquisition problem. If the Italian bipartition were just a marked language-specific phenomenon to be learned under direct exposure to the evidence, it would not be obvious why the passivization option is not extended by Italian children to the entire 'unaffected' class, instead of keeping it limited to a subset of the lexical items involved in English. We want to propose here a possible explanation for the English constraint and for the more complex situation observable in Italian. Consider the following examples:[36]

(68) a. la conoscenza dell'algebra
      b. the knowledge of algebra
(69) a. la sua conoscenza
      b. *its knowledge
      c. *algebra's knowledge

As shown by the examples, in English the object cannot appear in prenominal position, either as a pronoun, or as a possessivized full NP. In Italian, instead, it is perfectly possible to express the internal argument by means of a possessive. Other Nouns displaying this contrast pointed out by Cinque (1980) are *discussione* ('discussion') and *inseguimento/perseguimento* ('pursuit'), but the class is larger, as is revealed by the examination of the following items listed in Rozwadowska (1986), who credits them to Rappaport (1983):

(70) a. *John's sight
      b. *The event's recollection
      c. *The problem's perception
      d. *The picture's observation
      e. *The novel's understanding
      f. *The film's enjoyment
(71) a. A proposito di Gianni, la sua vista mi ha spaventato
         Concerning Gianni, his sight frightened me
      b. A proposito di quegli avvenimenti, il loro ricordo ancora mi
         spaventa

Concerning those events, their recollection still frightens me
c. A proposito di quel problema, la sua percezione varia da individuo a individuo
Concerning that problem, its perception varies from person to person
d. A proposito di quella fotografia, una sua attenta osservazione rivelerà molti particolari interessanti
Concerning that picture, its careful observation will reveal many interesting details
e. A proposito di quel romanzo, la sua comprensione richiede notevoli capacità ermeneutiche
Concerning that novel, its understanding requires remarkable hermeneutic skills
f. A proposito di quel film, il suo pieno godimento è certo riservato a pochi amatori
Concerning that film, its full enjoyment is certainly restricted to a few amateurs

We have already examined another case in which moving an object prenominally creates ungrammaticality in English NPs, but not in Italian, namely in Roeper's kind of sentences discussed in the previous sections. Therefore it seems natural to try to relate also this fact to our parameter, an idea additionally supported by the typological distribution of the phenomenon. In fact, it turns out that, with the possible exception of German which we will examine in section 10, the other Germanic languages, exemplified here by Norwegian, essentially behave like English, and the Romance ones like Italian, as already observed in Zubizarreta (1986). Consider, for instance, the following cases:

(72)   a. forståelsen av problemet
           the understanding of the problem
        b. *problemets forståelse
           the problem's understanding
(73)   a. French:
           (Ce problème est très difficile.) Sa compréhension exige beaucoup de travail
        b. Spanish:
           (Este problema es muy difícil.) Su comprensión exige mucho trabajo
           (This problem is very difficult.) Its understanding needs a lot of work

A good number of the contrasts of (70) and (71) go in the same direction. Our suggestion is the following: these data could be accounted for if the universal peculiarity of these Nouns, instead of consisting of the impossibility of moving the object, were rather the impossibility of obliterating the subject. Let us assume, in fact, that the subject of these Nouns has to be obligatorily present, even if not lexically realized. As a consequence, passivization would be impossible in English, where movement of the internal argument *does* obliterate the subject, given that the landing site, Spec, is the same as that occupied by the subject. In Italian, on the contrary, the prenominal position is still the landing site of the movement of the object, but such a movement does not interact with the subject, which may be preserved in the form of a pronominal empty category on the other side of N; therefore, in Romance, the subject can remain present in spite of passivization. Actually, a constraint of the kind required for our explanation has been independently proposed by Jaeggli (1986, p. 607) under the name of 'Affectedness Constraint'.[37]

(74)   If a complement of X is unaffected, it is impossible to eliminate the external θ-role of X

Jaeggli also makes the important suggestion that such a condition is likely to be derivable from a general theory of θ-assignment, yet to be developed, noting that the exact determination of the θ-role for 'unaffected' complements seems to be dependent on the nature of the external one: thus it is reasonable to suppose that the internal θ-role could not be assigned at all if the external one were not previously discharged.[38] Although, as noted by Jaeggli himself, the exact reason why the subject θ-role of these Ns cannot fail to be discharged is still a possible matter of research, such a condition seems to us to be independently motivated on the basis of another piece of evidence, originally pointed out by N. Chomsky and D. Pesetsky (p.c.). In English the existence of the phenomenon just discussed correlates with the impossibility for the corresponding Verbs to appear in the so-called 'middle' form (see also Rizzi 1986):

(75)   This book reads easily
(76)   a. *This subject knows easily
        b. *John sees easily in Paris
        c. *Such events recollect easily
        d. *This problem perceives differently from person to person
        e. *A picture like that observes easily
        f. *Those novels understand with great difficulty
        g. *Too many films do not enjoy easily nowadays

Contrary to the passive form, in such constructions, the external θ-role cannot be syntactically assigned at all, as suggested, e.g., by its inability to control (see Chomsky 1981; Manzini 1980). In the passive, according to the hypotheses put forth by Jaeggli (1986) and Roberts (1987), the external θ-role is assigned to the so-called -*EN* suffix of the Verb; in the examples (75) and (76), it cannot be assigned at all, since no suffix is present and the subject position is filled by the thematic object. If the Thematic Correspondence Hypothesis, inspired by Chomsky's (1970) lexicalist approach and explicitly suggested in chapter 1 for Nouns and Verbs, is interpreted in a broad sense, it will follow that a condition holding on the θ-grid of the Verb has to hold also on the θ-grid of the corresponding Noun and vice versa. Consequently, when the external θ-role must be assigned to a category represented in the syntax, this condition has to be satisfied both in the structure projected by the Verb and in the one projected by the Noun.

We will, then, assume that a class of lexical items, still unspecified with respect to $\pm N, \pm V$, universally obeys a condition along the lines of Jaeggli's (1986), requiring its external θ-role to be always syntactically realized.[39] This general constraint, independently suggested by examples like (76) in English, can still be satisfied under passivization of an NP in Romance but not in Germanic as a further consequence of the Head–Subject parameter. The different setting of the latter, suggested by quite substantial direct evidence, is thus the only difference between Italian and English which must be learned to master the phenomena discussed in this section.

This hypothesis, of course, does not apply to all the cases covered by Anderson (1979), but provides an explanation for a subset of them, namely the ones exhibiting the contrast between Italian and English. With respect to the other Nouns in question, those which resist passivization in either language (group), we will accept Anderson's (1979) original explanation, and provide further typological evidence in favour of it. Her idea was that with such Nouns the Preposition introducing the internal argument, even if it appears as *of*, as in the case of *fear*, is always a 'real' Preposition, i.e. not a bare Case-marker realizing Genitive Case (on this point see also Zubizarreta 1986). In other words, the internal argument of these Nouns would not be a true direct argument, but rather a prepositional complement. Since a possessivizable object has to be marked for Genitive, as discussed in chapter 2 above, the internal argument of *fear* cannot be possessivized. Some typological support for Anderson's original conclusions already comes from considerations internal to the comparison between English and Italian:[40] in fact, some 'unpassivizable' Nouns, apparently marking their internal argument for Genitive through *di* insertion in Italian, require a regular Preposition like *for*, and not *of*, in English, or vice versa:

(77) a. il desiderio di cioccolata
          the desire *for* chocolate
      b. il bisogno di cioccolata
          the need *for* chocolate
      c. il suo desiderio
          (* = the need for it)
      d. il suo bisogno
          (* = the need for it)
(78) a. the love of children
          l'amore *per* i bambini
      b. the hatred of Mary
          l'odio *per* Mary

Examining now languages other than Italian and English, we can see that it is most often the case that the internal argument of these Ns is introduced again by a visibly 'real' P, one which is morphologically different from the one used to realize adnominal Genitive. Consider, for instance, the word for *fear*; in languages as diverse as Spanish, Catalan, German and Swedish, the P introducing the object of such a Noun is not a mere Genitive Case-marker:

(79) a. German: die Angst *vor* Hans
          lit.: the fear in front of Hans
      b. Swedish: rädslan *för* Johan
          lit.: the fear in front of Johan
      c. Catalan: la por *envers/a* en Joan
          lit.: the fear toward/to Joan
          (cf. la por d'en Joan = 'Joan's fear')
      d. Spanish: el miedo *hacia* Juan
          lit.: the fear toward Juan
          (cf. el miedo de Juan = 'Juan's fear')

These data support Anderson's view and point to the conclusion that *di* or *of* in these cases are only homophonous with the Genitive Case-markers, but have different semantic properties, which make passivization impossible.

10   Markedness and the position of German

Some doubts on the unity of the phenomena which we have brought together under the Head–Subject parameter might be cast by the observation of the pattern provided by German (and by Dutch, which, wherever the comparison is possible, does not seem to differ from German in significant respects).[41] On the one hand, German seems to be a well-behaved Germanic language, like English and Scandinavian, with respect to our parameter. Nominal compounds are all head-final, referential Adjectives occur prenominally, as well as predicative ones:[42]

(80)   a. Arbeitgeberverband
            Workgivers' association
         b. der deutsche Einfluß/*der Einfluß deutsche(e)
            the German influence
         c. ein erfolgreicher Manager/*ein Manager erfolgreich(-er)
            a successful manager

Moreover, some forms of Genitive appear to be realized prenominally:

(81)   Ottos Beschreibung
         Otto's description

However, with respect to other properties following from the Germanic setting of the Head–Subject parameter, German appears to be potentially exceptional: first of all, it is always possible to express an external argument (either subject or possessor) by means of a postnominal realization of Genitive (bare Genitive, or *von* + Dat), independently of 'heaviness' or 'inanimacy' considerations:[43]

(82)   a. ein/das Buch von Peter
            a/the book of Peter
         b. (?)die Briefe Peters
            the letters of Peter

Second, it seems that two external arguments at the same time may be perfectly expressed on the right of the head Noun, as in Romance:

(83)   a. die Briefe Peters von seiner Mutter
            the letters of Peter of his mother
         b. die Briefe von Peter von seiner Mutter
            the letters of Peter of his mother

In (83)a the most natural interpretation is the one which assigns *Peters* the possessor role and *seiner Mutter* the agent one. This is consistent with the potentially universal Possessivization Hierarchy proposed in chapter 2, section 3, if we take the Genitive realization in *Peters* to be a form of possessive, as is natural given its possibility of occurring also prenominally. Accordingly, (83)b is more ambiguous, exactly like a corresponding Italian example with two Genitive Cases realized by *di* (see ch. 2, sect. 3): in fact, this is apparently the case also in German.

Third, the realization of Genitive Case in prenominal position appears to be much more constrained and different in nature with respect to the English/Scandinavian type (see also Haider 1987): the marker is more similar to a Case-ending occurring on the head Noun and some of its modifiers and is never found phrase-finally with the function of a postpositional head, as the English/Scandinavian *'s* was argued to be in chapter 2, e.g. in expressions like the following Norwegian NP and its gloss:[44]

(84)   kongen av Englands skokke
          the king of England's beard

Furthermore, only a very restricted class of Nouns, mostly limited to proper names, may occur as prenominal genitives in everyday modern German: branching phrasal constituents, even when not in violation of the Consistency Principle (see n. 15 above) as in (85), tend to be exceptional in the spoken language, even more so in the case of inanimate NPs, and real violations of the Consistency Principle are not tolerated:[45]

(85)   a. dieses Mannes Buch
           this man's book
        b. ?dieses Buches erste Seite
           this book's first page
        c. *des Mannes meiner Freundin Buch
           the husband of my friend's book

Fourth, it appears to be possible in German to possessivize unaffected objects, in examples like the following:

(86)   a. Was die Algebra betrifft, ist ihre Kenntnis sehr wichtig
           As far as algebra is concerned, its knowledge is very important
        b. Was diese drei Punkte betrifft, wird ihre Befolgung dir helfen
           As far as these three points are concerned, their following will help
           you

Finally, several speakers of German tend not to share the judgements concerning the effects of syntactic deactivation of the understood subject position noticed by Roeper under possessivization of the object in English and quite clearly attested in Scandinavian (see sects. 7–8 above):

(87)   a. die Zerstörung des Schiffes um die Versicherung zu kassieren
            the destruction of the ship to collect the insurance
        b. seine/?des Schiffes Zerstörung um die Versicherung zu kassieren
            its/the ship's destruction to collect the insurance
(88)   a. Das Ausprobieren dieser Droge an sich selbst machte Maria zu
            einer Invalide
            The testing of this drug on herself made Maria an invalid
        b. Ihr/?Dieser Droge Ausprobieren an sich selbst machte Maria zu
            einer Invalide
            Its/this drug's testing on herself made Maria an invalid
        c. Ihr Ausprobieren an einem selbst ist immer gefährlich
            Its testing on oneself is always dangerous

To summarize the results of the investigation about German, it appears that, of the properties deriving from the Germanic setting of the Head–Subject parameter, it fully retains the following:

(89)   a. head-final compounds
        b. no postnominal predicative APs
        c. no postnominal referential APs

On the other hand, it superficially patterns like Romance with respect to the following:

(90)   a. freedom of postnominal realization of Genitive
        b. cooccurrence of thematic subjects and possessors
        c. reduced 'Affectedness' restrictions
        d. lack of Roeper's effects

Finally, German seems to instantiate an intermediate case between Romance and Germanic with respect to:

(91)   Prenominal realization of Genitive (current with proper names, but
            not fully productive in the spoken language)

The latter property will be our starting point for the explanation we want to propose. Consider, thus, first of all, that the contrast between the properties in (89) and the property (90)a can be naturally treated in the framework of Koopman's (1984) and Travis's (1984) hypotheses concerning 'marked' word order: for instance, discussing the situation of Chinese VPs, where prepositionally introduced objects occur preverbally, but non-prepositional direct objects surface postverbally, Travis suggests that such an inconsistency could be easily described as a marked case where the direction of Case-marking and that of θ-marking by the same lexical unit diverge: the Verb would θ-mark to the left while Case-marking to the right, so that non-prepositional objects should move from left to right in order to receive their Case. This is supposed to be the only available case of markedness concerning word order of the complements within the same maximal projection.

Reasoning of a very similar kind seems applicable to the German case we are discussing: if our general parametric approach is correct, the generalizations (89) show that the direction of external θ-marking in German NPs is leftward, as in English. The scarcity of prenominal genitive phrases mentioned in (91), however, may be taken as suggesting that, productively, at least at a certain stylistic level, Genitive can only be realized as such rightwardly: to be concrete, we may assume that proper names and the limited number of genitive items occurring prenominally (e.g. *wessen, dessen,* 'whose') are intrinsically markable with Genitive morphology in the lexicon (apart from these, the only prenominal NPs are possessive pronouns, perhaps inherently marked for Genitive, but actually realizing the same Case as the head, under agreement, as in Romance), but that, in the syntax, Genitive may only be realized in postnominal position. This hypothesis leads us naturally to regard German NPs as marked cases, very much in the sense of Chinese VPs: nominal external arguments, when not marked Genitive in the lexicon, must move to the right in order to realize the Case they require: hence property (90)a. The obvious assumption here should be that such a rightward movement is licensed precisely by the unsatisfied need for Case realization. However, the proposed solution, though being probably on the right track, is still insufficient to account for properties (90)b, (90)c and (90)d. The behaviour of German in the latter cases presupposes that an external argument may be not just moved to the postnominal position, but even base-generated there: in other words, a postnominal overt or empty agent does not seem to require a trace, which, occupying the Spec along with, say, a possessor or a raised internal argument, could create a violation of the Uniqueness Condition discussed in section 6.

A slight elaboration of Travis's approach to markedness may provide us with a more satisfying solution: let us suppose that, when the direction of Case-marking and the direction of the corresponding θ-marking do not coincide, the latter may follow the former. Thus, since in German, at a certain level of abstraction, we may claim that Genitive Case only goes to the right of a head Noun, elements needing to bear a syntactic realization of such a Case not only must surface, but also may be θ-marked (hence base-generated) in such a position.[46] However, elements which do not syntactically realize Genitive Case, but bear an external semantic function, must appear to the left of the head, in accordance with the general Germanic setting of the Head–Subject parameter: hence the properties of Adjectives and nominal compounds in which German essentially coincides with English.

Along such lines of explanation it becomes necessary, in order to account for the lack of Roeper and 'affectedness' effects in German, to assume that the empty subjects of NPs normally need Genitive Case. This is so, because such subjects must be allowed to occur in D-structure to the right of the head, like their overt nominal correspondents and unlike Adjectives, even referential ones. That they must be assigned Genitive Case at D-structure, along with θ-assignment, already follows from Chomsky's (1986a) often mentioned Uniformity Condition: we may, thus, claim that the rightwardness of German Genitive concerns both assignment and realization.[47]

If the remarks of this section are on the right line, it appears that also for the Head–Subject parameter, as for other major cases of parametric variation, e.g. the Null Subject one, the occurrence of apparently intermediate cases between the two main values must not be taken as *prima facie* counter-evidence to the existence of the parameter itself and should not induce anyone to abandon the rational investigation of the phenomena. Rather, more often than not, it turns out that such intermediate cases represent instances of further, sometimes more marked, choices subject to highly detailed subregularities, whose study will much increase the typological accuracy and the predictive power of syntactic theory.[48] As a matter of fact, in this specific case, if the analysis proposed for German is tenable, it is also likely to extend to languages like the Slavic ones or, perhaps, modern Greek, where simple Adjectives, both of the predicative and of the referential type (the latter are particularly developed in Slavic, a phenomenon dating from the times of Old Church Slavonic), basically occur to the left of the head Noun, but Genitive arguments always appear postnominally.[49] According to our general approach, it is the position of referential Adjectives which represents the most direct surface mark of the direction in which external semantic functions are assigned: in fact, they require an external θ-role, but are not subject to constraints on Genitive realization and actually should be unable to move out of their base position, for the reasons discussed above. An important question which arises in connection with our analysis of the marked status of languages like German or the others mentioned, concerns the absence of corresponding (essentially mirror-image) marked cases among the

Romance languages: i.e. we may wonder why there exists no Romance variety with Adjectives basically occurring to the right but with most or all genitive NPs forced to surface prenominally owing to a lack of postnominal realization for their Case. With regard to this problem, we want to make the *a priori* most desirable suggestion, namely that such a gap in the typology is by no means due to chance. Consider, in fact, that in Romance languages, in which both the Head–Subject and the Head–Complement parameters are set to the right, an exclusively leftward Genitive-marking would represent a total divergence between the directions of Case- and θ-marking.

This is not the case in German, since there the rightward rule of Genitive-marking is consistent at least with the value of the Head–Complement parameter. Suppose now that, in order to constrain Travis's and Koopman's suggestions, we assume that the directions of θ- and Case-marking cannot be completely inconsistent, even in marked cases: now, the situation of German will represent a tolerable degree of markedness for a natural language, but any analogous reverse in Romance will be excluded in principle. The condition on markedness we have just proposed merely on the grounds of Romance and Germanic data is likely to make correct predictions over a larger typological domain, as was already the case with our hypotheses on the position of Adjectives in section 3 above. Consider that Hawkins (1983, 1985), who has extended Greenberg's fruitful typological approach to an expanded sample of about 350 languages and tried to avoid merely statistical claims by reinforcing the implicational structure of his statements, has proposed two potential universals such as these:

(92)   a. SOV→(A+N→GEN+N)
       b. VSO→(N+A→N+GEN)

Universal (92)a claims that if a language is basically SOV, then if its Adjectives normally precede the head Noun, then Genitive-marked arguments also will; (92)b essentially makes the mirror-image prediction about VSO languages. Consider now a possible theoretical interpretation of these principles. Assuming crosscategorial consistency in the direction of assignment of internal θ-roles in NPs and VPs as the unmarked case, then SOV and VSO might correspond in a good deal of cases to languages' projection of internal arguments of Nouns to the left and to the right respectively. We have already stressed how the position of attributive Adjectives, in particular of referential ones, represents under our approach the purest surface test to infer from a sample of data the setting of the Head–Subject parameter, since it cannot be influenced by Case considerations. So, if the positions of Genitive arguments and of Adjectives with respect to the head Noun diverge, this means in our framework that the direction of Genitive assignment and the value of the Head–Subject parameter diverge: according to the constraint on markedness put forth above, this will only be possible when the Head–Complement parameter also diverges from the Head–Subject one, which, by hypothesis, should not be the case in a consistent OV–AN language or vice versa. On the grounds of his extensive empirical coverage, Hawkins (1983) has also suggested two other tentative universals, similar to those of (92) except for the antecedent of the main implication:

(93)   a. Postpositions→(A + N→Gen + N)
        b. Prepositions→(N + A→N + Gen)

Again, assuming consistency in the setting of the Head–Complement parameter across PPs and NPs, Hawkins's implication (93) can be deduced from our hypotheses in the same manner as (92). Of course, predictions ensuing under our approach are weaker than those derivable from Hawkins's original formulation, since we must rely on the unwarranted assumptions of crosscategorial consistency. In other words, we make the prediction that violations of (92) and (93) can be found in some language where internal arguments of Nouns are projected inconsistently with respect to the internal arguments of Verbs or Prepositions. Such a prediction seems to be borne out. In fact, a typically inconsistent language like German, which is essentially OV in the VP but Noun–Complement in the NP, does instantiate a violation of (92)a, as is clear from the analysis of German NPs that we have provided in this section; however, it is consistent with our weakened approximation to that universal. The same reasoning extends to Dutch, which had already been noticed as a potential counter-example to (92)a by Coopmans (1984) and Hawkins (1985). In our framework such exceptions are reduced to the independent property of crosscategorial inconsistency of the Head–Complement parameter exhibited by these languages.[50]

As already argued in section 1, the more flexible hypotheses and the subtle distinctions provided by an abstract syntactic theory may sometimes prove able to increase the accuracy of typologically based predictions, even when starting from the observation of a relatively restricted sample of closely related languages (in this case, Germanic and Romance). Actually, the detailed comparison of a few diverging constructions in otherwise very similar languages often seems to lead to the 'right level of abstraction', the one on which further implicational properties can be captured by means of a stepwise extension of the typological coverage. This approach appears to us as a potentially very successful way of achieving that complementarity of methods in the search for principles and parameters of UG which Hawkins (1985) has very appropriately advocated.[51]

11   The possessive parameters

So far we have been treating possessive elements essentially as (genitive) NPs. This view, which appears to capture a semantic intuition, is partially correct, but somewhat simplistic, because there is some suggestive evidence for hypothesizing that the possessive is superficially realized as a kind of Determiner in English and French, and as an Adjective in Italian.[52] This distinction can be stated as a parameter which is orthogonal to the one we have proposed in the text. In addition, it is possible to identify another distinction, between strong and weak forms, cross-classifying both As and Ds, and determining language-internal alternations and further parametric variation.

Let us begin by noticing that Italian and English differ with respect to the distribution of articles and possessives within NPs.[53] Consider, for instance:

(94)   a. *the my book
         b. il mio libro

In English it is impossible to express both the article and the possessive, whereas in Italian this is perfectly acceptable. With respect to such a construction and to the other properties we are going to examine, French and German behave like English; Latin, although articleless, Portuguese and Catalan can be argued to behave essentially like Italian.[54] More generally, in fact, in English and French, possessive elements are in complementary distribution with a whole class of items that we may call Determiners; see e.g.:

(95)   a. *A my book
         b. *Each my book
         c. *This/that my book
         d. *Some my books
         e. *Three my books
         f. *Many my books
(96)   *Le mon livre

(97)   a. *Un mon livre
        b. *Chaque mon livre
        c. *Ce mon livre
        d. *Quelques mes livres
        e. *Trois mes livres
        f. *Plusieurs mes livres

all such phrases are acceptable in Italian:

(98)   a. un mio libro
        b. ciascun mio libro
        c. questo/quel mio libro
        d. alcuni miei libri/qualche mio libro
        e. tre miei libri
        f. molti miei libri

These differences between French and English, on one side, and Italian on the other, could be expressed by several more or less *ad hoc* rules. However, this property seems not to be an isolated one, but to correlate with others; by analysing all the potentially relevant properties together, it is possible to formulate a parametric theory with more explanatory power.

On the surface, there are at least three other properties which distinguish Italian from English and French possessives and *a priori* seem to be good candidates to cluster together with the one we have just illustrated. Let us examine them in turn. In Italian, possessive elements can also optionally occur in postnominal position, when focused or conveying contrastive information, whereas this is impossible in English and French:

(99)   a. il libro mio
        b. *the book my
        c. *le livre mon

Furthermore, only in Italian is it possible to use a possessive as a predicate in various constructions:

(100)   a. Questo libro è mio
        b. *This book is my
        c. *Ce livre est mon
(101)   a. Questo libro sembra mio
        b. *This book seems my
        c. *Ce livre semble mon
(102)   a. Lo considero mio
        b. *I consider it my
        c. *Je le considère mon

Finally, as observed by G. Cinque (p.c.), only Italian possessives may cooccur with a gapped head Noun:

(103)   a. Metti i tuoi libri vicini ai miei
         b. *Put your books next to my
         c. *Mets tes livres près de mes

Let us give a theoretical account of the phenomena just illustrated. Our first proposal is that an open parameter of UG which differentiates Italian from English and French can be identified and formulated as follows:

(104)   Possessive elements are syntactically specified to be realized on the surface either as As (as in Italian), or as Ds (as in English and French).[55]

The parameter just formulated can simply account for the contrast between (98), on the one hand, and (96) and (97) on the other, because there is evidence that only one overtly realized Determiner may appear for each NP, whereas no constraint exists on combining a Determiner and an Adjective.[56] In fact, Determiners cannot be multiplied:

(105)   a. *il ciascun libro
         b. *the each book
         c. *le chaque livre

However, as we have said, As can freely cooccur with a Determiner, both in Italian and in English, or French:

(106)   a. Un buon libro
         b. A good book
         c. Un bon livre

The distribution illustrated in (99) follows directly instead from the observation that Adjectives, unlike Determiners, may superficially occur in Italian on both sides of a head Noun:

(107)   a. un ottimo libro
         b. un libro ottimo
            a very good book
(108)   a. ciascun libro
         b. *libro ciascuno
            each book

With respect to this property, the typologically most crucial case appears

to be French, since, as we know, in English there is in any event no
postnominal position for simple Adjectives to surface, exactly as for
Determiners, as we have discussed in the text:

(109)   a. this book
         b. *book this
(110)   a. the nice boy
         b. *the boy nice
         c. the boy nicer than me

Therefore (99)b might be ruled out even if possessives were Adjectives in
English too. On the other hand, although French displays the Italian value
with respect to the Head–Subject parameter, hence to the properties
illustrated in (107) and (108), still in French a possessive cannot appear in
postnominal position:

(111)   a. un très bon livre
         b. un livre très bon
         c. ce livre
         d. *livre ce

Since the contrasting behaviour of Italian and French can be explained by
our hypothesis, it seems legitimate to relate the ungrammaticality of (99)b
to the ungrammaticality of (109)b rather than to that of (110)b.

A further difference between Italian and the other two languages also
follows from our hypothesis: in fact, not only is it the case that Italian may
use phrases like (94)b, but, apart from very few lexical exceptions, it *must*
resort to such phrases to express the definite meaning typical of (94)a and
of *John's book*, or of French *mon livre*.[57] In other words, while English and
French articleless NPs with a possessive are semantically determined like
those containing a definite article, and may occur as referential arguments
in thematic positions, Italian *mio amico* is not (see Lyons 1984, 1986).
Rather, it is completely indeterminate and, in the singular, may normally
occur just in non-thematic positions, as in vocative, predicative and
exclamatory contexts:

(112)   a. Amico mio, vieni qui!
            my friend, come here!
         b. Gianni è mio amico
            Gianni is my friend
         c. Dio mio!
            My God!

(113)   a. *Ho visto mio amico
          I saw my friend
         b. *Mio amico mi ha telefonato
          My friend phoned me

In other words articleless singular NPs containing a possessive tend to pattern, in Italian, like singular countable common Nouns occurring unmodified or anyway without a Determiner; the latter, in fact, cannot function as arguments (in either Italian or English; for this generalization, see also Renzi 1985a):[58]

(114)   a. Amico caro, vieni qui!
          Dear friend, come here!
         b. Gianni è grande amico di Maria
          Gianni is great friend of Maria
         c. Dio santo!
          Holy God!
(115)   a. *Ho visto caro amico
          I saw dear friend
         b. *Grande amico di Maria mi ha telefonato
          Great friend of Maria phoned me

It seems to us that, in languages with a full system of Determiners, the overt presence of such elements is often necessary to saturate internally a Noun Phrase (in the sense of Rothstein 1983; Higginbotham 1985), at least in the singular, and make it into an argument.[59] We must, then, conclude that French and English possessives are able to saturate an NP, as members of the class of Determiners can, but Italian possessives cannot, behaving exactly like Adjectives also in this respect. Such a conclusion immediately derives, with no stipulation, from our categorial hypothesis.

The categorial approach turns out to be insufficient, however, to account for the distinctions exemplified in (100)–(103). The reasons are the following: in both types of languages there exist items which, according to the distributional and semantic tests of the previous discussion, should be categorized as Determiners, yet they frequently occur in all or some of the environments available to *mio* and unavailable to *my*, *mon* in (100)–(103). Such is the case, for example, of demonstratives like Italian *questo* ('this') and of the other possessive forms of English, the so-called 'pronominal' ones *mine*, *yours*, etc.:[60]

(116)   a. Il libro di Gianni è questo
          The book of Gianni is this

b. Metti i tuoi libri vicino a questi
   Put your books next to these

(117)   a. This book is mine
         b. This book seems mine
         c. I consider it mine
         d. Put your books next to mine

In order to understand the paradigm (100)–(103) consider, then, that among both As and Ds we find items differing with respect to what can be referred to as 'strong' and 'weak' distribution. A weak position, in the relevant sense, can be defined as a prenominal position in an NP with a lexically realized head. Strong positions would be all the others *a priori* accessible to Ds or As (postnominal positions), predicative ones and the occurrence in an NP with an empty head. Clearly, there exist Determiners which only occur in weak position, like Italian and English articles, and in Italian the reduced demonstrative *quel* ('that') or the quantifier *qualche* ('some', sg.):

(118)   a. *Uno di questi ragazzi è il
            One of these boys is the
         b. *Mary met a
         c. *Gianni ha letto quel
            Gianni has read that (reduced form)
         d. *Qualche mi ha telefonato
            Some has phoned me

The natural conclusion is that English *my* and French *mon* belong to this class of weak Determiners, whereas Italian *questo* and English *mine* do not. The partitioning of (possessive and non-possessive) Determiners arrived at so far, however, cannot exhaust the discussion of the properties of English *mine*. In fact, the Determiners of this class, unlike Italian *questo*, appear to occur *only* in strong positions (namely predicative and next to an empty N); in other words (119)a contrasts with b:

(119)   a. questo libro
            this book
         b. *mine book

It seems plausible, then, to admit of the possibility of two types of non-weak Determiners, one occurring just in strong positions, the other allowed to appear in either strong or weak environments. The latter should also include, in addition to certain demonstratives like *questo*, one possessive Determiner of English, namely *his*, which is neutral between the purely strong (*mine, yours, hers, ours, theirs*) and the purely weak (*my, your, her, our, their*) class, occurring both in prenominal and in predicative and headless contexts:

(120)   a. his book
       b. the book was his
       c. mine is better than his

Adopting a feature system we might classify *my* as [−strong], *mine* as [+strong] and *his* as [±strong]. This last specification is certainly represented among non-possessive Determiners as well, as is exemplified not only by Italian *questo*, but also by English *this* or *that*.[61] The purely [+strong] kind might be instantiated by French 'pronominal' demonstratives like *celui* ('that').[62]

Consider now how the feature classification may apply to Adjectives as well. Let us begin with the non-possessive ones. Clearly [−strong] adjectival items are represented in Italian by such reduced forms as *bel* ('beautiful'), *buon* ('good'), *gran* ('great, big'), which only occur prenominally. The last Adjective has a [±strong] corresponding form *grande*. The other two, instead, have corresponding allomorphs which might perhaps be classified just as [+strong], *bello* and *buono* respectively, with the provisos already discussed in note 11. The best results of the proposed feature system are achieved, however, with possessive Adjectives. Standard Italian has only one possessive series, which, as we have seen, is categorized as adjectival: given their distribution, which exhausts the possible contexts for possessives, such items must all be assigned the neutralized feature [±strong]. Other languages, however, display more than one possessive series: we have already seen that English possessives, though all being categorized as Determiners, bear distinct feature specifications, namely [−strong] (e.g. *my*), [+strong] (e.g. *mine*) and even [±strong] (in the case of *his*). A partially similar multiplicity of feature specifications can also be found among adjectival possessives: many northern Italian and Tuscan dialects display two different possessive forms, one occurring in strong environments, the other, phonologically reduced, only in prenominal position (see Rohlfs 1949). Consider the following examples from Paduan, provided by P. Beninca (p.c.):

(121)   a. el me libro/*el mio libro
          my book
       b. el libro mio/*el libro me
          my book
       c. el mio/*el me
          mine

d. Sto libro ze mio/*me
This book is mine

The prenominal form, as can be seen, occurs along with a Determiner, hence must anyway be categorized as an Adjective, of the [−strong] type, of course. It is also *a priori* conceivable that a language may have distinct possessive series, one falling into the class of Determiners and the other into the class of Adjectives. As a matter of fact, when this situation arises, the languages here considered seem to further distinguish the two series by means of the [+strong]/[−strong] specification and invariably associate the [+strong] feature with the Adjective and the [−strong] one with the Determiner. This appears to be the case in German with the *mein/meinig* forms, and, we may argue, also in modern French; in this language, the series represented by *mon* (i.e. a [−strong] Determiner) is paralleled by that exemplified by (*le*) *mien*. The latter must be classified as adjectival, as shown by its (obligatory) occurring with the article, but also as [+strong], since it occurs with gapped head Nouns. The modern French system is, however, largely defective, since the adjectival series *mien* has a very restricted distribution, and tends to be found only in the just-mentioned context of an empty nominal head (for some exceptions, rare after the sixteenth century, see Grevisse 1975, pp. 392 and 494).[63] We will not investigate the nature of such additional restrictions, whose existence does not seem to affect the value of the system so far developed, which yields further explanatory results. In fact, recognizing the existence of the descriptive correlation between the A/D parameter and the [+/−strong] classification allows us to deal in a revealing way with the 'mixed' behaviour of the Spanish possessive system: the latter includes a [−strong] possessive determiner, only occurring in phrases like (122)a and a [+strong] possessive Adjective, occurring in all the other environments:

(122)   a. mi libro/*el mi libro/*el mio libro
my book
b. un libro mio/*un libro mi[64]
a book of mine
c. el mio/*el mi
mine
d. Este libro es mio/*mi
This book is mine

Thus, the proposed feature system provides a neat account of an otherwise complex distributional problem. The main result achieved in this section about possessives can be usefully summarized in the following chart:

(123)	Determiners	Adjectives
−strong	Engl. *my*, Fr. *mon*, Sp. *mi*	Paduan *me*
+strong	Engl. *mine*	Fr. *mien*, Sp. *mio*, Paduan *mio*
±strong	Engl. *his*	It. *mio*

Further possible neutralizations are sporadically found: French *leur* ('their') and Spanish *nuestro*, *vuestro* ('our', 'your') appear to neutralize the two major series, lexically realizing, at the same time, a [+strong] Adjective and a [−strong] Determiner, but still respecting the observed correlation between the values of the two choices.

12   The structural properties of the possessive

Pursuing the analysis of possessives, in this section we will provide further evidence in favour of the presence of empty subjects of NPs. Actually, the discussion of more complex cases of binding and control by understood arguments of N will offer an even less theory-internal argument supporting the existence of empty categories in general. Finally, some conclusions will be drawn about the possible targets of syntactic movement and the functioning of the Projection Principle.

Let us start by considering now the question of the thematic properties and hierarchical positions of the possessive. Within the NP a possessive can express either a 'possessor' (a bare R-relation in Higginbotham's sense; see above) or a thematic 'subject', or an 'object', as in the following cases:

(124)   a. il mio libro/il libro mio
            my book
         b. il mio regalo a Maria/il regalo mio a Maria
            my present to Maria
(125)   a. la mia cattura/la cattura mia
            my (theme) capture
         b. la mia descrizione/la descrizione mia
            my (agent or theme) description
         c. la mia partenza/la partenza mia
            my departure

As shown, the Italian possessive can appear (most often immediately, like other Adjectives) to the right of the head, in all these cases. The problem we want to address now concerns the level of attachment of the possessive. Let us consider first (124)a and (124)b. According to the

Head–Subject hypothesis, the θ-position of these elements in Italian is always postnominal; therefore we can suppose that the possessive originates there at D-structure, and that it can either surface there or move prenominally. This is due to the fact that in Italian it is an Adjective, as we have just proposed. In French, too, we have to suppose that the possessive originates on the right of N, but it cannot surface there, since the relevant feature 'possessive' can only be realized by a Determiner, hence in prenominal position. According to this reasoning, the two relevant surface structures in Italian should be the following (overlooking for simplicity the distinction between the two positions external to N', the one for agents/experiencers and the one for possessors, and also the possibility that binary branching forces the AP position in Spec to hang from a higher node than the external thematic NPs):

(126)a.

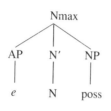

b.

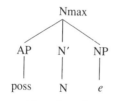

However, consider also the cases given in (125): the possessive may or must express an internal argument and, again, it can appear either pre- or postnominally. Structurally, there are two reasons suggesting that it must in either case raise from within N' to a higher position, one theoretical and one empirical: the first is that, being an Adjective, it will have to pick up the agreement features outside N', analogously to other Adjectives, as we have proposed in section 4. The other reason is that a possessive anaphor cannot be bound by an internal argument either on the left, as was shown by Giorgi in chapter 1, or on the right of N (see also n. 19 to this chapter):

(127)   a. la descrizione di se stesso$_i$ a Gianni$_i$
            the description of himself to Gianni
         b. *la propria$_i$ descrizione a Gianni$_i$
            self's description to Gianni

c. *la descrizione propria$_i$ a Gianni$_i$
the description self's to Gianni

As has already been argued in chapter 1, this effect cannot be due simply to a principle C violation, but has to be attributed to principle A as well. Therefore, if *proprio* were allowed to appear under N′, it would be properly bound by its supposed antecedent and (127)c should be grammatical. Since it is not, we may conclude that the possessive has necessarily to move from N′ to a higher projection.

A reasonable hypothesis is that the obligatoriness of such a movement (which is likely to fall under the same generalization as the obligatorily external occurrence of referential Adjectives discussed in sec. 4) is a consequence of the need for a possessive to receive a Case (to realize its inherent Genitive) under agreement with the head, a process that we have suggested to be only possible outside the N′ node, i.e. the domain of internal arguments.

When the possessive appears prenominally, we assume that it moves to Spec, a 'core' case of movement. But which position does it raise to, when it appears on the right of the head N? First of all, let us remark that it is quite unlikely that the surface position of possessives on the right of the Noun is an adjoined one: apart from the implausible conclusion that agreement would take place between the head and an adjoined phrase, we should also face the consequence that it would become impossible to explain the difference between, say, English and Italian, or French and Italian, with respect to such a rightward occurrence of the possessive. In other words, we could not maintain the principled parametric explanation we suggested before for the contrasts of (99): in fact, while there is independent evidence that the two language types differ with respect to the surface categorization of possessives, there is no apparent reason why they should differ with respect to the possibility of rightward adjunction to N projections. If the surface distribution of possessives in Italian follows from the fact that in such a language they are realized as Adjectives, it must be the case that a possessive raised to the right of N′ from an internal position moves to the normal position of postnominal Adjectives. The very existence of such a movement in languages like Italian has an important theoretical consequence: it suggests that the target of substitution rules is not generally limited to Spec, as is usually maintained (see Chomsky 1986b), but must be extended to include other non-subcategorized positions, i.e. not projected as a consequence of the Projection Principle. This conclusion reinforces the fundamental distinction between external positions (base positions for external thematic arguments, even on the opposite side of Spec, and also targets of movement) and other thematic positions, which is so basic to our present approach.

We may wonder, now, whether, by raising to the right of the head, an Italian possessive necessarily interferes with an empty pronominal subject, as a mirror image of what seems to happen in Spec in the English examples pointed out by Roeper (1984). Actually, it appears that the understood subject retains its properties of syntactic activity:

(128)   a. (?)A proposito di quei farmaci e della possibilità di una sperimentazione loro sugli uomini, il parere della commissione è stato negativo
Concerning those drugs and the possibility of their testing on humans, the opinion of the committee was negative

b. (?)A proposito di quei farmaci, una sperimentazione loro su di sé comporta sempre gravi rischi
Concerning those drugs, their testing on oneself always implies serious risks

c. (?)A proposito di quei farmaci, una sperimentazione loro allo scopo di ottenere nuovi risultati sarebbe pericolosa
Concerning those drugs, their testing in order to achieve new results would be dangerous

All these sentences are slightly marked, a frequent consequence of the appearance of a postnominal possessive without a licensing context, e.g. being informationally and intonationally focused; however, the options of binding and control seem not to be affected, as shown in (b) and (c). The conclusion must thus be that on the right of the head both a PRO-like empty category and a raised possessive can survive. This is not surprising: in fact, Adjectives, with which possessives share the surface distribution, and overtly realized thematic subjects may easily cooccur in Italian on the right side of an NP:

(129)   le sperimentazioni segrete del dottor Frankenstein
the secret experimentations of doctor Frankenstein

Furthermore, and more importantly, it is clear, as we have already noticed in section 6, that no Uniqueness Requirement on arguments holds on the right side of NPs. Thus the results of (128) are exactly what we may expect: the landing site of the possessive raised to the right does not, in simple cases, necessarily coincide with the external argument position; let us consider, however, a more complex and subtle prediction. Recall that in sentential structures the PRO subject of certain adverbials can be controlled by the direct object from the surface position occupied after passivization, but not from its VP-internal base position, perhaps for reasons of c-command (see Manzini 1983a):

(130)   a. Gianni$_i$ fu giustiziato dopo PRO$_i$ aver subito un regolare processo
            Gianni was executed after facing a regular trial
         b. *Hanno giustiziato Gianni$_i$ dopo PRO$_i$ aver subito un regolare processo
            They executed Gianni after facing a regular trial
         c. Hanno giustiziato Gianni$_i$ dopo che pro$_i$ aveva subito un regolare processo
            They executed Gianni after he had faced a regular trial

A roughly analogous contrast (although often less sharp) can be found within nominals:

(131)   a. La sua$_i$ esecuzione dopo PRO$_i$ aver subito un processo irregolare rimarrà un'infamia
            His execution after facing an irregular trial will remain a disgrace
         b. ?*L'esecuzione di Gianni$_i$ dopo PRO$_i$ aver subito un processo irregolare rimarrà un'infamia
            The execution of Gianni after facing an irregular trial will remain a disgrace
         c. L'esecuzione di Gianni$_i$ dopo che pro$_i$ aveva subito un processo irregolare rimarrà un'infamia
            The execution of Gianni after he had faced an irregular trial will remain a disgrace

Compare also the contrast in the following pairs:

(132)   a. ?*L'assassinio di Moro$_i$ da parte delle Brigate Rosse dopo PRO$_i$ essere stato rapito sarà ricordato nei libri di storia
            The murder of Moro by the Red Brigades after being kidnapped will be mentioned in history books
         b. Il suo$_i$ assassinio da parte delle Brigate Rosse dopo PRO$_i$ essere stato rapito...
            His murder by the Red Brigades after being kidnapped...

(133)   a. ?*L'assunzione di nuovi professori$_i$ dopo PRO$_i$ essere stati esaminati è l'obiettivo dei ministri competenti del governo
            The hiring of new professors after being examined is the aim of the relevant ministers of the government
         b. La loro$_i$ assunzione dopo PRO$_i$ essere stati esaminati...
            Their hiring after being examined...

The plausible suggestion in the presence of such contrasts consists of three assumptions:

(134)   a. The infinitival adverbial clause of these examples cannot hang from N′
         b. The *di* + NP phrases, unlike possessives, can hardly raise to positions external to N′
         c. C-command is required for these cases of control

Actually, all these assumptions are likely to be independently needed. We have, in fact, already suggested in the text the possibility that N′ is the domain of all and only the internal arguments of the head; as for (134)b, it may follow from Chomsky's (1986a) Last Resort Principle, which essentially rules out instances of movement to an A-position if not for reasons of Case-marking: in fact *di* + NP phrases may realize Genitive under N′ as such, so that they have no reason, hence are not allowed, to raise outside it; possessives, instead, have to, if, as we have suggested before, Case agreement with the head is only possible under higher projections of N.[65] Finally, the need for (134)c may be inferred from the analogous pattern of control in sentences referred to above.

However, notice that control in sentences seems to take place only from A-positions: thus, cliticization or wh-movement of the object in sentences like (130)b, unlike NP-movement, do not help it to better control the PRO of the adverbial. The prenominal non-thematic position of possessives cannot count as an A one in Italian, but might rather be assimilated to a sort of clitic position. Then, we may wonder whether movement from an internal position in (131)a, (132)b and (133)b was direct to Spec or can rather have been mediated by a postnominal A-position actually counting as the controller.

We have suggested before that an internal argument raised as a possessive to the right of N′ does not necessarily interfere with a pronominal empty category in subject position, arguably because, being surface Adjectives, possessives may occupy an adjectival postnominal position of their own. However, it is doubtful that such an adjectival position may always count as a real A-position; it is true that it seems sometimes to receive a θ-role, as discussed in the text with respect to referential Adjectives; consider, however, the following fact:

(135)   a. l'appello presidenziale al paese
            the presidential appeal to the country
         b. l'appello presidenziale di Reagan al paese
            Reagan's presidential appeal to the country

While *presidenziale* ('presidential') in (135)a seems to be a real thematic argument, the agent, meaning 'of/by the president', in (135)b it cannot have such an interpretation because a real genitive argument is present (here, the Adjective roughly means 'as the president', and it has a predicative interpretation): thus, when a nominal subject is present, no external θ-role may ever be assigned to the adjectival position as a consequence of the θ-criterion. Technically speaking, the latter position is not, in such cases, a potential θ-position, hence an A-position, and it should not count as valid for binding. The reasoning can probably be generalized and the analysis made more plausible by admitting that the adjectival position in question is never a θ- and A-position and that in examples like (135)a and similar ones the referential AP moves string-vacuously from the subject θ-position to the adjectival one. If this is the case, an internal argument realized as a possessive, whatever its final surface position, will have to raise through the external A-position of subject NPs (thus filling it with its trace and preventing a PRO from occurring there) at least in one case: namely, when such a possessivized internal argument must control the subject of an adverbial which it may not control from the D-structure object position, as in (131)–(133) above. As indeed already pointed out, control, like binding, may only take place from A-positions.[66] This subtle and intricate prediction of our approach is strikingly and significantly correct, reinforcing the analysis proposed in sections 8–9 above. Consider in fact the following sentences:

(136)   a. ?*Disapprovo l'attribuzione del premio a Maria dopo essere stato a lungo in ballottaggio tra i due concorrenti
           I disapprove of the attribution of the prize to Maria after being long at stake between the two candidates
       b. A proposito del premio, disapprovo la sua attribuzione a Maria dopo essere stato a lungo in ballottaggio tra i due concorrenti
           Speaking of the prize, I disapprove of its attribution to Maria after being long at stake between the two candidates

(137)   a. L'attribuzione del premio a se stessa ha fatto di Maria un tipico rappresentante della corruzione odierna
           The attribution of the prize to herself made Maria into a typical representative of today's corruption
       b. A proposito del premio, la sua attribuzione a se stessa ha fatto di Maria un tipico rappresentante della corruzione odierna
           Speaking of the prize, its attribution to herself made Maria into a typical representative of today's corruption
       c. *A proposito del premio, la sua attribuzione a se stessa dopo essere stato a lungo in ballottaggio fra i due concorrenti ha fatto di

Maria un tipico rappresentante della corruzione odierna
Speaking of the prize, its attribution to herself after being long at
stake between the two candidates made Maria into a typical
representative of today's corruption[67]

Examples (136)a and b show that control of the subject of the adverbial
is only possible from a prominent position outside N′ (see above); the
paradigm (137) suggests that such a position must be that of external
thematic NPs, dethematized and filled by the possessive on its way to
Spec, so that a trace of the latter crucially excludes the PRO-like element
from it in the (c) example. The natural structure of (136)b would, then, be
the following (irrelevant details omitted):

(138)   [La sua$_i$ [$_{N'}$ attribuzione t_i a Maria] t_i [dopo PRO$_i$ essere stato...t_i]]
          Its attribution to Maria after being...

where the highest t is the only c-commanding A-position available for the
control of PRO. Example (137)c, on the other hand, would be associated
with either of the following ungrammatical structures:

(139)   a. [La sua$_i$ [$_{N'}$ attribuzione t_i a se stessa$_j$] PRO$_j$ [dopo PRO$_i$ essere
             stato...]
             Its attribution to herself after being...
         b. [La sua$_i$ [$_{N'}$ attribuzione t_i a se stessa$_j$] t_i [dopo PRO$_i$ essere stato...]
             Its attribution to herself after being...

Structure (139)a is excluded by the lack of a c-commanding controller in
A-position for the *PRO*$_i$ subject of the adverbial infinitive (*sua*$_i$ in Spec is
in A′-position, t_i does not c-command beyond N′); (139)b is straightforwardly ruled out by principle A of the Binding Theory, since the
anaphor *se stessa* has no antecedent.

Notice that it is not the case that a possessivized object and an
understood subject cannot be syntactically active (in the sense of binding
or controlling), hence realized, at the same time. In fact, this situation may
arise when the trace of the object within N′ suffices to establish the binding
or control relation in question and, thus, no higher A-position is required
for this:

(140)   a. Una rapida restituzione di Maria a se stessa per riscuotere il
             compenso pattuito è l'obiettivo dello psicoanalista
             A quick restoration of Maria to herself in order to receive the
             honorarium agreed upon is the psychoanalyst's goal
         b. Una sua rapida restituzione a se stessa per riscuotere il compenso
             pattuito è l'obiettivo dello psicoanalista
             Her quick restoration to herself in order to receive the honorarium
             agreed upon is the psychoanalyst's goal

In both (140)a and b the psychoanalyst is the one who wants to do the restoration and is supposed to collect the payment: he seems, thus, to be denoted both by a PRO-like subject of *restituzione* and the one subject of *riscuotere*. Since the anaphor is an internal argument contained within N′, the trace of the possessive in object position suffices to c-command and A-bind it: hence the raising of the possessive to Spec may be direct, without interfering with the postnominal subject position filled by a pronominal empty category. The same reasoning can be reproduced with a case of control in which the PRO can be directly controlled from the object position (arguably, because the infinitival complement occurs within N′, or within V′, in sentences):

(141) a. La condanna di Maria a scontare tre anni di carcere senza averle
          dato la possibilità di difendersi mi ha scandalizzato
          The conviction of Maria to serve three years in prison without
          giving her a chance to defend herself scandalized me
       b. La sua condanna a scontare tre anni di carcere senza averle dato la
          possibilità di difendersi mi ha scandalizzato
          Her conviction to serve three years in prison without giving her a
          chance to defend herself scandalized me

Here the object controls the PRO subject of *scontare* ('serve') and the understood arbitrary subject of *condanna* ('conviction') may control the other PRO subject of the *without* clause. Hence both the subject and the object of the NP are syntactically active.

The further prediction is that with head Nouns like *conoscenza* ('knowledge'), which, according to the theory developed in the text, always require a syntactically realized subject, the object should never improve its control capabilities through possessivization. This seems to be the case, contrary to what happens in sentences (where, as we have said, the subject θ-role remains syntactically realized on the *-EN* passive morpheme):

(142) a. *Non è possibile conoscere l'algebra senza essere studiata bene
          It is not possible to know algebra without being studied well
       b. Non è possibile che l'algebra venga conosciuta senza essere
          studiata bene
          It is not possible that algebra comes to be known without being
          studied well
(143) a. *Non è possibile la conoscenza dell'algebra senza essere studiata
          bene
          Knowledge of algebra without being studied well is not possible
       b. *Non è possibile la sua conoscenza senza essere studiata bene
          Its knowledge without being studied well is not possible

(144) a. *E' raro osservare un tale fenomeno senza essere stato predetto da una teoria
It is rare to observe such a phenomenon without having been predicted by a theory

b. E' raro che un tale fenomeno venga osservato senza essere stato predetto da una teoria
It is rare that such a phenomenon is observed without having been predicted by a theory

(145) a. *E' rara l'osservazione di un tale fenomeno senza essere stato predetto da una teoria
The observation of such a phenomenon without having been predicted by a theory is rare

b. *E' rara la sua osservazione senza essere stato predetto da una teoria
Its observation without having been predicted by a theory is rare

Summarizing now the results of this section, we have been led to the following conclusion:

(146) a. Possessive forms, which are genitive NPs at D-structure, surface with the distribution either of Adjectives (e.g. in Italian) or of Determiners (e.g. in English); in both cases they must occur at S-structure outside N', binding a trace therein if interpreted as internal arguments.

b. The θ-position for subjects on the postnominal side of Italian NPs behaves like other non-strictly subcategorized A-positions (e.g. subjects of sentences) in being a target for movement (raising of a possessive object), although not necessarily the only possible one; on the other hand, it is the only possible A-position, hence the only one available for binding and control outside N'.

c. Unlike possessives, internal arguments of the form $di+$NP never surface higher than N', i.e. never undergo raising to the subject position, probably as a consequence of Chomsky's (1986a) Last Resort Principle (to be understood as discussed in n. 65 above).

As a consequence, the effect of the Projection Principle must be so understood as to enforce the projection of internal (subcategorized) arguments of heads, but also to optionally base-generate external positions, not necessarily coinciding with Spec, even without actually θ-marking or interpreting them. In the course of the derivation such dethematized positions will either be filled by A-movements or remain empty, being filtered out as ungrammatical, in the latter case, by the θ-criterion and the conditions on the nature and distribution of empty categories.

An approach based on these conclusions, as well as on the others reached throughout the present work, is, thus, able to derive a wide range of intricate and correct consequences in the domain of binding and control within NPs. More generally, it seems clear to us that no theory dispensing with the postulation of distinct empty categories like traces and PROs, and of designated A- and θ-positions at distinct levels of structural embedding within NPs could account for this array of facts in a principled or even descriptively adequate way.

Appendix: The Head–Subject parameter across categories

An obvious question which arises, in the framework of the Head–Subject hypothesis, is whether the proposed parameter also extends to govern the internal structure of the other major lexical phrases, like APs and VPs. Consider, in fact, that most of the languages here considered are, to a very large extent, crosscategorially consistent with respect to the more easily checkable value of the Head–Complement Parameter. Furthermore, if some independent notion of Spec can be defined (see n. 3 above for discussion), it is rather clear that Spec is ordered before the head in all phrases of Romance and Germanic languages. It is thus tempting to assume crosscategorial consistency also for the Head–Subject parameter. Let us consider whether such an hypothesis can be corroborated on empirical grounds, starting by examining the case of APs. The latter, of course, never contain a subject in the sense of an external thematic argument, or a possessor. However, the existence in English of an essentially productive system of pre-head adjectival (or adverbial) compounding, as in *language-specific(-ally*) or *water resistant*, suggests that the Head–Subject parameter could be active within APs (and derived adverbial phrases) as well. Unfortunately, we lack, in this case, the expected counter-check provided by Romance, since in this language group real adjectival compounds seem to be very restricted or even missing at all. A possible example, going in the expected direction from the point of view of the parameter, could be provided by the case of modified colour Adjectives, suggested to us by S. Scalise (p.c.):

(147)   a. verde bottiglia
             lit.: green bottle (bottle-green)
         b. rosso pomodoro
             lit.: red tomato (tomato-red)

However, it must be noticed that such structures are never inflected for gender and number, but always stay in the masculine singular form:

(148)   a. i vestiti verde/*-i bottiglia
             bottle-green (singular/plural) dresses
         b. Una gonna rosso/*-a pomodoro
             a tomato-red (masculine/feminine) skirt

It is conceivable, then, that when so modified these colour names are substantivized, losing their Adjective status and entering a sort of potentially recursive nominal compound (e.g. N–N–N), as in (148)). The lack of adjectival compounding in Romance could perhaps be attributed to some stricter interpretation for Adjectives of the contradictory requirements mentioned in note 25 above (inflection on the compound head vs inflection final). In any event, the consequence is that we cannot find in this case totally convincing comparative evidence for the Head–Subject parameter. It seems very likely that it can account, as was suggested in chapter 2, for the distribution of measure phrases selected by the head (thus, neither purely adverbial in nature nor θ-marked as internal arguments):

(149)   a. alto due metri/*due metri alto
          b. two metres tall/*tall two metres

If the suggested analysis is correct, we have, then, some comparative evidence in favour of the application of the Head–Subject parameter within APs. The next natural problem to be addressed concerns the possibility for the Head–Subject parameter to constrain the position of subjects of Verb Phrases in IPs. We may assume with Travis (1984) that on the surface the position of external arguments of VPs is governed by a parameter concerning the direction of predication (cf. Rothstein 1983). But the interesting question is whether the D-structure position in which external θ-roles of Verbs are assigned is determined by the Head–Subject parameter. The latter conjecture has become especially interesting and plausible since the appearance of certain hypotheses, most carefully worked out in Koopman and Sportiche (1988), according to which the subject of sentences is base-generated within VP and then raised to the Spec of IP. We will not reproduce here the empirical data supporting Koopman and Sportiche's approach, but will only sketchily point out some conceptual and empirical advantages which could be derived by combining their hypothesis with our Head–Subject parametrization. Koopman and Sportiche argue, in fact, that external arguments of unergative Vs are always base-generated in the Spec of VP, where, at least in a class of languages including the most common European varieties, they cannot survive, for Case reasons; thus they must raise to the Spec of IP in order to be marked Nominative under agreement. However, if our Head–Subject hypothesis is correct, we should perhaps expect to find the external θ-position of Vs in Spec of VP in the Germanic languages, but on the right of the head, although still outside V′, in Romance. Furthermore the latter position should be a possible target of A-movement for lower arguments of the Verb, on the analogy of what seems to happen in NPs (see section 12 of this chapter). This approach immediately presents some obvious conceptual advantages. The first is represented by the regularization of the internal phrase structure of the major lexical categories: in principle, VPs, as well as NPs and APs, could now consist at D-structure of at least two distinct argument levels, one for internal θ-roles and one for the external one, and the directionality of assignment of such roles would be crosscategorially consistent. Consider next the possibility that Italian and English (and, perhaps, all languages) may be identical in not allowing any instance of Case-marking in the Spec of VP (see Koopman and Sportiche 1988), but also in allowing some form of Nominative assignment or transmission to the right of V′.[68] Although not easy to formulate theoretically, this assumption is quite plausible: the idea that no unnecessary difference must be postulated between the two languages is the null hypothesis; as for the curious distribution of Case alluded to, it is hardly unexpected if I is assimilated to a raising predicate, as in Koopman and Sportiche's proposal: for true raising Verbs do not allow Nominative marking of the embedded subject in the Spec of the IP they govern, but they do in the inverted position:

(150)   a. *Sembrano i ragazzi aver telefonato
             Seem the boys to have called up
         b. Sembrano non aver telefonato neppure i ragazzi
             Seem not to have called up the boys either

(in which prefixing *neppure* ('either') to the inverted subject ensures that it will have to occur in the c-domain of the negation, hence in the embedded VP and not just in the matrix one). If both Nominative Case and θ-role can be assigned to an NP right sister of V′, then the so-called inverted subject of unergative Verbs in sentences like (151)

(151)   ha telefonato Mario
         has called up Mario

could precisely occupy the position in question, and not necessarily a VP-adjoined one. From this hypothesis another obvious conceptual advantage ensues: according to the analysis developed in Rizzi (1982b), the trace of subject wh-movement in languages with free inversion (e.g. standard Italian and most of its dialects) is left in the inverted position; if this position is an adjoined one, hence an A′ one, it becomes difficult to maintain the conceptually appealing notion of variable as always occurring in A-position. Of course, this problem is automatically overcome by the proposed suggestion, which could assign (151) the analysis in (152) and represent (153)a roughly as in (153)b:

(152) $[_{IP}\text{pro}[_{I'}\text{ha}[_{VP}[_V\text{telefonato}]\text{Mario}]$
         has called up Mario

(153)   a. Chi ha telefonato?
             Who has called up?
         b. $[\text{Chi}[_{IP}\text{pro}[_{I'}\text{ha}[_{VP}[_V\text{telefonato}]t]$

Here *t* is the variable and occurs in a θ-, hence A-, position. Of course, postulating a structure like (152) in Italian as a consequence of the Romance setting of the Head–Subject parameter immediately suggests a possible connection, in English, between the ungrammaticality of the corresponding inversion and the opposite value of the parameter. In other words, apparent inversion could be allowed in Italian and other Romance languages as a case of surfacing of the subject in the base-generated θ-position predicted by the head–subject order, whereas it would be ungrammatical in English as a function of the subject–head value. As is known, however, the inversion of subjects of unergative Verbs has often been related to the null-subject parameter: more precisely, most approaches to Null-subject phenomena, since Taraldsen's (1978) paper, admit, with the notable exception of Safir (1984), that for a language to display empty pronominal subjects is a sufficient condition to have free inversion of the subject also with unergative Verbs. If this is the case, the only possible testing ground for our hypothesis about the relevance of the head–subject value for inversion will be provided by the comparison of English with a Romance variety like French, which is not a null-subject language. As a matter of fact, French appears to contrast with English roughly in the expected way, since it displays certain instances of subject inversion with unergative verbs; we are thinking in particular of the construction usually termed

Stylistic Inversion (see Kayne 1972; Kayne and Pollock 1978):[69]
(154)   a. le jour où ont téléphoné tous mes amis
         b. il faut que téléphonent tous mes amis
(155)   a. *the day when have called up all my friends
         b. *it is necessary that call up all my friends
In French, under certain circumstances (essentially, presence of a wh-moved phrase or of a subjunctive mood) studied in the references cited, it is possible to have an empty category in the Spec of IP and the subject in postverbal position. So far, no explanation has ever been provided for why the same conditions do not have a comparable licensing effect for inversion in English. The best possible assumption would be, of course, that the licensing conditions operative in French are, by and large, universally available and that their not being manifested in English is a consequence of some independently motivated parameter. Our Head–Subject hypothesis, in conjunction with the already mentioned idea that Nominative can crosslinguistically appear on a right sister of V' (but not on a left sister or on an adjoined position), provides an immediate solution: the only difference between the two languages would be that the subject is base-generated as a right sister of V' in French and may surface there whenever the Spec of IP is allowed to remain empty by certain potentially universal licensing conditions, whereas in English it is generated in Spec of VP, and therefore it must raise to the Spec of IP, *à la* Koopman and Sportiche, for Case reasons.

The situation is, however, slightly more complex than that. The reason is that in French Stylistic Inversion also affects the subjects of ergative Verbs, while even this option is ungrammatical in English:
(156)   le jour où est arrivé Jean
(157)   *the day when arrived John
Now, according to Burzio's (1986) ergative hypothesis, the subjects in (156) and (157) should both be base-generated in postverbal position as internal arguments, so that, under a linear parametrization approach, we might expect (157) to be grammatical in English. The traditional answer to the question of the status of (157) consists of saying that English is independently known not to have a Stylistic Inversion rule. Since our aim is precisely that of eliminating this rule in favour of an independent parametric account, we cannot adopt such a solution literally. However, notice that the traditional approach regarding the grammaticality of (156) in French as the same phenomenon as the grammaticality of (154) is certainly correct in one sense, namely that the position of *Jean* in (156) is exactly the same as the position of *tous mes amis* ('all my friends') in (154) and differs from the regular position of internal arguments. This is directly supported by the following evidence, discussed by Kayne (1981a) in part on the grounds of previous work by Obenauer (1978) and of other references cited there:
(158)   a. ?*un cinéma où sont beaucoup passés *e* de films bulgares
            a movie theatre where have many played (of) films Bulgarian
         b. Il a été beaucoup *e* de films bulgares
            It has been many played (of) films Bulgarian
The contrast of (158) can be straightforwardly explained, in Kayne's terms, if the empty QP in the Spec of the NP (*e de films bulgares*) is allowed to meet its proper government requirements through external government by the Verb in (158)b, but

not in (158)a. In other words, (158) can be taken to suggest that a postverbal subject of an ergative predicate remains in its internal argument base position (cf. the equal acceptability of *On a beaucoup passé de films...* 'One has many played of films...') in the *il* construction, but moves to a 'less governed' position in the Stylistic Inversion cases. Recall, at this point, our conclusion in chapter 2 that the inverted subject position of an unergative Verb is properly governed by it, but its Spec is not, and consider that the position in question is now likely to be precisely the right sister of V' hypothesized directly above. Recall also the other conclusion arrived at in section 12 of this chapter, namely that the external argument base position, generated in Romance as the right sister of N', can also be left empty and dethematized at D-structure and in such a case it can sometimes serve as the landing site of an internal argument raised from a lower position under N'.

Combining all these insights together, we may propose that Stylistic Inversion for subjects of ergative Verbs is precisely raising to NP1 from NP2 in the following structure:

(159)

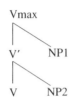

If such raising is obligatory, say for Case reasons, it will be immediately explained why (157) is ungrammatical in English (i.e. for lack of the landing site, due to the value of the Head–Subject parameter) and (158)a in French (i.e. because the empty QP in the Spec of the 'inverted' NP will not be accessible to external government by the Verb *passés*). We should assume, then, again, that the only position within the VP where Nominative can be assigned or transmitted is the right sister of V', excluding thus the right sister of V, as well as Spec and any adjoined position.[70] This hypothesis is for now provisional and needs to be analysed in detail in further work: if it turns out that it can be maintained, though, it will be possible to assume it crosslinguistically and, as we have shown, the only parametric distinction needed to account for the French–English contrast with respect to Stylistic Inversion is the one provided by the Head–Subject parameter.

4* Null pronominals within NPs and the syntax of DPs

A. GIORGI AND G. LONGOBARDI

Introduction

In chapter 3 we have provided some arguments in favour of the presence within NPs of syntactically active empty categories with the function of pronominal subjects. In order to strengthen our conclusion we will present here new empirical evidence suggesting that such elements exist and may naturally fall into the already established theory of empty categories. In particular, we will show that their distribution and interpretation as subjects of NPs closely resembles the one found in infinitival clauses, therefore further confirming our main claim that the structure of NPs is governed by roughly the same general principles governing sentential structures. The null element in subject position, in fact, will be shown to have the same control properties as PRO in sentences and we will conclude, therefore, that it is precisely PRO, a possibility already suggested in Chomsky (1981).

We will first give a set of additional arguments in favour of the idea that, when necessary, an empty subject *can* be syntactically represented within NPs; later, we will suggest that with a subset of Nouns it *must* obligatorily be represented, namely with the class of Nouns with unaffected objects (see also ch. 3, sect. 9) in Anderson's (1979) sense. Then we will also discuss some evidence pointing to the existence of another empty pronominal in object position with properties rather similar to those of the empty object of Verbs identified by Rizzi (1986). Finally, we will address the question of the position of Determiners and the structure of their projections, bringing to light the conclusions that the results achieved throughout the book allow one to draw about this much-debated issue.

1 Additional arguments for the existence of null subjects within NPs

It is a well-known fact that the so-called long-distance anaphors are subject-orientated. The Italian possessive anaphor *proprio* ('self's'), belongs (also) to this class, as discussed in Giorgi (1984):

(1) Gianni$_j$ ha informato Maria$_i$ che il proprio$_{*i/j}$ avvocato avrebbe seguito il processo
Gianni informed Maria that self's lawyer would follow the trial

Consider now, in this light, the following examples:

(2) a. Ho consigliato a Maria$_i$ un'attenta indagine sui fatti che avevano portato all'arresto dei propri$_i$ genitori (da parte della polizia)
I recommended to Maria a careful investigation about the facts which led to the arrest of self's parents (by the police)
b. *Ho consigliato a Maria$_i$ un'attenta indagine da parte del suo avvocato sui fatti che avevano portato all'arresto dei propri$_i$ genitori
I recommended to Maria a careful investigation by her lawyer about the facts which led to the arrest of self's parents
c. *Ho promesso a Maria$_i$ un'attenta indagine sui fatti che avevano portato all'arresto dei propri$_i$ genitori
I promised Maria a careful investigation about the facts which led to the arrest of self's parents

In (2)a *proprio* can refer to an indirect object, an unusual behaviour for a long-distance anaphor. A plausible hypothesis is that binding is not direct, but mediated by an empty category coindexed with *Maria* in the subject position of the NP. The judgement in (2)b confirms this idea: if we overtly express the agent of the NP headed by *indagine* ('investigation'), *Maria* is no longer a possible antecedent, whereas the expressed agent is an acceptable one. In (2)c, where the agent of the investigation is no longer understood as coreferential with *Maria*, since a Verb like *promettere* tends to refuse object control, *propri* cannot refer back to it. This contrast is the same as that found in the corresponding sentences:

(3) a. Ho consigliato a Maria$_i$ di indagare attentamente sui fatti che avevano portato all'arresto dei propri$_i$ genitori
I recommended to Maria to carefully investigate about the facts which led to the arrest of self's parents
b. Ho consigliato a Maria$_i$ che il suo avvocato$_j$ indagasse attentamente sui fatti che avevano portato all'arresto dei propri$_{j/*i}$ genitori

I recommended to Maria that her lawyer carefully investigate
about the facts which led to the arrest of self's parents

c. *Ho promesso a Maria di indagare attentamente sui fatti che
avevano portato all'arresto dei propri genitori
I promised Maria to carefully investigate about the facts which led
to the arrest of self's parents

In (3)a a non-subject, *Maria*, appears to be a possible antecedent for
propri, owing to the intervention of a subject, PRO, coreferential with it.
In (3)b this option is no longer available and only *il suo avvocato* can bind
propri; in (3)c, which is a structure of subject control, PRO controlled by
a first-person subject cannot bind *propri*, since the latter is exclusively a
third-person anaphor. With respect to this bridge property, therefore, the
unexpressed subject of an NP is as syntactically active as PRO in
sentences.

Another argument in the same vein concerns the possibility of split
antecedents. In English PRO of infinitives may take a split antecedent at
least in a context of non-obligatory control (see Chomsky 1986a, p. 126)
and in Italian also in some contexts of obligatory control, but only if both
antecedents c-command it:[1]

(4)   a. Gianni voleva che Maria si convincesse che era ora di PRO
liberare se stessi da quell'imbarazzante situazione
Gianni wanted Maria to be convinced that it was time to free
themselves (masc.) from that embarrassing situation

b. La madre di Gianni voleva che Maria si convincesse che era ora di
PRO liberare se stesse/*se stessi da quell'imbarazzante situazione
Gianni's mother wanted Maria to be convinced that it was time to
free themselves (fem.)/themselves (masc.) from that embarrassing
situation

c. Gianni$_i$ ha proposto a Maria$_j$ di PRO$_{i+j}$ partire insieme per
Casablanca
Gianni proposed to Maria to leave together for Casablanca

d. [La madre di Gianni$_j$]$_k$ ha proposto a Maria$_i$ di PRO$_{i+k/*k+j}$ partire
insieme per Casablanca
Gianni's mother proposed to Maria to leave together for
Casablanca

In (4)a, apart from the arbitrary reading, the masculine plural anaphor *se
stessi* may take *Gianni* and *Maria* as its reference; this is impossible in (4)b,
which is therefore ungrammatical with *se stessi* except in the mentioned
arbitrary reading; it is acceptable with the feminine form of the reflexive,
se stesse, and *Maria* and *la madre di Gianni* as split antecedent. Since split
antecedents are usually forbidden for lexical anaphors, the possibility of
the latter reading must be imputed to the PRO subject of the infinitive.[2]

A similar test is provided by *insieme* ('together'), a predicative adjunct, which requires a local non-split plural antecedent.[3] Now, exactly the same paradigm holds with NPs, therefore suggesting an analogous explanation:

(5)   a. Gianni$_i$ voleva che Maria$_j$ sapesse che era arrivata finalmente l'ora della liberazione di se stessi$_{i+j/arb}$ dalla schiavitù
         Gianni wanted Mario to know that the time of the liberation of themselves from slavery had finally arrived

      b. [La madre di Gianni$_i$]$_k$ voleva che Maria$_j$ sapesse che era arrivata finalmente l'ora della liberazione di se stesse$_{i+k}$/*se stessi$_{i+j/arb}$ dalla schiavitù
         The mother of Gianni wanted Maria to know that the time of the liberation of themselves (fem. plur.)/(masc. plur.) from slavery had finally arrived

(6)   a. Gianni$_j$ ha proposto a Maria$_i$ un viaggio insieme$_{i+j}$ a Casablanca
         Gianni proposed to Maria a trip together to Casablanca

      b. [La madre di Gianni$_j$]$_k$ ha proposto a Maria un viaggio insieme$_{k+j/*j+i}$ a Casablanca
         Gianni's mother proposed to Maria a trip together to Casablanca

Another case where the understood subject of Noun Phrases is crucially active to bridge an illicit antecedent–anaphor relation is represented by instances of 'backward' control like the following ones:

(7)   a. Conoscere se stesso è stato molto utile a Mario
         To know himself has been very useful to Mario

      b. La conoscenza di se stesso è stata molto utile a Mario
         The knowledge of himself has been very useful to Mario

(8)   a. Conoscere se stesso è stato molto utile alla carriera di Mario
         To know himself has been very useful to Mario's career

      b. La conoscenza di se stesso è stata molto utile alla carriera di Gianni
         The knowledge of himself has been very useful to Gianni's career

(9)   a. Conoscere se stesso sarà molto utile per la carriera che Mario si prefigge
         To know himself will be very useful to the career that Mario plans for himself

      b. La conoscenza di se stesso sarà molto utile per la carriera che Mario si prefigge
         The knowledge of himself will be very useful to the career that Mario plans for himself

(10) a. * Conoscere se stesso è stato molto utile alla madre di Mario
         To know himself has been very useful to Mario's mother

      b. *La conoscenza di se stesso è stata molto utile alla madre di Mario
         The knowledge of himself has been very useful to Mario's mother

(11) a. *Conoscere se stesso è stato molto utile alla carriera della madre di Mario
         To know himself has been very useful to the career of Mario's mother

    b. *La conoscenza di se stesso è stata molto utile alla carriera della madre di Mario
       The knowledge of himself has been very useful to the career of Mario's mother

(12)   a. *Conoscere se stesso sarà molto utile per la carriera che la madre di Mario si prefigura per lui
       To know himself will be very useful for the career that Mario's mother plans for him

    b. *La conoscenza di se stesso sarà molto utile per la carriera che la madre di Mario si prefigura per lui
       The knowledge of himself will be very useful for the career that Mario's mother plans for him

In these examples the behaviour of infinitives and Noun Phrases is exactly identical: the lexically unexpressed subject of a subject phrase may be controlled by a non-c-commanding antecedent within the corresponding VP, but only if it is the least embedded *animate* NP. The coincidence of behaviour with respect to such a peculiar condition provides us with a very strong argument suggesting that an empty subject is present in these Noun Phrases and actually functions like PRO. Notice that no direct binding of the anaphor by *Mario* would *a priori* be possible in such cases, for lack of the required prominence of the understood antecedent. It is, in fact, true that anaphors in comparable positions may, in certain examples, be bound by a non-c-commanding object NP, a fact especially stressed by Manzini (1983a), but such a binding relation is fully acceptable only with so-called psychological Verbs and, more importantly, for no speaker is it ever possible when the antecedent is embedded *within* an object. Consider the following examples with the Italian possessive anaphor *proprio* itself playing the subject role, thus excluding the possibility of an empty local binder, as pointed out in Giorgi (1984):

(13)   a. Il proprio stato di salute preoccupa molto Mario
       Self's health condition worries Mario a lot

    b. ?Il proprio stato di salute può favorire Mario
       Self's health condition may favour Mario

    c. *Il proprio stato di salute può favorire la carriera di Mario
       Self's health condition may favour Mario's career

    d. *Il proprio stato di salute può favorire la carriera che Mario si prefigge
       Self's health condition may favour the career that Mario plans for himself

The ungrammatical sentences of (13) obviously become grammatical if the possessive pronoun *suo* is substituted for the anaphor *proprio*. These examples and their contrast with the ones in the preceding paradigm show that an empty subject must be possible in the latter, to mediate the relationship between the antecedent and *se stesso*.

A fourth phenomenon which can be explained by adopting our view has to do with the possibility for anaphors embedded within an NP to acquire an arbitrary interpretation under circumstances which would be inexplicable otherwise. Consider, for instance, the following contrast:

(14)   a. *Dio conosce se stessi
             God knows oneself
         b. PRO_{arb} conoscere se $stessi_{arb}$ è importante
             To know oneself is important

If the lexical anaphor *se stessi* is not bound by an arbitrary element, as in (14)b, it cannot receive the arbitrary interpretation by itself. In the light of this consideration we are led to the conclusion that in the following examples an arbitrary element is present which is able to assign reference to the anaphor:

(15)   a. Mario ti convincerà dell'importanza della conoscenza di se $stessi_{arb}$
             Mario will convince you of the importance of the knowledge of oneself
         b. Gianni ritiene che la conoscenza di se $stessi_{arb}$ sia importante
             Gianni believes that the knowledge of oneself is important

In order to account for these facts we have to hypothesize the existence of an arbitrary empty category in the subject position of *conoscenza*. Once again, we can find an interesting parallelism between the behaviour of this empty element and PRO in infinitival clauses:[4]

(16)   a. Mario ti convincerà dell'importanza di PRO_{arb} conoscere se $stessi_{arb}$
             Mario will convince you of the importance of knowing oneself
         b. Gianni ritiene che PRO_{arb} conoscere se $stessi_{arb}$ sia importante
             Gianni believes that knowing oneself is important

2   Control of null subjects in sentences and Noun Phrases

The previous tests have established that the presence of a syntactically realized null subject in NPs must be allowed in a variety of cases; now we must push still further the comparison of its control properties with those of PRO in infinitives.

Like PRO in sentences, such an empty element, apart from the cases of backward control, is sensitive to c-command:

(17)   a. $Gianni_i$ persegue la conoscenza di se $stesso_i$
             Gianni pursues the knowledge of himself

b. *La sorella di Gianni_i persegue la conoscenza di se stesso_i
   The sister of Gianni pursues the knowledge of himself

The ungrammaticality of example (17)b shows that the control of an empty subject, which could mediate the relationship with the only feature-compatible NP, is subject to a c-command constraint. Consider the parallelism with control in clauses:

(18)   a. Gianni_i pensa di PRO_i conoscersi_i/conoscere se stesso_i
          lit.: Gianni thinks to know himself
          Gianni thinks he knows himself
       b. *La sorella di Gianni_i pensa di PRO_i conoscersi_i/conoscere se stesso_i
          lit.: the sister of Gianni thinks to know himself
          Gianni's sister thinks he knows himself

Local direct or indirect objects are likely to be possible antecedents as well:

(19)   a. Ho incoraggiato Gianni_i alla conoscenza di se stesso_i
          I encouraged Gianni to the knowledge of himself
       b. Ho raccomandato a Gianni_i la conoscenza di se stesso_i
          I recommended to Gianni the knowledge of himself

Once again control of PRO in sentences behaves in the same way:

(20)   a. Ho incoraggiato Gianni_i a PRO_i partire
          I encouraged Gianni to leave
       b. Ho raccomandato a Gianni_i di PRO_i partire
          I recommended to Gianni to leave

However, most prepositional objects cannot be coreferential with the understood subject of an NP, or with PRO, perhaps for lack of c-command:

(21)   a. Ho deciso con Gianni_i la consegna di me stesso/*se stesso_i alla polizia
          I decided with Gianni the delivery of myself/himself to the police
       b. Ho deciso con Gianni_i di consegnare me stesso_i/*se stesso alla polizia
          I decided with Gianni to give myself/himself up to the police

Finally, if the NP in question is less locally embedded with respect to the expected antecedent, once again we find behaviour typical of PRO:

(22)   a. Gianni_i ritiene che [la conoscenza di se stesso_i] sia importante
       b. Gianni_i ritiene che sia importante [la conoscenza di se stesso_i]
          Gianni believes that the knowledge of himself is important

    c. *Gianni$_i$ ritiene che Maria non apprezzi [la conoscenza di se stesso$_i$]
       Gianni believes that Maria does not appreciate the knowledge of himself

(23) a. Gianni$_i$ ritiene che [PRO$_i$ conoscere se stesso$_i$] sia difficile
    b. Gianni$_i$ ritiene che sia difficile [PRO$_i$ conoscere se stesso$_i$]
       Gianni believes that to know himself is difficult
    c. *Gianni$_i$ ritiene che Maria non desideri [PRO$_i$ conoscere se stesso$_i$]
       Gianni believes that Maria does not wish to know himself

If the empty category is embedded inside a preverbal or inverted subject it can be coreferential with *Gianni*, but if it is embedded within an object, it undergoes the usual opacity effects induced by the subject (see Manzini 1983a).

From the examples given so far we could conclude that the null subject of infinitival clauses has exactly the same interpretative properties as the phonetically null subject of NPs. However, a potential difference between the two patterns may arise when we examine the distribution of the arbitrary reading. Consider, first of all, that even in this domain null subjects of NPs and of infinitives pattern alike to a certain extent:[5]

(24) a. Ho ordinato a Maria$_i$ la consegna di se stessa$_i$/*se stessi alla polizia
       I ordered Maria the delivery of herself/oneself to the police
    b. Ho deciso la consegna di me stesso/*se stessi alla polizia
       I decided the delivery of myself/oneself to the police
    c. Mario$_i$ pensò solo alla protezione di se stesso$_i$/*se stessi
       Mario thought only of the protection of himself/oneself
    d. Mario ti convincerà dell'importanza della conoscenza di te stessa/se stessi
       Mario will convince you of the importance of the knowledge of yourself/oneself
    e. Gianni$_i$ ritiene che la conoscenza di se stesso$_i$/se stessi sia importante
       Gianni believes that the knowledge of himself/oneself is important

(In all these examples, the arbitrary anaphor is understood as coreferential with an equally arbitrary null subject of the NP.)

(25) a. Ho ordinato a Maria$_i$ di consegnare se stessa$_i$/*se stessi alla polizia
       I ordered Maria to consign herself/oneself to the police
    b. Ho deciso di consegnare me stesso/*se stessi alla polizia
       I decided to consign myself/oneself to the police
    c. Mario$_i$ pensò solo a proteggere se stesso$_i$/*se stessi
       Mario thought only of protecting himself/oneself

    d. Mario ti convincerà dell'importanza di conoscere te stessa/se stessi
       Mario will convince you of the importance of knowing
       yourself/oneself
    e. Gianni$_i$ ritiene che conoscere se stesso$_i$/se stessi sia importante
       Gianni believes that knowing himself/oneself is important

In other cases, however, with the appropriate lexical choices, null subjects of NPs admit of the arbitrary reading also in the context where infinitival PRO is usually submitted to obligatory control, namely as the subject of a phrase in complement position:

(26)   a. Socrate$_i$ voleva/amava anzitutto la conoscenza di se stesso$_i$/se stessi
       Socrates mainly wanted/loved the knowledge of himself/oneself
    b. Gianni$_i$ odia la paura di se stesso$_i$/se stessi
       Gianni hates the fear of himself/oneself
    c. Socrate esortava ogni discepolo$_i$ alla conoscenza di se stesso$_i$/se stessi
       Socrates encouraged every disciple to the knowledge of himself/oneself
(27)   a. Socrate$_i$ voleva/amava anzitutto conoscere se stesso$_i$/*se stessi
       Socrates mainly wanted/loved to know himself/oneself
    b. Gianni odia temere se stesso/*se stessi
       Gianni hates to fear himself/oneself
    c. Socrate esortava ogni discepolo a conoscere se stesso/*se stessi
       Socrates encouraged every disciple to know himself/oneself

Even with Verbs not allowing minimal contrasts with infinitival PRO, because they do not take sentential arguments, the behaviour of the null subject of complement NPs is often free (hence also arbitrary) and is subject to obligatory control only depending on the semantic properties of specific lexical items:

(28)   a. Gianni ha sempre provato una grande paura di se stesso/*se stessi
       Gianni always experienced a big fear of himself/oneself
    b. Gianni ha sempre apprezzato la paura di se stesso/se stessi
       Gianni always appreciated the fear of himself/oneself

Therefore the only difference in control possibilities between null pronominal subjects of NPs and infinitival sentences concerns certain (lexically conditioned) cases in which the NP, or sentence, occurs in complement position: the subject of NP may still be arbitrary, in cases where that of IP is in a situation of obligatory control.[6] Actually, the lack of parallelism is, in part, only apparent; in fact, it is not the case that every PRO subject of an infinitive in complement position undergoes obligatory control. As especially stressed by Manzini (1983a), the presence of a fronted wh-phrase may suffice to protect PRO from obligatory control. Compare the following pair:

(29)　　a.　Gianni$_i$ pensa di conoscere se stesso$_i$/*se stessi
　　　　　　lit.: Gianni thinks to know himself/oneself
　　　　　　Gianni thinks he knows himself
　　　　b.　Gianni$_i$ pensa a come conoscere se stesso$_i$/se stessi
　　　　　　Gianni thinks of how to know himself/oneself

We refer the reader to Manzini (1983a) for more details and for a possible approach; we simply note that the behaviour of the empty subject of complement NPs is still analogous to that of some infinitival PROs in corresponding positions, namely to that of PROs protected by a fronted wh-phrase. We will leave open here the question of why this is so.

3　　Control under reconstruction

Another apparent difference can be reduced to the conclusion reached above that the understood subject of NPs can be arbitrary more often than PRO in sentences. Consider the following examples:[7]

(30)　　a.　La sorella di Gianni$_i$ non apprezza la conoscenza di se stesso$_i$ che
　　　　　　lui$_i$ ha raggiunto
　　　　　　Gianni's sister does not appreciate the knowledge of himself that
　　　　　　he has attained
　　　　b.　Gianni$_i$ sostiene che Maria non apprezza la conoscenza di se
　　　　　　stesso$_i$ che lui$_i$ ha raggiunto
　　　　　　Gianni believes that Maria does not appreciate the knowledge of
　　　　　　himself that he has attained

Examples (30) represent at first sight a violation of the control principles so far assumed; in (30)a no c-commanding antecedent exists and in (30)b the c-commanding antecedent is opacized by a non-local subject.

Our suggestion is that in these sentences the empty subject contained in the NP is interpreted under 'reconstruction', i.e. in its D-structure position. In fact, if the whole NP is viewed by control theory as the object of the relative clause, a local c-command relation does hold between the pronoun *lui* and the controlled empty category.[8]

That the pronoun *lui* is the actual controller is made clear by the fact that, if the latter does not corefer with *Gianni*, the understood subject of the NP fails to do so as well, and indeed corefers with the pronoun:

(31)　　　　La sorella di Gianni$_i$ non apprezza la conoscenza di se stesso$_j$/*$_i$/*$_k$
　　　　　　che lui$_j$ ha raggiunto
　　　　　　Gianni's sister does not appreciate the knowledge of himself that
　　　　　　he has attained

Analogous ungrammaticality arises if the pronoun is not in a locally c-commanding position even at D-structure:

(32)   a. *La sorella di Gianni non apprezza la conoscenza di se stesso che
           lui crede che Maria abbia raggiunto
           The sister of Gianni does not appreciate the knowledge of himself
           that he believes that Maria attained
        b. *La sorella di Gianni non apprezza la conoscenza di se stesso che
           sua cognata ha raggiunto
           The sister of Gianni does not appreciate the knowledge of himself
           that his sister in law attained

The case of relativization does not appear to differ in this respect from those of topicalization, clefting or question formation:

(33)   a. LA CONOSCENZA DI SE STESSO credo che Gianni abbia raggiunto!
           The knowledge of himself I think that Gianni has attained!
        b. E' la conoscenza di se stesso che credo che Gianni abbia raggiunto
           It is the knowledge of himself that I think that Gianni has attained
        c. Che grado di conoscenza di se stesso credi che Gianni abbia
           raggiunto?
           Which degree of knowledge of himself do you think that Gianni
           attained?

These facts suggest, thus, that control of the understood subject of NPs, while retaining the usual basic properties displayed at S-structure (roughly locality and c-command), may also apply with reference to D-structure configurations (under reconstruction of wh-movement). It is likely that the same is true of NP-movement in examples like the following:[9]

(34)   La conoscenza di se stesso$_i$ sembra t essere stata proposta t da
        Socrate ad ogni discepolo$_i$ come il più alto obiettivo
        The knowledge of himself seems to have been proposed by
        Socrates to every disciple as the highest goal

Now we may raise, once again, the usual question: do these properties of control in NPs extend to PRO in sentences? In cases in which an infinitival sentence moves to a position which is not one of control at S-structure, it seems that the interpretation of PRO is always sensitive to D-structure configurations, as in the case of subjects of NPs:

(35)   CONOSCERE SE STESSO$_i$ credo che Gianni$_i$ desideri!
        To know himself I believe that Gianni wishes!
(36)   E' conoscere se stesso$_i$ che credo che Gianni$_i$ desideri
        It is to know himself that I believe that Gianni wishes

However, in the case of relativization, a contrast appears between sentences and NPs. The test must be performed with appositive relative clauses, introduced by a wh-word like *il che* (lit.: 'the which'), since a true restrictive interpretation with a sentential head is hardly possible.

If PRO within the head of a relative clause is in a position of obligatory control at S-structure, it may never be controlled in the same way as if it were contained in the position of trace of relativization:

(37)   *Gianni desidera [conoscere se stessa]$_i$, il che Maria forse non vorrebbe e_i
         Gianni wishes to know herself, which Maria perhaps would not want

However, marginal acceptability is found when no obligatory control context is defined at S-structure and provided that a controller under reconstruction is available:[10]

(38)   a. ?Gianni pensa che [conoscere se stessa]$_i$ il che Maria desidera da molto tempo e_i, sia un'impresa psicologicamente difficile
            Gianni thinks that to know herself, which Maria has wished for a long time, is a psychologically difficult task
         b. *Gianni pensa che [conoscere se stessa] sia un'impresa psicologicamente difficile
            Gianni thinks that to know herself is a psychologically difficult task

The conclusion that we may draw is, thus, that control under reconstruction does not distinguish subjects of NPs from subjects of infinitival sentences, i.e. nominals pattern with (38)a and not with (37): in both cases the option of satisfying control within the head of a relative clause under reconstruction is available only if no obligatory control requirement is imposed by the S-structure configuration. The asymmetry represented by the wider acceptability of control under reconstruction with NPs is, then, just another consequence of the already discussed fact that nominal complements, unlike non-wh-infinitival sentences, do not necessarily create environments of obligatory control for their empty subjects.[11]

4   The subject with 'unaffected' objects

So far we have shown that the option of having a null pronominal subject in NPs is always available. Now we will argue that, for a given class of NPs, such an option *must* be chosen. The NPs in question are those we have analysed in chapter 3, section 9, i.e. those headed by Ns with 'unaffected objects' such as *knowledge* and *fear*.[12] In fact, here we will provide further evidence in favour of the idea that the external θ-role of these Nouns, or rather of these X^0 categories, must always be discharged, unlike that of other Nouns, and thus forces the syntactic realization of a subject. We will start by recalling a basic argument, first given by Ross (1969), then mentioned in Koster (1984) and Chomsky (1986a). The argument is based on the consideration of the same backward control structures analysed before, this time replacing the reflexive by a pronoun: unexpectedly the latter turns out to be disjoint from the non-c-commanding controller.

Consider the following contrast:

(39)   a. Una migliore conoscenza di lui e della natura del problema
           avrebbe giovato alle decisioni di Mario
           A better knowledge of him and of the nature of the problem
           would have helped Mario's decisions
        b. Una migliore conoscenza di se stesso e della natura del problema
           avrebbe giovato alle decisioni di Mario
           A better knowledge of himself and of the nature of the problem
           would have helped Mario's decisions

(40)   a. Quella gran paura di lei non gioverà certo alla carriera politica di
           Maria
           That great fear of her certainly will not help Maria's political
           career
        b. Quella gran paura di se stessa non gioverà certo alla carriera
           politica di Maria
           That great fear of herself certainly will not help Maria's political
           career

In (39)a the pronoun cannot be coreferential with *Mario*, at least in the natural situation in which it is *Mario* who should know himself; this would appear as a surprising fact, were it not for the *obligatory* presence of an empty subject, controlled in this reading by *Mario*. No comparable problem arises in (b), of course. Analogous are the judgements and the contrast in (40). The contrast of (39) parallels, then, the one found in infinitival sentences:

(41)   a. Conoscere meglio lui e la natura del problema avrebbe giovato alle
           decisioni di Mario
           Better knowing him and the nature of the problem would have
           helped Mario's decisions
        b. Conoscere meglio se stesso...
           Better knowing himself...

Notice, however, that this contrast does not show up with Ns not belonging to the class in question, as illustrated by the following examples:

(42)   a. Quella fotografia di lui$_i$ in divisa ha giovato molto alla carriera di Gianni$_i$
       That picture of him in a uniform helped Gianni's career very much
      b. Quella fotografia di se stesso in divisa...
       That picture of himself in a uniform...[13]

In this case, the option of having a pronoun coreferential with *Gianni* can be chosen imagining that the person taking the picture was *Gianni* himself; this fact suggests that in (42)a *no* empty category is present, so that any interpretation (even no interpretation at all) about the author of the picture is possible. In (42)b, instead, an agent coreferential with *Gianni* is obligatorily understood: in fact a subject empty category is required to bind the anaphor. In such cases a contrast arises with the corresponding sentential structures:

(43)   a. Fotografare lui in divisa ha giovato molto alla carriera di Gianni
       Photographing him in a uniform helped Gianni's career very much
      b. Fotografare se stesso in divisa ha giovato molto alla carriera di Gianni
       Photographing himself in a uniform helped Gianni's career very much

In (43)a, in fact, *lui* is clearly disjoint from *Gianni* via the PRO subject of the infinitive, which is obligatorily controlled by the latter. The difference between sentences and NPs of this second class must probably be traced back to the obligatoriness of a realized subject position for sentences: theoretically, such a generalization, expressed by Chomsky (1982) in his Extended Projection Principle, is now derivable from Rothstein's Predication Principle, which imposes the presence of a subject for non-argument maximal projections, like VP, but not for non-maximal phrases, like intermediate projections of N. The effects of this difference between clauses and Nouns Phrases are likely to be independently manifested by another well-known contrast: the lack in NPs of expletives or meteorological quasi-arguments, overtly required by clausal expressions in certain languages:

(44)   a. *(It) is raining
      b. (*It's) rain
(45)   a. *(There) were discussed many problems
      b. (*There's) discussion of many problems[14]

With items like *paura* ('fear'), or *conoscenza* ('knowledge'), on the other hand, where the pronoun is accepted only if the subject is understood as disjoint, the obligatoriness of a syntactic subject follows from the thematic principle elaborated by Jaeggli (1986) and adopted by us in chapter 3, section 9.

The contrast between (46)c, on one side, and (46)a and b on the other, points to the same bipartition of the class of Nouns:

(46)   a. Gianni$_i$ ricorda la paura di lui$_i$ (subj. $\neq$ i)
            Gianni remembers the fear of him
        b. Gianni$_i$ ricorda la paura di se stesso$_i$ (subj. $=$ i)
            Gianni remembers the fear of himself
        c. Gianni$_i$ mi ha mostrato dei ritratti di se stesso$_i$ in divisa
            (subj. $=$ i/j)
            Gianni showed me some portraits of himself in a uniform[15]

Here *Gianni* c-commands the pronoun/anaphor, but is external to the first potential binding domain. Again, the results in (46)a and b are only compatible with the hypothesis that discharging the subject θ-role on an empty pronominal is obligatory in such cases. The optional lack of a subject in (46)c, however, extends the binding category of the reflexive to the whole sentence.

Another argument in favour of the obligatory presence of a subject with *conoscenza* comes from the following examples:

(47)   a. Mario$_j$ ha incoraggiato Gianni$_i$ alla conoscenza di se stesso$_{i/*j}$
            Mario encouraged Gianni to the knowledge of himself
        b. Mario$_j$ ha incoraggiato Gianni$_i$ a PRO$_i$ conoscere se stesso$_{i/*j}$
            Mario encouraged Gianni to know himself

In (47)a we find the same possibilities of coreference we have in (46)b, namely the anaphor cannot refer to the subject *Mario*. In (47)b we can attribute this fact to constraints due to control, that is to lexical requirements imposed by the Verb *incoraggiare* on the subject of its prepositional complement. The obvious suggestion is to extend this explanation to (47)a, claiming that there is an empty subject behaving like PRO. In fact, if in this case the option could be taken of not syntactically realizing the subject, as in (46)c above, *Mario* would certainly be a possible antecedent. In this case, the least CFC containing a possible antecedent would be the whole sentence and therefore *Mario* should qualify as such.[16]

As a conclusion, the facts discussed in this section clearly confirm the assumption made in chapter 3 (sect. 9), on the grounds of Jaeggli's (1986) proposal, that the most salient feature of NPs with unaffected objects is the obligatoriness of the syntactic discharging of the subject θ-role.

5   The PRO theorem

The set of arguments given in the previous sections strongly support, then, the two following conclusions:

(48)   a. Understood subjects of Noun Phrases may be syntactically realized as pronominal $[_{NP}e]$ categories
b. The assignment of reference to such empty categories observes exactly the pattern imposed by Control Theory on PRO subjects of infinitives

On the grounds of these observations we will propose that Chomsky's hypothesis (see 1981, p. 156; 1986a) that empty pronominal subjects of NPs are actually instances of PRO is correct. The latter assumption, which immediately accounts for the properties of this element discussed throughout the section, raises, however, the question of why PRO may survive in what appears to be a context of government by a lexical head (N). An environment of this type should be forbidden for PRO as a consequence of Chomsky's (1981) so-called PRO-theorem: since the binding domain for an anaphor or a pronoun must apparently contain such an element as well as its governor, the possibility of having a governor must be blocked for PRO; otherwise it will be assigned a binding domain (a governing category) in which, as a pronominal anaphor, it will be subjected to the contradictory, hence unsatisfiable, requirements of the binding principles A and B at the same time.

Although the formal derivation of such a theorem had to be slightly modified with the recent developments in the theory of binding and the introduction of the notion of licensing (see Chomsky 1986a), the logic of the argument remains almost unchanged and should rule out PRO inside a lexical category. The crucial assumption for the derivation of the PRO theorem is that the governor of an anaphor or a pronoun must be included in its binding domain. We may thus wonder what sort of evidence, independently of the PRO theorem, supports this crucial assumption. In the most recent version of the binding principles, as presented in Chomsky (1986a), mention of the governor appears still to be motivated by one fact: namely, that a subject pronoun in the following examples is disjoint from the subject of the matrix clause, identifying the latter, and not the embedded IP, which does not contain its governor, *believe* or *for*, as the relevant binding domain:

(49)   a. John believes [$_{IP}$ him to be intelligent]
        b. John would prefer for [$_{ip}$ him to win]

Consider now the type of government instantiated in (49): according to standard assumptions, in both cases the Verb *believe* and the complementizer *for* are heads (i.e. X⁰s) governing and Case-marking the pronoun across their complement IP, i.e. under c-command and not just under m-command (in the sense of Chomsky 1986b); in other words, the pronoun is contained within a branching V′, or C′, respectively (see again Chomsky 1986b for the phrase structure). Instead, PRO as the subject of an NP, according to the internal structure evidenced in chapter 1, would occur outside N′, hence it would not be c-commanded but just m-commanded by the head N (we assume this to be true even in the cases where N′ does not branch). On the basis of this observation we will define two kinds of government: namely (1) c-government, for which the governee β has to be contained in all the projections containing the governor α; and (2) m-government, for which β is contained in all the *maximal* projections containing α. Now we may claim that the kind of government crucially mentioned in the binding conditions and thus relevant to the derivation of the PRO theorem is the more restricted one: precisely c-government by an X⁰ category.[17] This is not implausible, since also the notion of c-command involved in binding has been argued to be c-command and not m-command, in particular in Chomsky (1986b; see also ch. 1). As a consequence of this approach, PRO is still disallowed in complement position everywhere, but is available as an external argument (i.e. outside N′) inside NPs.[18] A minimal and conceptually natural sharpening of the existing notion of government is thus sufficient to accommodate the current theory of PRO distribution with the empirical results suggested in this chapter.[19]

6   A pronominal empty object

From this approach it follows, then, that control PRO cannot occur as an internal argument of a head Noun, exactly as in the corresponding position of other categories, e.g. Vs, As and Ps. There is, however, some evidence suggesting that a kind of pronominal empty category does appear as an internal argument of N in certain cases; consider the following example:

(50)   A proposito di quel famoso psicoanalista, la tecnica della sue
          riconciliazioni con se stessi è veramente perfetta
          Speaking of that famous psychoanalyst, the technique of his
          reconciliations with oneself is really perfect

In this sentence, the anaphor *se stessi* is understood as referentially dependent on an arbitrary antecedent corresponding to the genitive internal argument. The external θ-role of agent of *riconciliazioni* is borne by the possessive pronoun in Spec, i.e. *sue*. It appears, then, that an arbitrary empty category of some sort must occur also as a genitive internal argument, hence presumably under the N′ node (see ch. 1), in order to bind the anaphor. One fact immediately suggests, however, that the properties of such a category cannot be fully assimilated to those of the empty pronominal subject of NP, which we have recognized as PRO.

In fact, while the control properties exemplified for the subject empty category seem to hold crosslinguistically, the occurrence of the arbitrary object is clearly parametrized; in English it is totally impossible, as shown by the ungrammaticality of the gloss of (50). The contrast between (50) and its gloss immediately recalls the analogous ones arising in sentences (example adapted from Rizzi 1986):

(51)   Un bravo psicoanalista può riconciliare con se stessi
          A good psychoanalyst can reconcile with oneself

According to the analysis proposed in Rizzi (1986), many Italian Verbs, unlike the corresponding English ones, are able to license the occurrence of an empty category in object position, which, lacking an antecedent or a coindexing relation with a set of identifying features, is restricted to the arbitrary interpretation. Such a category, being certainly governed, cannot, according to Rizzi, bear the feature conjunction [+anaphoric, +pronominal] typical of PRO; Rizzi proposes, then, that it may be identified with Chomsky's (1982) *pro*, i.e. a [−an, +pr] category, whose occurrence would be constrained in general by the following licensing condition:

(52)   *pro* is Case-marked by X^0_y

where y freely ranges parametrically over the features identifying the various lexical and non-lexical heads. Rizzi gives examples of languages choosing, as licensers of *pro*, V and I, like Italian, V and P (and perhaps subjunctive I), like French, and no head at all, like English. If the Italian empty object of N is really to be assimilated to the empty object of Verbs, it is plausible that some stronger condition may be imposed on the variation of the feature *y*. We can hypothesize, in fact, that the possible values of *y* are not just A, V, N, P, I (to say nothing about C) or any combination of them, but rather that, in the spirit of Chomsky's (1970) Lexicalist Hypothesis, the major lexical heads, A, V and N, form a natural class with a unitary behaviour with respect to the parameter. Therefore, if V is a licenser for *pro* in a language, also N and, in principle, A will be such licensers.[20] This approach captures the intuition that the grammaticality of both (50) and (51) in Italian and the corresponding ungrammaticality of their glosses in English constitute a genuine generalization of comparative syntax.[21]

Extending Rizzi's approach to the empty object of N and assuming, then, that it is [−an, +pr] the prediction ensues that it will exhibit the disjointness effects with respect to its subject manifested by the local verbal counterpart. As Rizzi notices, in fact, even two *arb* indices may be forced to be referentially independent as a consequence of principle B of the Binding Theory; consider, therefore, the following example:

(53)   a. Riconciliare _ con se stessi è spesso un'operazione molto difficile
        To reconcile with oneself is often a very difficult operation
       b. Pensare che uno psicoanalista possa sempre riconciliare _ con se stessi è pura follia
        To believe that a psychoanalyst may always reconcile with oneself is mere craziness

The arbitrary object locally binding the anaphor and the arbitrary subject of the infinitive can denote the same set of (arbitrary) persons in (b), but not in (a), where they are clausemates. In other words, the agent of the reconciling must necessarily be distinct from the patient of it in (53)a. However, contrary to the expectation, no such intuition is carried on to the corresponding nominalization:

(54)   La riconciliazione con se stessi è spesso un'operazione molto difficile
       The reconciliation with oneself is often a very difficult operation

Here it is possible to understand the three roles contained in the θ-grid of the head as played by the same individual. To be precise, (54) is ambiguous between a reading analogous to that of (53)a (especially when followed by an utterance like ' ... therefore it must be practised only by an expert psychoanalyst') and a reading analogous to the 'middle' one of (55):

(55)   Riconciliar*si* con se stessi è spesso un'operazione molto difficile
       To reconcile +*refl clitic* with oneself is often a very difficult task

In fact, (55) has a reflexive reading, identical with that of its non-cliticized version (56):

(56)   Riconciliare se stessi con se stessi...
         To reconcile oneself with oneself...[22]

i.e. with three referential arguments all coreferential; but it also displays an interpretation which may be called 'middle', with the agent θ-role left unsaturated in the syntax, hence neither necessarily coreferential, nor necessarily disjoint from the arguments bearing the other two roles.[23] This appears to be the second reading available for (54). We suggest, then, that the fact that the empty object of N is not disjoint from the agent, unlike its sentential counterpart, is just another consequence of the non-obligatoriness of syntactic realization for such agents within NPs. Thus, the difference in nature between the empty object of Nouns and the one of Verbs is likely to be only apparent.

Consider now the question of the control properties displayed by the empty object; as is known, Rizzi's object *pro* can only be arbitrary and never has a personal antecedent:

(57)   a. *Io credo che quello psicoanalista possa riconciliare con me stesso
            I believe that that psychoanalyst may reconcile with myself
        b. Credere che uno psicoanalista possa riconciliare con se stessi è
            ingenuo
            Believing that a psychoanalyst may reconcile with oneself is naive

The understood object cannot be controlled by the first-person higher subject in (57)a, but can be understood as coreferential with the equally arbitrary and non-local PRO subject of *credere* in (57)b. Essentially the same happens in NPs with an expressed subject:

(58)   a. *A proposito di quello psicoanalista, credo nel successo della sua
            riconciliazione con me stesso
            Speaking of that psychoanalyst, I believe in the success of his
            reconciliation with myself
        b. A proposito degli psicoanalisti, credere nel successo delle loro
            riconciliazioni con se stessi$_{arb}$ è ingenuo
            Speaking of psychoanalysts, believing in the success of their
            reconciliations with oneself is naive

However, non-arbitrary control of an understood thematically internal argument appears to be possible in NPs without an overt genitive subject:

(59)   a. Quella riconciliazione con se stesso ha finito per giovare alla
            carriera di Mario
            That reconciliation with himself ended up helping Mario's career

b. Luisa vorrebbe ricordare a Maria che è venuto il momento di una riconciliazione con se stesse
   Luisa would like to remind Maria that the moment has come for a reconciliation with themselves

In (59)a the anaphor is, as usual, understood as coreferential with the direct internal argument of the Noun. The latter must be syntactically present in the form of an empty pronominal, since the reflexive could not be bound by a non-c-commanding or split antecedent.

Again, we propose to maintain the hypothesis that the empty object of N is identical with that of Vs and to attribute this difference as well to the non-obligatoriness of a syntactically realized agent within such NPs. It is, in fact, reasonable to suppose that in (50) it is the internal argument which behaves as the subject of the NP from the viewpoint of control theory: for example, control of such an internal argument seems to fail in those cases where normal control of PRO subjects, in NPs and infinitival clauses, usually fails:

(60)   a. ?*Quella riconciliazione con se stesso ha finito per giovare anche alla carriera della moglie di Mario
          That reconciliation with himself ended up helping the career of Mario's wife as well
       b. ?*Il fratello di Giovanna spera ancora in una riconciliazione con se stessa
          Giovanna's brother still hopes for a reconciliation with herself

This pattern may be interpreted as suggesting that the empty category in question in these examples is to be identified with PRO and not with *pro*, at least in a theory distinguishing between these two categories along the lines of Rizzi (1986). We have claimed above that *pro*, but not PRO, may occur in the internal position under N' c-governed by the head: since the internal θ-role has been shown in chapter 1 to be discharged only under N', if PRO occurs bearing this role, it must appear at S-structure in a higher position as a result of movement. Conceptually, this would be analogous to what happens to PRO with passive (with the difference of the overt verbal morphology) or ergative infinitives. Actually, in chapter 3, we have suggested that raising from the object to the subject θ-position in NPs is indeed possible, subject, however, to some version of Chomsky's Last Resort Principle: namely, it is grammatical only for those genitive NPs whose realization under N' is impossible (e.g. possessives). Thus, since PRO has been assumed to be unable to surface under N', it must almost automatically be expected to undergo raising to the subject θ-position outside N′, as its 'last resort'.[24] If our reasoning is correct and sentences like (60) actually do not contain a *pro* in object position but rather a PRO, bearing their internal θ-role, though raised to the subject position at S-structure, this hypothesis should be confirmed by independent evidence. In chapter 3, we have argued that only an internal argument raised to the subject A-position outside N′ may control inside an adverbial clause modifying the NP, essentially the analogue of a phenomenon well attested by active/passive contrasts in sentences; consider now the following examples:

(61)   a. (*) Quello della cattura di Gianni prima di aver potuto varcare la
            frontiera è il maggior pericolo da evitare
            That of the capture of Gianni, before being able to cross the
            border is the highest danger to avoid
       b. (?) Quello della sua cattura prima di aver potuto varcare la
            frontiera...
            That of his capture before being able to cross the border...
       c. (?) Quello della cattura prima di aver potuto varcare la
            frontiera...
            That of the capture before being able to cross the border...[25]

These examples show that the arbitrary empty internal argument of (61)c is treated on a par, as a controller, with a possessive pronoun, which can be argued to raise outside N′ (see ch. 3). This confirms that it may be PRO in subject position at S-structure, not *pro* in object position. Notice also that there is direct evidence that an arbitrary empty object cannot function as a controller into an adverbial in the cases where it cannot be recognized as PRO raised to the subject position; this happens when an overt phrase bearing the external θ-role is expressed:

(62)   *A proposito di quello psicoanalista, le sue riconciliazioni con se
        stessi dopo essere stati analizzati sono terapie lunghe e costose
        Speaking of that psychoanalyst, his reconciliations with oneself
        (masc. plur.) after being analysed (masc. plur.) are long and
        expensive therapies

The contrast between (61)c and (62) parallels, then, the same one found with control in clausal structures like the following:

(63)   a. Essere catturati prima di poter varcare la frontiera sarebbe triste
            Being captured before being able to cross the border would be sad
       b. *Uno psicoanalista può riconciliare con se stessi dopo essere stati
            analizzati
            A psychoanalyst may reconcile with oneself after being analysed

To conclude, it appears once again that the argument frame of NPs displays many of the properties typical of active/passive VPs and clauses: such a parallelism has been shown here to hold with respect to object empty categories as well as to subject ones.[26]

7   The syntax of DPs

In this chapter we have substantiated the hypothesis of the existence of PRO as the subject of NPs on the grounds of arguments which can be easily reproduced for all the languages here considered. Now, we want to further clarify the structural conditions under which it can appear in a language, say, like English. As we have claimed, in Germanic languages, PRO must appear prenominally; we know independently that in such a prenominal position an 'Argument Uniqueness' principle holds, perhaps universally (see ch. 3, sect. 6); namely, only one element bearing a θ-role can occur there. Therefore, when PRO occurs no other thematic argument should appear prenominally. Parallel to such a generalization, another one holds concerning the uniqueness of Determiners; in fact, another obvious observation made in chapter 3 is that elements functioning as Determiners can never cooccur, in any reciprocal order.[27] Consider the following examples:

(64)   a. the/a book about World War Two
        b. John's book about World War Two
        c. my book about World War Two
        d. *a my book
        e. *a John's book
        f. *my John's book

These two principles seem to be sufficient to describe the occurrences of elements in the prenominal position; notice that the prediction which follows from the conjunction of the two generalizations is that among elements with a Determiner function a non-argument one can cooccur with PRO, but one which receives a θ-role, such as a possessive pronoun or a prenominal genitive phrase in English, cannot. Consider, in fact, the following cases, whose acceptability levels have been motivated by the complex evidence discussed in chapter 3 above:

(65)   a. yesterday's PRO attempt to leave
        b. the PRO attempt to leave
        c. *John's/my PRO attempt to leave[28]

PRO is obviously a θ-marked argument, but does not function as a

Determiner, *the* or *yesterday's* do (they syntactically 'close' or 'internally saturate' the NP as an argument; see ch. 3, sect. 11) but are not arguments, *my* and *John's* are both thematic arguments and have Determiner functions. Notice that the two Uniqueness Principles might be different in nature. The one concerning Determiners is presumably related not (or not only) to an incompatibility of structural position, given the seemingly wide categorial variety of items involved, but rather to the fact that an NP can be determined from the semantic point of view only once: it is plausible, in fact, that elements with the function of Determiners are licensed precisely by each introducing a distinct NP. From this point of view such a constraint would be similar to the ban against vacuous quantification, holding generally in natural languages and preventing, among other things, two operators from binding the same variable.

On the other hand, the constraint relative to Argument Uniqueness is perhaps related to the existence of a single structural slot for nominal expressions in the Spec of NP. Such a generalization is reminiscent of the well-known Doubly Filled Comp Filter which, analogously, captures the generalization that in the Spec of Comp only one empty or realized argument is possible, and it is likely that given an appropriate formulation both constraints may be subsumed under a single general condition.[29]

At this point we are naturally led into the question of the precise structural positions to be assigned to Determiners and all other items occurring to the left of head Nouns. Let us begin, as usual, by analysing Italian structures. Some relevant evidence can be provided by considering coordinate constructions; it is well known, in fact, that coordination provides a very good test for constituency, given the general constraint that only phrases can be coordinated. Consider in this light the following examples:

(66)   a. la [mia nuova efficiente segretaria] e [tua ottima collaboratrice]
          lit.: the my new efficient secretary and your very good collaborator
     b. la mia [nuova efficiente segretaria] e [ottima collaboratrice]
     c. la mia nuova [efficiente segretaria] e [ottima collaboratrice]
          lit.: the my new efficient secretary and very good collaborator
     d. la mia nuova efficiente [segretaria] e [collaboratrice]
          lit.: the my new efficient secretary and collaborator

Example (66)a shows that, since it is possible to coordinate whole nominal expressions with another one, excluding only the article, there must be a single node dominating the rest of the phrase. Sentence (66)b shows that there must be another constituent excluding the possessive but including all other Adjectives; moreover, the possibility of the interpretation in (66)c, in which the denoted individual is intended to be 'new' both as an efficient secretary and as a very good collaborator, suggests that Adjectives can be semantically ordered with respect to each other: the reading is most naturally encoded by a constituent structure like (66)c. Finally, (66)d shows that also heads, as is obvious, can be coordinated. A very plausible structure is therefore the following:

(67)   [la [mia [nuova [efficiente [segretaria]]]]]
        lit.: the my new efficient secretary

From these examples, notice also the special function of the Determiner, here the Italian article *la*, in defining the referential force of the expression: all the examples in (67) introduced by a singular Determiner denote, in fact, a single individual; only when it is the Determiner that is repeated does the reference immediately become plural:

(68)   La mia nuova efficiente segretaria e la tua ottima collaboratrice
        stanno uscendo/*sta uscendo
        lit.: The my new efficient secretary and the your very good
        collaborator are going out/*is going out

We should now assign categorial labels to the structure in (67). Let us start from the position of the Determiner. In order for the X-bar approach to syntactic structures to be completely general, along the lines suggested by Chomsky (1986b), each word must be the head of a phrasal constituent; consequently, Determiners, as far as they represent a distinct category, must also project a Determiner Phrase. Notice now that there are two *a priori* possible labellings for structures such as $[D [...N...]]$ which we were led to hypothesize:

(69)   a. $[_{Nmax} [_{DP}D] [_{Nmax-1}...N...]]$
        b. $[_{DP}D [_{Nmax}...N...]]$

The choice between the two structures is apparently underdetermined to a large extent in Romance and not obviously decidable in many Germanic languages: in particular, most basic generalizations we have captured throughout this book can apparently be formulated in either framework and are thus rather neutral with respect to the choice. For this reason, we have not yet addressed the question and, whenever necessary, we have assumed, without argument, the more traditional structure in (69)a. However, we should consider the possibility that the representation in (69)b is the more correct one; this is particularly plausible on the basis of some evidence recently discussed from the Semitic languages (see Ritter 1986 and Ouhalla 1988) and Scandinavian (Taraldsen 1989).[30] The latter, which we will examine directly, is especially relevant since it may constitute the clearest case, if not the only one, in which the adoption of one of the two alternatives turns out to be more readily compatible with our previous results than the choice of the other. Such analyses seem to suggest that the head D must c-command the head N, a possibility not admitted in (69)a under any definition. The structure of the argument basically runs as follows, in the three cases: in the languages in question the head N can sometimes precede all other elements in the NP, resulting in a surface NSO order. The simplest hypothesis compatible with the data always turns out to be the one according to which the head N is moved in pre-possessive position; since it is a head, to obey the constraint imposed by structure preservation, it has to be moved into another head position: the only obvious candidate is therefore the head D. The consequences are that such a head (D) must c-command the other one (N), as a result of the constraints on antecedent–trace relations, and that, accordingly, only (69)b is a possible structure.[31] For instance in Norwegian (Taraldsen 1989) the following orders are possible:

(70)   a. hans bøker om syntaks
           his books of syntax
    b. bøkene hans om syntaks
        lit.: book-the-s his of syntax

This situation is apparently unexpected, given the analysis of Norwegian as a well-behaved Germanic language with respect to the Head–Subject parameter, provided in chapter 3. The possessive, however, cannot appear phrase-finally:

(71)   *bøkene om syntaks hans
       lit.: book-the-s of syntax his

Moreover, Taraldsen (1989) shows that, applying essentially the c-command tests elaborated by Giorgi in chapter 1 above, it turns out that the possessive pronoun is in either case higher in structure than the complement, so that the surface NSO order of (70)b must be the product of some movement rule not affecting the basic c-command relations. Therefore, he argues that (70)a essentially represents the base structure, in agreement with the predictions of our Head–Subject parameter of chapter 3 and with Giorgi's thematic Correspondence Hypothesis in chapter 1 (i.e.

with a structure [hans [bøker om syntaks]]): (70)b would then be derived by moving the head N and adjoining it to the article in D, i.e. to the next head higher up, according to the constraints imposed on this kind of movement (see Chomsky 1986b). Notice that Heavy NP Shift of the subject, introduced now by the Preposition *til*, is also possible, as it is in English; consider the following example:

(72)   bøkene om syntaks til den gutten som står der borte
         the books of syntax of the boy who is there

This evidence, while confirming the correctness of the approach we propose in chapter 3, constitutes obvious evidence that the head D c-commands the head N, and, thus, the whole NP. Similar conclusions can be drawn from the mentioned studies about Semitic languages.

   Notice that, if this is really the case, some minor qualifications, never affecting the substance of our argumentation, are needed to accommodate some of the Germanic and Romance facts presented in the preceding chapters, and both sources of evidence become relevant to further selection among the possible variants of structure (69)b. Consider first the latter point. In fact, three different conceptions of a $[_{DP}D [_{NP}...N...]]$ structure are possible: of the three layers of argument structure of a head N defined in our two initial chapters and tentatively identified as N' (the domain of internal arguments), N'' (the domain of the external thematic argument) and N''' (the domain of the possessor or R-relation) respectively, NP could now include just the lowest or the two lower ones or all three. In the first two alternatives, the remaining one(s) would then hang from a (maximal or intermediate) D projection. However, such alternatives (one of which had been proposed in Abney 1986) are immediately and trivially falsified by the evidence provided by most Romance languages. As we have seen in the previous chapter, in fact, according to the Head–Subject parameter, the base position for the external argument is on the left in Germanic and on the right in Romance (recall also that this generalization holds both for the R-related phrases, in the sense defined in Higginbotham 1983 and in the preceding chapters, and for the external thematic arguments proper). In Romance, then, prenominal possessives are necessarily derived via movement. In languages like Italian, moreover, where articles and possessives may cooccur, as a consequence of the values of the other parameters introduced in chapter 3, section 11, the first element appearing on the left of the nominal head is always the article, which also precedes the possessive pronoun:

(73)   a. il mio libro
           lit.: the my book
        b. *mio il libro
           lit.: my the book

Now, the definite article is the most obvious candidate to be a head D. Consequently, in Romance, if one hypothesizes that the element bearing the external θ-role or the R-relation is generated under DP, to obtain the linear order of (73)a, one must lower it to the Spec of NP for it to appear on the right of D and on the left of N, violating again the c-command condition on movement: therefore we can straightforwardly exclude this kind of derivation. In Romance, therefore, also the base position of the external arguments must be included inside NP. It is plausible to suppose that Germanic must obey the same thematic constraints as Romance, especially in the light of the parametric approach extensively motivated in chapter 3. Therefore, in Germanic too, the element expressing the external θ-role and the R-relation must be generated inside NP, contrary to the proposal made by Abney (1986).

A priori, a question analogous to that raised by the choice between (69)a and b presents itself with respect to [A[N]] structures, exemplified in (67) as well. The right labelling could either be the more traditional (74)a or (74)b, suggested in Abney (1987):

(74)   a. $[_{Nmax} [_{AP}A] [_{Nmax-1}N]]$
        b. $[_{AP}A[_{Nmax}N]]$

Now, it is clear that, given the standard conditions on structure preservation and movement of heads, (74)b is straightforwardly incompatible with the movement derivation of prenominal Adjectives in Romance empirically motivated in detail in chapter 3. The choice of (74)b, which, among other things, would make it impossible to deduce the positional properties of Adjectives from the Head–Subject parameter, can thus be considered immediately falsified by the Romance evidence we have discussed in chapter 3.

The next natural question concerns the meaning of the parametric distinction between D possessives and A possessives discussed in chapter 3, section 11. If we want to maintain that the same semantic roles are always assigned inside the same phrases, possessive pronouns must be projected as arguments of N, i.e. within NP. In languages such as Italian they would surface as APs, exactly as proposed in chapter 3 section 11; in French or in English they would not be literally categorized as Ds, as suggested earlier, but would rather be even on the surface genitive NPs able, by virtue of some special feature, to determine (internally saturate) the whole nominal expression.[32] For this reason, they would make an element of the category D unnecessary, hence, semantically unlicensed and, ultimately, impossible.

Adopting a $[_{DP}D\;[_{NP}...N...]]$ structure also requires a slight modification of the approach to extraction from Romance NPs proposed in chapter 2. In fact, according to the evidence provided there, the extraction-through-Spec analysis crucially requires that a trace be left in the Spec of Nmax and properly governed by the Verb selecting the entire nominal expression, now the DP. Therefore, the trace in Spec of NP should be governed across DP and NP, even in the presence of an overt D:

(75)   Gianni, di cui ho conosciuto $[_{DP}$un $[_{NP}t$ fratello $t]]$
          Gianni, of whom I have met a brother

This situation would represent a clear violation of many, if not all, current definitions of government, in particular, of the minimality requirements on government (see ch. 2, sect. 12). A possible way out, assuming the structure in (75), consists of hypothesizing the occurrence of two intermediate traces, one in the Spec of NP and one in the Spec of DP. The presence of the former would be motivated by the data concerning Cinque's generalization on extraction and enforced by the non-structural nature of N as a governor (see the extensive discussion in ch. 2); that of the latter is suggested by the sensitivity of extraction to government by a higher Verb, displayed in the examples of chapter 2, section 6. By which principle could the presence of such a trace be enforced and, moreover, how could the other trace in Spec of NP satisfy the head-government requirements, imposed by the CC in the framework of chapter 2? Consider that, according to the definition of government postulated there, the head D, being non-lexical, can govern the trace in the Spec of its complement NP just in case it is coindexed with it. Now it is likely that such coindexing may only arise through Spec–Head agreement in DP: thus, a higher trace in the Spec of DP could share its index with the head D, allowing this latter to govern the lower coindexed one in the Spec of NP. This would provide a unified and theoretically natural answer to the two questions raised above: the process would, in fact, represent a further instance of the one probably operative with the head C in the French *que–qui* rule and in other cases considered, again, in chapter 2, section 5.

By this last move, all the basic generalizations we have tried to capture in the present book become compatible with the DP structure represented in (69)b.

Notes

Introduction

1 The term 'thematic relation' has been introduced mainly by Gruber (1965) and Jackendoff (1972).

2 According to recent hypotheses, however, all the θ-roles of a given head, also the subject role of Vs, are assigned internally to its maximal projection and subsequent movement raises the subject to the Spec of IP. See especially Koopman and Sportiche (1988). Notice that such an idea would provide an elegant solution to the locality anomalies discussed directly below in the text, making the whole θ-process homogeneous: no long-distance θ-assignment, in fact, would ever occur, but only a strictly local one plus raising to the external subject position. On some interactions of our proposals with these hypotheses, see chapter 3 and the appendix.

3 The inflectional features (present tense, third person singular) are presumably encoded in the tree under I; on new developments of the theory with respect to this point, see Pollock (1989) and Chomsky (1988).

4 Two nodes in a tree are said to be sisters if and only if they hang directly from the same node, i.e. are immediately dominated by it.

5 Expletives remain outside this classification, in the sense that there is no principle concerning them. The hypothesis suggested by Chomsky (1986a) is that at LF they disappear, i.e. the expletive is replaced by the element which is coindexed with it. If this is the case, only principles applying at levels other than LF can be relevant for the distribution of expletives.

6 Notice that in this case PRO can have arbitrary reference:

(i) PRO_{arb} to behave oneself is important

We will not further discuss this matter here; for an interesting theory on this topic, see Manzini (1983a).

1   On NPs, θ-marking and c-command

* Preliminary versions of this paper have been presented at NELS XVI, Montreal, and in a seminar held at the Fundación Ortega y Gasset, Madrid, 1986. A previous version of section 6 appeared as a Squib in *Linguistic Inquiry* (1987) 18, 3; the present one has been enlarged and revised in the light of subsequent developments.

1 In this work we therefore distinguish two notions of command, i.e. the one involved in binding and the one involved in government. For the same proposal, see Chomsky (1986a). For a different approach to binding within NPs, see Hellan (1986).

2 According to this line of reasoning, we might also expect principle C to be violated in (1) and (2), since *di* fails to block c-command of the R-expression by the anaphor or the pronoun. However, the data do not fulfil this expectation, given that the examples in (1) are grammatical. The reasons for this are quite complex, and some constitute the central point of this work. In sections 2, 3 and 4 it will be shown, in fact, that there is no c-command from the anaphor toward the R-expression, independently of the properties of *di*.

3 Notice that structures such as (3)a and (4)a again raise some problems for principle C of the Binding Theory. In fact, on the one hand the R-expression c-commands the anaphor, but, given the properties of *a* and *di*, the anaphor also c-commands the R-expression. We will show in section 4 that these problems extend to principle B and that, unlike those mentioned in the preceding note, they cannot be circumvented by any particular formulation of the notion of c-command, but require a reinterpretation of the meaning of the binding principles.

4 *A* and *di* can be considered pure Case-markers here; *di* realizes Genitive and *a* Dative. If the following principle is tenable:

(i)   Bare Case-markers do not block c-command

we can account, on this basis, for the difference between *a*, *di* and other Ps, such as, for instance, *con* ('with'). The latter, in fact, delimits a c-domain, presumably projecting a PP node with all the relevant properties of a maximal projection:

(ii)   a. la mia riconciliazione di Gianni$_i$ con se stesso$_i$
          my reconciliation of Gianni with himself
       b. *la mia riconciliazione di se stesso$_i$ con Gianni$_i$
          my reconciliation of himself with Gianni

(iii) a. Ho riconciliato Gianni$_i$ con se stesso$_i$
          I reconciled Gianni with himself
       b. *Ho riconciliato se stesso$_i$ con Gianni$_i$
          I reconciled himself with Gianni

The (b) examples can also be construed as cases of principle C violation, since again the anaphor c-commands the R-expression. However, we will show that this factor would probably be insufficient by itself and that their ungrammaticality is likely to be primarily due to a violation of principle A; see section 4 of this chapter. In order to establish which Prepositions are bare Case-markers and which are not, it will be sufficient for our purposes to adopt an intuitive criterion of 'semantic' content. However, on some occasions, such a criterion can give rise to uncertainties. For our purposes here, anyway, it can be considered sufficiently discriminative even if more problematic cases deserve further attention.

5 Aoun and Sportiche's (1982) definition of c-command is the following:

(i) α c-commands β if
every maximal projection dominating α also dominates β

Reinhart's (1976) first definition is the following (p. 32):

(ii)   Node A c[onstituent]-commands node B iff neither A nor B dominates the other and the first branching node which dominates A dominates B

In the course of the discussion she modifies her definition as follows (p. 148):

(iii)   Node A c[onstituent]-commands node B iff the first branching node α dominating A dominates B or is immediately dominated by a node α' which dominates B, and α is of the same category type as α'.

Notice that (iii) is closer to Aoun and Sportiche's (1982) definition and therefore it shares with it part of the shortcomings we are discussing in the text.

6 The Italian possessive pronoun is morphologically very similar to regular Adjectives. It agrees in gender and number with the head Noun; conversely, it does not agree in gender with its antecedent:

(i)   a. la sua casa
(the) his/her (fem. sing.) house (fem. sing.)
b. il suo cane
(the) his/her (masc. sing.) dog (masc. sing.)

Moreover, as shown by the examples, it displays syntactic properties of Adjectives, since it is not in complementary distribution with articles and other Determiners. For further arguments concerning the adjectival status of the Italian possessive, see chapter 3. For a slightly different treatment see Lyons (1984). Although the possessive in Italian can also appear postnominally, e.g. *il libro mio* ('the book my'), its binding properties are not affected by this linear ordering: whatever is suggested in this chapter with respect to any sentence containing a possessive in prenominal position holds for the corresponding one with the possessive in postnominal position.

7 Notice also that there is a class of Nouns (see Cinque 1980, 1981a; Anderson 1979), which cannot be passivized, such as *desiderio*:

(iii)   a. il tuo desiderio
your desire (only experiencer)
b. il desiderio di te
the desire for (lit. of) you (only theme)

To explain these data, Anderson (1979) proposed the so-called 'affectedness constraint'. For a development of Anderson's explanation see chapter 3; for additional discussion see also section 3 below, Grimshaw (1986), Jaeggli (1986), Rozwadowska (1986), Zubizarreta (1986) and Safir (1987).

8 Notice that θ-marking of the external argument must be claimed to be compositional, i.e. performed by the head along with its internal arguments,

in other words by N′, in order to maintain that θ-assignment generally takes place under sisterhood.

9 We are disregarding here the structure of the Spec of the NP. By 'Spec' we refer to the syntactic position(s) on the left of N, without specifying their content or hierarchical organization (see also Chomsky, class lectures, autumn 1986).

10 Chomsky (1986b) distinguishes m-command in the sense of Aoun and Sportiche (1982) from c-command, which he defines as follows (p. 8):

(i)   α c-commands β iff
       α does not dominate β and every γ that dominates α dominates β
       Where γ is restricted to maximal projections we will say that α m-commands β

This definition of c-command is more restrictive than the one of Reinhart (1976) adopted here in the text, because it does not make any reference to branching. As we said directly in the text, no empirical difference seems to arise between the two definitions with respect to the data discussed in this work.

11 The only relevant factor in this discussion is the hierarchical structure, which should not vary across languages. As for the irrelevance of linear order, see the discussion above in the text.

12 Notice that two readings are also excluded by independent considerations (Williams, 1977). In fact, sentence (29), owing to some parallelism condition, cannot mean:

(i)   a. *I revealed to you Gianni's$_i$ opinion about his$_i$ wife, but not his$_j$ wife's opinion about Franco$_j$
       b. *I revealed to you his$_i$ wife's opinion about Gianni$_i$, but not Franco's$_j$ opinion about his$_j$ wife

θ-role assignment, in other words, cannot be 'switched' in the two conjuncts.

13 In this work we are mainly concerned with subject–object asymmetries within NPs. Another set of considerations holds with respect to the distribution of bound elements inside non-subcategorized phrases, such as relative clauses and by-phrases (on the status of by-phrases in clauses and NPs, see Jaeggli, 1986; Zubizarreta 1985; Baker 1985), perhaps because the level of attachment of these elements can be subject to a certain degree of variation. Notice first that the basic observation about these facts in Italian seems to be that clear judgements are very hard to obtain and that tendentiously all examples are considered marginal. Consider the following sentences:

(i)   a. ?L'offerta di ogni impiegato$_i$ che il suo$_i$ datore di lavoro
          maggiormente gradisce è quella di fare lo straordinario gratis
          The offer by (lit.: of) every employee that his employer likes most
          is the one of doing overtime without pay
       b. L'offerta ad ogni impiegato$_i$ che sua$_i$ moglie attende più
          impazientemente è quella di un aumento
          The offer to every employee that his wife is most impatiently
          waiting for is the one of a salary raise

In the first case the quantified NP expresses the subject θ-role and therefore is attached at a higher level, whereas in the other case it is an indirect object and therefore hangs from N'. Since (i)b appears to be less acceptable than (i)a, we might conclude that at least there is a preference to attach a relative clause at a level higher than N'. Notice that the phenomenon cannot be influenced by a possible reconstruction of the NP into the gap position of the relative clause (cf. Vergnaud 1974; Cinque 1982), since in that case an equal weak crossover violation should arise. In English the same structures seem to be much more acceptable and apparently there is no clear contrast between a quantified subject and a quantified indirect object; the reasons for this are unclear. Consider now the distribution of *by*-phrases:

(ii)   a.   la descrizione di ogni ragazzo$_i$ da parte di sua$_i$ madre
            the description of every boy by his mother
       b.   la presentazione di una bella ragazza a ogni studente$_i$ da parte dei suoi$_i$ amici
            the introduction of a pretty girl to every student by his friends

In this case, the two phrases seem not to contrast, but they are both quite marginal. If we consider them to be more on the side of grammaticality, we could argue that the *by*-phrase has the possibility of being attached under N'; if we conclude that they are ungrammatical, we have to say that the *by*-phrase hangs at a level such that the arguments of the head cannot c-command it. We are more inclined to this second solution, because there is converging evidence that the *by*-phrases in nominals do not belong to the argument structure of the head (see also ch. 2 below), a fact that in terms of attachment could be expressed by assigning it to a higher position in the structure. If so, however, it is not clear why these phrases are not more sharply ungrammatical.

14 There may be some apparent counter-examples to the generalizability of our definition of c-command to structures with prepositional complements. It could be argued, in fact, that certain PP complements are attached under X" and, therefore, binding should not be possible from an object hanging from X' toward the PP complement. Yet, such structures are acceptable as illustrated by the example in (i):

(i)   The psychoanalyst turned Mary against herself

However, in this case the simplest solution is to assume that *against herself* hangs from a level that allows binding, namely that the PP must be dominated by a node lower than V", i.e. V'; arguments to this effect can be found in Giorgi (1987b). Consider also the following piece of evidence:

(ii)   The psychoanalyst turned Mary against him/*himself

If the binding problem in (i) could just be solved by adopting a 'command' solution, we should expect the same distribution of anaphors and pronouns with respect to both antecedents, since the subject also certainly 'commands' the anaphor in any possible specification of such a notion. We will not give a theoretical account of these cases here, but will simply suggest that the object and the PP are sisters and moreover that *Mary + against NP* somehow constitute the relevant domain for the binding of anaphors, one which excludes the subject of the sentence (see Chomsky 1981; Bouchard 1984). Analogously, in a structure like (iii), there is reason to claim that the locative PP, inside VP, is not higher than the direct object:

(iii)   The police surprised Bill in his office, but not John

Under the sloppy reading of the pronoun, we must assume c-command of the PP by the direct object. The simplest idea compatible with our hypothesis is that there exists mutual c-command or even that *Bill* and *in his office* constitute a small-clause-type structure. Furthermore, it could be objected that elements preposed in CP which can be bound by subjects constitute a counter-example to this theory, given the intervention of an IP node between the binder and the bindee. Consider, for instance, the following examples, which would anyway represent an exception also for an approach *à la* Aoun and Sportiche (1982) (if IP is really maximal):

(iv)   a. About himself John can talk forever
       b. Which papers of each other do they like most?
       c. Near him$_i$, everyone$_i$ keeps a gun

However, in such cases it can be argued that the binding relations may also be computed under reconstruction, as illustrated by the fact that a higher sentence can be interposed between the anaphor (or bound pronoun) and the antecedent:

(v)   a. About himself, I think that John can talk forever
       b. Which papers of each other do you think they like most?
       c. Near him$_i$, I think that everyone$_i$ keeps a gun

Hence, these sentences are no counter-examples to any theory of c-command.

15 Longobardi (this vol., ch. 2) notices another fact which suggests that claiming maximality for N' without revising Aoun and Sportiche's definition of c-command would not be the theoretically correct move; namely, that the asymmetry between external and internal arguments can be reproduced for the external argument and the possessor. This means that an intervening node has to constitute a c-domain including the external argument and excluding the possessor. If this is the case, then, (at least) two projections of N block c-command and it would be simply *ad hoc* to assume that just one of them is maximal, i.e. the one corresponding to N'. Moreover, there would be only one head to project two Xmax.

16 On the distribution of modifiers within NPs in English, see the interesting analysis by Safir (1987). The ungrammaticality of (37)b and (38)b is probably due to the impossibility of extracting only the head from this kind of genitive NP. These structures would then be ruled out for the same reason that rules out the (b) and (c) sentences derived from (a) in the following examples:

(i)   a. Ho incontrato il ragazzo che Maria amava
           I met the boy who Maria loved

          b. *E' il ragazzo che [ho incontrato che Maria amava]
              It is the boy that I met who Maria loved
          c. *L'ho incontrato che Maria amava
              I him (clitic)-met that Maria loved
 (ii) a. Ho incontrato un ragazzo alto
              I met a tall boy
          b. *Il ragazzo che ho incontrato alto
              The boy whom I met tall
          c. *L'ho incontrato alto
              (I) him (clitic) met tall

In these structures, comparable to the ones given in the text, both cliticization and wh-movement are starred. We can conclude that movement to the Spec position of the NP obeys whatever constraint is relevant in the cases given here. Notice that Cinque in his papers also accepts the phrase *la descrizione di te* (the description of you), where *te* (you) is a theme; we agree that when the form di + NP expresses the internal θ-role of a 'transitive' N, the ungrammaticality is less severe, but, still, such a phrase seems to be highly marginal.

17 Notice that we are assuming that the inherent Case feature of the possessive pronoun is different from the Case feature it receives *via* agreement with the head. This situation is not exceptional, since also the number-feature is 'doubled' in the same way: *suoi* (*libri*) ('*his* + *masc. plur.* books') is a third person *singular* (= the number of the antecedent) pronoun, agreeing, however, in gender and number with the head N ($-i =$ masc. plur.). See the following chapters for a more detailed formalization of these ideas.

18 Italian uses the same pronominal possessive form in NP-internal position as in postcopular position; English has two distinct pronominal forms. Notice, however, that this contrast is not directly relevant to the issue discussed here; it is in fact a consequence of the independent parametrization proposed for possessives in chapter 3.

19 Notice that the point of this section will not undercut the explanation provided for the ungrammaticality of structures like (9)a, (10)a and (11)a under the interpretation in which *di lui* is assigned the external θ-role; even if the form di + pronoun could be replaced by a possessive and is therefore ungrammatical, an account of this kind is still insufficient. In fact, in cases where there is no coreference between the pronoun and the R-expression, as in (33)a, the resulting ungrammaticality is often less severe than that of a binding violation: furthermore it can be completely rescued under one of the licensing factors exemplified in (35) and in (37)–(38), which is never possible in cases like (9)–(11).

    Recall also that, obviously, Cinque's filter, and the proposed revision, could not account for the *contrasts* in (9)–(11), since the absence of a principle C violation in the (a) phrases of the pairs should still be captured; our hypothesis in section 2 is therefore independently needed.

20 Lasnik and Barss (1986) convincingly show that in English double-object

constructions c-command is asymmetric; only the leftmost object c-commands the other. The structural solution to this problem remains to be worked out. Note that in English c-command is not symmetric in DO–IO constructions either:

(i)   a. I introduced John and Mary to each other
       b. *I introduced each other to John and Mary
(ii)   a. In my dreams, I introduced John to himself
       b. *In my dreams, I introduced himself to John
(iii) a. I returned each book to its owner
       b. *I returned his book to each student
(iv)   a. I described Mary to her husband, but not Susan (sloppy)
       b. I described her husband to Mary, but not to Susan (non-sloppy)

There is no contrast in the Italian counterparts to these examples:

(v)   a. A quella festa in maschera, ho finito col presentare Maria a se stessa
          At that fancy dress party, I ended up introducing Maria to herself
       b. A quella festa in maschera, ho finito col presentare a Maria se
          stessa
          At that fancy dress party, I ended up introducing to Maria herself
(vi)   a. Ho restituito ogni libro$_i$ al suo$_i$ proprietario
          I returned each book to its owner
       b. Ho restituito i suoi$_i$ libri ad ogni$_i$ studente
          I returned his books to every student
(vii) a. Ho descritto MARIA a suo marito, ma non Susanna
          I described MARIA to her husband but not Susanna (sloppy)
       b. Ho descritto A MARIA suo marito, non a Susanna
          I described TO MARIA her husband, not to Susanna (sloppy)

In principle, these cases could be accounted for by claiming that *to* blocks c-command in English, whereas *a* does not in Italian; however, this line of explanation is very problematic because of the grammaticality of the following sentence:

(viii)   I talked to John and Mary about each other

See Larson (1988) for an interesting approach to these constructions in English.

21   The existence of mutual c-command in Italian poses a problem for Kayne's (1984) theory of binary branching. Under such an approach phrases must be represented by binary trees, unlike the representation we propose in (47). Our hypothesis and our data could be made compatible with a binary branching approach while retaining the notion of c-command based on branching, as in (15). However, this move would require a modification of Kayne's mechanism of Case assignment. The examples in (i) and (ii) could be assigned the structures in (iii) and (iv):

(i)   Una lunga terapia psicoanalitica restituì Maria a se stessa
       A long psychoanalytic therapy restored Maria to herself

(ii)   la restituzione di Maria a se stessa da parte dello psicoanalista
the restoration of Maria to herself by the psychoanalyst

(iii)

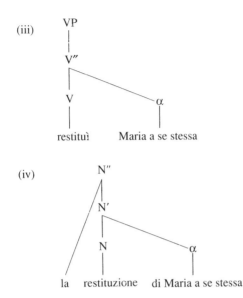

(iv)

In (iii) and (iv) the structure branches in a binary fashion and c-command can be reciprocal (on the unavailability of reciprocal c-command in English, see n. 20). The phrase α, despite certain analogies, presents different properties with respect to typical small-clause (SC) constituents like complements of a Verb such as *ritenere*:

(v)   Gianni$_i$ ritiene Mario$_j$ orgoglioso di se stesso$_{j/*i}$
Gianni considers Mario proud of himself

In (v), in fact, the SC is the binding domain for the anaphor. In a way to be specified, this fact could be related to the different thematic properties of the Verbs in question; i.e. *ritenere* θ-marks the SC as a whole, while *restituire* seems to θ-mark both complements separately; further study is necessary.

22 It is well known that in Italian the cliticized version of sentences like (51)a is ungrammatical:

(i)   *Si$_i$ ho restituito Maria$_i$
lit.: I to herself (clitic) restored Maria
I restored Maria to herself

At first sight this fact could be taken to be a counter-example to the claim that no binding violation arises from c-command by an anaphor of its antecedent (see Rizzi 1982b). However, several scholars (Burzio 1981, 1986; Manzini 1983b; Cinque 1987) have tried to unify the various uses of Italian *si* by postulating the existence of a privileged relation between *si* and the subject position, which must always hold if the structure is to be considered grammatical. Therefore, to exclude the sentence above we need not resort to principle C, but rather may appeal to a more general condition on the third person anaphoric clitic, i.e. *si* must be linked to the subject. For more details, see the cited references. Consider also the grammaticality of the following sentence:

(ii)   Una lunga terapia psicoanalitica le$_i$ ha restituito se stessa$_i$
         A long psychoanalytic therapy to her (clitic) restored herself

(For a similar example, see also Rizzi 1986, p. 551, ex. 110a.) Therefore, according to a theory like Rizzi's (1982b), where (i) is excluded by disjointness, it is necessary to assume also that the clitic position is not c-commanded by the direct-object position; otherwise (ii) would be excluded. But, under this assumption, the whole reliance on disjointness becomes superfluous, even in Rizzi's framework, since (i) is independently ruled out by principle A for lack of c-command on the part of the supposed antecedent. Hence, the exclusion of (i) on the grounds of a principle C violation appears not to be a theoretically necessary hypothesis.

23 For further discussion, see, among others: Reinhart (1983, 1987); Sells (1986); Higginbotham (1983).

24 Since in (63)a the possessive originates from an internal position, we must rule out the possibility of binding the anaphor under 'reconstruction' i.e. in its D-structure position. Such an option is sometimes allowed in cases of NP movement, in fact. Recall that a direct object can be bound in its thematic position under N', as is the case in example (4)a. However, there is some reason (see ch. 3) to believe that in Italian the possessivization alternation *di se stesso/proprio* is a movement process analogous to cliticization (*si/se stesso*); now, it is well known that the binding possibilities of *si* are not the same as those of *se stesso* (see Burzio 1981, 1986; Rizzi 1982b):

(i)   a. Gianni$_i$ è stato affidato a se stesso$_i$
            Gianni was entrusted to himself
        b. *Gianni$_i$ si$_i$ è stato affidato

Such examples suggest that cliticization is not subject to binding reconstruction. It is also plausible that the reconstruction process between the two positions in examples like (63)a is prevented by the formal difference in the realization of the anaphor: as a possessive Adjective vs a *di* + NP phrase.

25 Notice that sentence (65) cannot be excluded by our principle (4) concerning the appearance of a form *di* + pronoun/anaphor simply because the prenominal possessive anaphor in this case is not available:

(i)   *La propria$_i$ telefonata a Gianni$_i$
        Self's phone call to Gianni

As shown in section 4, this case also involves a violation of principle A.

26 Consider that the same pattern arises also in the following cases of inherently 'passive' Nouns (see Cinque 1980, 1981a):

(i)   a.   la cattura degli afgani da parte dei russi
           the capture of the Afghans by the Russians
      b.   *la cattura afgana da parte dei russi
           the Afghan capture by the Russians

Cattura ('capture') only has the passive form, since its θ-roles can just be expressed as in (i)a, which contrasts with both the forms (ii)a and b:

(ii) a.   *La cattura degli afgani dei russi
           the capture of the Afghans of the Russians
      b.   *la loro cattura dei russi
           their capture of the Russians

27 Notice that, intuitively, the externalized argument of VPs headed by certain ergative Verbs can be interpreted as more 'agentive' than with other Verbs in the same class. For instance, *Gianni* in *Gianni è intervenuto alla festa* ('Gianni intervened at the party') seems more agentive than in *Gianni è morto ieri* ('Gianni died yesterday'). For an analysis of the thematic values assigned by ergative Verbs see Gràcia (1986) and references cited there. Such a higher degree of agentivity appears to be correlated with the level of acceptability of a referential Adjective in the corresponding NPs:

(ii) a.   L'intervento papale alla conferenza per la pace sorprese tutti
           The papal intervention at the conference for peace surprised
           everybody
(ii) a.   *L'improvvisa morte papale sorprese tutti
           The sudden papal death surprised everybody
      b.   L'improvvisa morte del Papa sorprese tutti
           The sudden death of the Pope surprised everybody

Therefore, this may suggest that lexical items like *intervenire*/*intervento* coming out in Italian as ergative according to the usual tests for Verbs, such as *ne* extraction and auxiliary choice, apparently can also assign an agentive external θ-role, which is thus realized outside X′, at least in nominal projections. These lexical items presumably have the possibility of assigning the relevant θ-role either internally, or externally to X′, according to the semantic value prevailing in the interpretation of the argument. A similar hypothesis is actually put forward by Gràcia (1986), who shows that in Catalan *ne*-extraction from a postverbal subject of unaccusative Verbs is sensitive to a more or less agentive interpretation of the NP (from Gràcia, p. 350, exx. (39)b and (40)b):

(i)   a.   Del Barça, demà en$_i$ vindran [$_{NP}$ els jugadors e_i]
           Of the Barcelona, tomorrow of it-will come the players
      b.   Ara en$_i$ ve [$_{NP}$ el temps e_i] (de la caiguda del cabell)
           Now of it-comes the time (of the fall of the hair)

28 The same distribution of anaphors and pronouns obtains in the following cases:

(i)   a. *il suo$_i$ libro su se stessa$_i$ che Moravia aveva scritto/scritto da Moravia
          Her book about herself which Moravia had written/written by Moravia
      b. il suo$_i$ libro su di lei$_i$ che Moravia aveva scritto/scritto da Moravia
          her book about herself which Moravia had written/written by Moravia

(ii) a. *Moravia è l'autore di tutti i libri di Maria$_i$ su se stessa$_i$
          Moravia is the author of all the books of (poss.) Maria about herself
      b. Moravia è l'autore di tutti i libri di Maria$_i$ su di lei$_i$
          Moravia is the author of all the books of Maria (poss.) about her

To account for these facts, we can hypothesize the presence of an empty agent position within the NP coreferential with *Moravia*, so that the structure will have an indexing I, BT-compatible with the pronoun but not the anaphor. Conversely, such a hypothesis also makes the correct predictions in the following examples:

(iii) a. Quel libro su se stesso$_i$ che Moravia$_i$ aveva appena finito di scrivere non mi piacque affatto
          I did not like that book about himself that Moravia had just written
      b. *Quel libro su di lui$_i$ che Moravia$_i$ aveva appena finito di scrivere non mi piacque affatto
          I did not like that book about him which Moravia had just written

In the fourth chapter we argue, following Chomsky (1981, 1986a), that with this class of Nouns the realization of the subject is in general not obligatory; its obligatoriness in (i) and (ii) should, then, be due to the presence of a relative clause (or of a modifier, a superordinate sentence, etc.), overtly containing a potential 'controller', i.e. an element which imposes a fixed semantic and thematic interpretation on such an empty argument of N. It seems, in fact, that, if in the sentence there is no mention of such a possible 'controller', both the anaphor and the pronoun are (almost) acceptable with the indicated reading, showing that the hypothesis suggested in Chomsky (1986a) and developed in chapter 4 below is basically correct:

(iv) a. ?Le sue$_i$ (poss) foto di se stessa$_i$ (theme) in costume sono molto belle
          Her (poss.) photos of herself (theme) in a bathing suit are very nice
      b. ?Le sue$_i$ (poss.) foto di lei$_i$ (theme) in costume sono molto belle
          Her (poss.) photos of her (theme) in a bathing suit are very nice

The acceptability of examples (iv) is predicted by the BT proposed in Chomsky (1986a), supplemented by the revision which we are going to develop in the text.

29 Notice that under some version of the so-called DP hypothesis these facts could be captured in an analogous way (see Abney 1986 and Ritter 1986). Here, however, we do not have in mind Abney's version (namely that our N′ is equal to NP and is the complement hanging from D′), but a possible revision of it; i.e. the complement of D′ would be our N″, thus including the θ-grid but excluding possessors. The resulting structure is therefore the following:

(i)

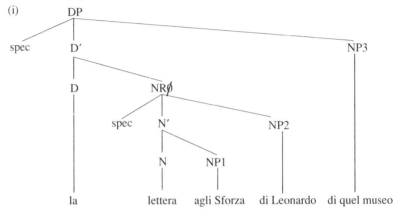

The 'least CFC' for NP1 is NP∅, whereas DP, though a CFC, is not the 'least' one for such an NP. This way, the two CFCs would both correspond to maximal projections. However, from a conceptual or empirical point of view, this solution does not add anything new to what we are saying. Consider, moreover, that the adoption of this version of the DP hypothesis (as well as Abney's one) raises a problem concerning linear order. In chapter 3 below we argue that the base positions in Romance are only to the right of N. If this is the case, the prenominal position of a possessive is derived via movement, i.e. *la mia lettera agli Sforza di Leonardo* ('my letter to the Sforzas by Leonardo') is derived moving the 'possessor' from right to left. The landing site, according to the DP hypothesis specified as in (i), has to be the Spec of DP. This way, however, the possessive should precede the article, an option always impossible in Italian; see chapter 4 for a more detailed discussion of these issues.

30 The following phrases are ungrammatical:

(i)   a. *il suo$_i$ libro di se stesso$_i$
          his (poss.) book by himself (agent)
      b. ??il suo$_i$ libro di lui$_i$
          his (poss.) book by him (agent)

Both structures are predicted by our hypotheses to be acceptable, since the anaphor should be bound in the maximal projection and the pronoun should be free in the domain defined by the θ-roles selected by the head, that is, excluding the 'possessor'. However, they are both excluded, though the pronoun seems to be slightly more acceptable.

Such judgements can be due to the interaction of completely independent factors. We argued in the text that non-possessive pronouns or anaphors in NPs are generally marked and functionally disfavoured with respect to the possessive ones. But, even in the cases where no alternative option with a possessive is available, pronominal external arguments are much harder to accept in the non-possessive form than internal ones. Consider, in fact, the following paradigm:

(ii) a. *Ho perso il mio libro di te sulla seconda guerra mondiale
          I lost my (possessor) book of you (agent) on World War Two
      b. Ho perso il mio libro della Morante sulla seconda guerra mondiale
          I lost my (possessor) book of Morante (agent) on World War Two
      c. ?Ho perso quella mia descrizione di te
          I lost my (agent) description of you (theme)

i.e. also independently of binding and possessivization processes, the option di + pronoun is a very marked way of realizing an agent, as illustrated by the contrast between (ii)a on one hand and (ii)b and c on the other. The same clear contrast arises also with anaphors:

(iii)   Gianni mi ha mostrato una descrizione di se stesso
          Gianni has shown me a description of himself (?theme/*agent)

For a discussion of the impossibility of anaphors as agents of NPs, see Graffi (1987).

31 An alternative way of looking at these facts could be to hypothesize that a possessor is not in a true A-position, hence is in a position from which binding cannot obtain. This idea is not on the right track, as is shown by the fact that when the possessor is a quantified NP, it can bind a pronoun as a variable. Consider the following contrast:

(i)   a. I libri di ogni$_i$ biblioteca sul suo$_i$ fondatore sono moltissimi
          The books of every library about its founder are many
      b. *I libri del suo$_i$ fondatore su ogni$_i$ biblioteca sono moltissimi
          The books of its founder about every library are many

Example (i)a shows that binding of a pronoun by the possessor, *ogni biblioteca* ('every library'), is possible, whereas it is excluded in the other direction. As expected, (i)b is ungrammatical both under the interpretation in which *suo fondatore* is the 'possessor' and under the interpretation in which it refers to the writer. Such ungrammaticality is due to the lack of c-command from the quantifier towards the pronoun.

32 Examples (93)b, (94)b and (95)b could be irrelevant, if the anaphor were bound by the 'agent' collapsed within the head N, as, for instance, in the following cases:

(i)   a. Un buon giudice$_i$ di se stesso$_i$ è sempre molto severo
           A good judge of himself is always very severe
       b. Un ammiratore$_i$ di se stesso$_i$ ha pochi amici
           An admirer of himself has few friends

Notice, however, that in other cases it is apparent that the antecedent of the anaphor is the subject of the clause which receives the agent θ-role from the head of the predicate:

(ii)   Quella donna è il miglior giudice di se stessa/*se stesso
        That woman is the best judge of herself/himself

In this example the anaphor has to be feminine singular, agreeing with *donna* ('woman'), and cannot be masculine, i.e. it cannot agree with *giudice* ('judge'), as is, however, possible and obligatory in (i). Recalling also that anaphors always agree in gender and number with the antecedent, we can conclude that in cases like (ii), the antecedent is *donna* and not *giudice*.

2   Extraction from NP and the proper notion of head government

* A version of this work was presented in a lecture given in Madrid in February 1986; for this opportunity I am indebted to the Fundación J. Ortega y Gasset and to the organizers V. Demont and M. Fernández Lagunilla.

1 A partially similar view is defended in work in progress by E. Torrego (see also Torrego 1986), who analyses the main properties of extraction from NP in Continental Spanish. Although the Spanish facts presented by Torrego differ in various respects from the equivalent structures in Italian, she shows anyway that the basic schema of extraction from NP through Spec can be assumed for Spanish as well, a significant convergence which reinforces the basic hypothesis here discussed. Actually, the empirical arguments that we present for Italian in the text in favour of the extraction-through-Spec hypothesis apply, as far as we could test, in the other Romance languages.

2 The conclusion appears now to be strengthened by converging evidence presented in the recent literature: see especially Aoun *et al.* (1987).

3 Longobardi (1985b) proposed essentially the following definition of proper government:

α properly governs β iff
α governs β
    and
α licenses (or selects) β or γ, γ containing β

As a basic hypothesis of the paper, we assumed proper government to be needed both for a trace and for any maximal projection containing such a trace free (elaborating, thus, on Huang's (1982) work on the Condition on Extraction Domains, henceforth CED). This twofold requirement was also shown to be subsumable under a proper formulation of Kayne's (1983) Connectedness Condition (CC). While essentially accepting Kayne's original formulation of the constraint, as in (i) below, we advocated, in fact, the slight modification of the definition of g-projection given in (ii):

(i)   Given a set of empty categories $\beta_1 \dots \beta_n$ all locally bound by α, the union of the g-projection sets of every β must form a subtree with $\{\alpha\}$.

(ii)   Z is a g-projection of β iff Z is an X′ projection of γ, γ a proper governor of

      1. β

      2. a g-projection of β (only if β has a structural governor)

For the empirical motivation behind the proposed definitions of proper government and g-projection see also Longobardi (1983 and forthcoming).

4 By frame of N we refer to the set of elements (arguments, adverbials, relative clauses, adjectival phrases and other modifiers) complementing the head of the NP.

5 Here, and in the rest of the chapter, we will often give examples of wh-extraction via relativization as incomplete sentences just including the head and the relative clause.

6 With the meaning of 'possessor' the genitive clitic *ne* and the possessive tend to be complementary with respect to the feature of animacy: so *ne* usually pronominalizes inanimate NPs (like *la fondazione* ('the foundation') as in (11)c), while a possessive may better pronominalize animate ones (like *mia sorella* ('my sister') as in (11)b). No such specialization arises when these expressions bear a real thematic interpretation (e.g. agent, theme).

7 Longobardi's (1985b) argument is based on the observation that, while wh-traces contained within *by*-phrases in sentences are normally possible and may even act as licensing gaps for parasitic ones outside the *by*-phrase, empty categories embedded in *by*-phrases of NPs can only be parasitic exactly as gaps contained within adverbials. The contrast is shown in the following paradigm whose second pair is from D. Pesetsky (1982):

(i) a. A person who everybody is usually upset by *e* very quickly

    b. *A person who everybody who meets *e* is upset before talking to *e*

    c. ?A person who everybody who meets *e* is upset by *e* before talking to *e*

(ii) a. *Which topic would you approve a discussion of set theory by a specialist in *e*

    b. ?Which topic would you approve a discussion of *e* by a specialist in *e*

Cinque (p.c.) also points out that in Italian *by*-phrases of nominals occur even with certain head Nouns which can hardly be considered 'passivized', as they are not related to any transitive predicate: cf. e.g.

(iii)   La possibilità da parte vostra di superare l'esame

       The likelihood by you to pass the examination

8 A defence of the opacity approach, however, could be and, in fact, was attempted in the framework of Aoun's Generalized Binding (cf. Aoun 1985). An empirical advantage of our proposal over Aoun's analysis of extraction from NP will be pointed out in sect. 6 below.

9 By the label Spec we never refer to a particular category but simply to the (set of categories occurring in) prehead position of Italian or English XPs. See also Chomsky (class lectures, autumn 1986). Some speculations on the possible structure of this syntactic position will be made in chapters 3 and 4.

10 Since French, as described in particular by Milner (1982), appears essentially to obey Cinque's generalization and thus to be largely reducible to our extraction-through-Spec analysis, we must suppose that the ban against, e.g. the cooccurrence of *le + son* (the + his) in the Det position, does not apply to an article and a phonetically null element, here a trace of extraction (in the following chapters we show that the same can be argued in the case of an empty pro subject). In other words, the non-occurrence of an article with an overt possessive must be a special property of the surface realization of the latter (see chapters 3 and 4). The Spanish definite article (but not the indefinite one) seems instead to have more constraining effects on extractions, but Torrego (1986) argues that this is due to independently observable properties which distinguish it from the French and Italian one (see also Brucart and Gràcia 1986). Finally, in the spirit of the strictly structural approach taken in the present work, one would wish to provide a configurational solution to the question of the effects of demonstratives on extractability. It is apparent however that the facts in question can hardly be collapsed with Cinque's generalization and our account of it. In fact, extraction over a demonstrative yields sharply different results with questions and with relativization or cliticization:

(i)   a. *Di chi conosci questa descrizione?
          Of whom do you know this description?
      b. Gianni, di cui conosco questa descrizione...
          Gianni, of whom I know this description...
      c. A proposito di Gianni, ne conosco questa descrizione
          Speaking of Gianni, I of-him know this description

It seems also that the usual 'opacity' effect, which *questa* ('this') does not suffice to induce in (i)b and (i)c, regularly reappears when a real subject is present:

(ii)   Gianni, di cui/ne conosco questa descrizione di Maria...
          Gianni, of whom/of him I know this description of Maria...

Thus, in (ii) *Maria* can only be understood as the thematic 'object' of the description. Notice that the ungrammaticality of (i)b and (i)c also embarrasses the traditional 'Specificity' account for the effects induced by demonstratives: at least in (i)b, in fact, the specific NP appears to freely contain a variable, the one left by relativization. Some insight into the nature of the relevant constraint may be provided by the behaviour of topicalization or clefting, as suggested by N. Chomsky (p.c.): these two rules, which in Italian only front focused (informationally new) phrases, cannot extract out of an NP introduced by a demonstrative:

(iii) a. *DI GIANNI conosco questa descrizione
          OF GIANNI I know this description
       b. *E' di Gianni che conosco questa descrizione
          It is of Gianni that I know this description

Question formation would, then, obey the same restriction essentially because, unlike relativization, it is likely to imply a certain degree of contrastive (new) information for the involved phrases. In the formulation of the relevant restriction, some notion akin to Specificity still seems to play a role, because the same paradigm of extractability reappears with NPs which do not contain demonstratives, but are made highly specific by other kinds of modifiers:

(iv) a. *Di quale autore hai letto il libro che ti ho prestato ieri?
          Of which writer did you read the book that I lent you yesterday?
      b. ?*DI GIANNI ho letto il libro che mi hai prestato
          OF GIANNI I read the book that you lent me yesterday
      c. *E' di Gianni che ho letto il libro che mi hai prestato ieri
          It is of Gianni that I read...
(v)   a. Gianni, di cui ho letto il libro che mi hai prestato ieri
          Gianni, of whom I read...
      b. Ne ho letto il libro che mi hai prestato ieri
          I of-him read...

The role played by Specificity is also confirmed by this fact: the forbidden cases of extraction over a demonstrative are improved when the NP refers more generically, e.g. to a general kind:

(vi)   (?)Di quale autore hai letto questi libri con la copertina blu, ma non quelli con la copertina rossa?
          Of which writer did you read these books with the blue cover, but not those with the red cover? (uttered pointing to a pile of blue books)

It appears, then, that some notion of referential specificity intervenes in constraining the observable outputs of extraction from NP in Italian, but it applies only to movement of phrases focused or contrastively interpreted. If the patterns exemplified in this note are taken to be representative, then, the constraining effects of demonstratives on extraction from NP are hardly an argument for extraction-through-Spec (unlike those discussed in the text) and the desired structural account for such effects, if it can be found, can hardly be collapsed with Cinque's generalization and the explanation we propose for it.

11 For the anaphoric nature of *proprio* see Giorgi (1983); for the conditions on bound pronouns see Reinhart (1976; 1983).

12 See chapter 1 for discussion of this point. Structural conclusions similar to the ones reached here were arrived at also by Milner (1982), relying, however,

precisely on considerations of linear order, which, as we said, often express just preferences and may always be affected by stylistic rearrangements. The data provided in (28)–(29) are thus, to our knowledge, the most direct evidence available in favour of the structural asymmetry between agents and possessors, and, consequently, in favour of the Possessivization Principle (31).

13 As also noticed by Torrego (1986) for Spanish, structures like (32)c are more degraded in acceptability than those like (32)b; thus, although possessivization of a direct object is still quite severe, possessivization over a possessor of a subject yields a normally milder violation. This fact could be related to the closer affinity between thematic subjects and possessors in NPs, as both 'external' arguments opposed to the internal ones (see on this point chapter 3 below). As usual, the same degrees of contrast found with possessivization are reproduced by extraction.

14 For the distinction between the modern German and the Latin/Greek way of realizing genitive see chapter 3, section 10.

15 The whole question of the categorial status of the latter elements will be addressed in detail in section 11 of chapter 3.

16 As a descriptive generalization and on the grounds of the argumentation provided in the following chapter, it is possible to identify the elements to be called 'possessives' in the Germanic and Romance languages, as a (negatively defined) natural class: the class of those arguments of N whose way of realizing the inherent Genitive Case is excluded from the N' domain, for reasons of linear order or of Case agreement. See chapters 1 and 3 for the relevant facts and arguments.

17 In order to derive all the content stated in principle (31) from this formal machinery, it is necessary to add a uniqueness requirement on the feature [Poss], i.e. each NP must have at most one such specification (also none, of course, in case no possessive appears). However, the exceptional behaviour of referential Adjectives must be noted, in this regard; for it is possible to find a possessive pronoun cooccurring with a referential Adjective:

(i)   La sua segretaria francese
        his/her French secretary

In this sense, referential Adjectives appear to escape a strict uniqueness formulation of the Possessivization Principle, although they must be characterized as possessive expressions obeying the principle because of the behaviour displayed in (13) of the text and in such cases as the following:

(ii)   Tutti i miei dipinti francesi
        all my French paintings

Thus, (ii) is promptly understood as referring to paintings which I own and were painted by French artists, but rather more marginally as referring to paintings which I painted and are owned, say, by the French government or by French museums, or just are in France. This fact may suggest that, if an Adjective like *French* is interpreted as a possessor, it tends to prevent possessivization of a lower argument, such as a thematic agent. More available seems, in fact, the interpretation of *French* as possessor (in the usual extended sense) when the agent is not possessivized:

(iii)   tutti i dipinti francesi di Leonardo
         lit.: all the French paintings of Leonardo

We could then say that such Adjectives must receive and absorb the feature [Poss] if they express the highest argument but, in the cases in which this feature is assigned to a higher phrase, they must have some other way of realizing their inherent Case, which still allows them to surface. For the differences between these Adjectives and possessive pronouns/anaphors and for the unclear status of an A like *diffuso* ('widespread, common') see chapter 3.

18 *Cui* is analogous in its distribution to normal pronominal or anaphoric possessives with the difference that it never occurs postnominally (see Cinque 1981b for details):

(i)   *Gianni, il figlio cui...
         Gianni, the son whose...

The same form *cui* may also appear as the complement of a preposition and in that case some fixed expressions where it may assume pro-sentential meaning exist, like *da cui*, *per cui* ('from which', 'for which').

19 Infinitives are apparently Genitive marked, in the sense of being introduced by *di*, when they occur as complements of Nouns, but still they cannot be possessivized or extracted:

(i)   a. La probabilità di scamparla non si può valutare facilmente
            The probability of escaping cannot be evaluated easily
         b. *Scamparla, la cui probabilità non si può valutare facilmente, sarebbe bello
            Escaping, whose probability cannot be evaluated easily, would be wonderful
         c. *La morte, di scampare alla quale non si può valutare facilmente la probabilità...
            Death, of escaping which cannot be evaluated easily the probability...

It is highly unlikely that the option of possessivization here is blocked by an understood subject of the head Noun, required as a controller for the PRO of the infinitive (cf. ch. 3). Other possibilities are conceivable, however, and worth exploring: for instance, *di* might fail to count as a mark of Genitive for the Possessivization Principle, since here it probably heads CP and not the usual PP, as is argued in Cinque (forthcoming).

20 Spec–head agreement in CP is independently argued to give rise to government by C into IP in Longobardi (forthcoming), in order to account for the classical Comp–trace phenomena with subject extraction.

21 If Koster (1978) is right, subject sentences would not be in Spec of IP, but

rather in TOP, a position which might now be identified with the Spec of another CP. This latter (with an empty head) should probably be taken as a complement by the first C, thus assuming structures of the form:

(i)   [wh-phrase C[$_{CP}$ TOP C [$_{IP}$ ...]]]

Obviously nothing would really change with respect to the theoretical conclusions we draw. As pointed out by G. Cinque (p.c.) such structures could be required anyway, to account for certain similarly weakened violations with extraction from preposed adverbials, which may very naturally be in TOP:

(ii)   ??Gianni, al quale penso che, parlando *e*, non otterremo nulla
        Gianni, to whom I think that, talking, we will not obtain anything

22 The weakness of the CED violation in such extractions from preverbal subjects extends to corresponding cases in various other languages (we tested Spanish, French and, with less clear results, English) and, within Italian, to some cases where the sentential subject in question is tensed, provided at least that the independently excluded clash between two adjacent complementizers can be avoided:

(i)   a. ???Gianni, a cui penso che, in fondo, che tu parli non sia biasimevole
          Gianni, to whom I think that, all in all, that you talk is not lamentable
       b. *Gianni, a cui penso che che tu parli non sia biasimevole
          Gianni, to whom I think that that you talk is not lamentable
       c. Penso che, in fondo, che tu parli a Gianni non sia biasimevole
          I think that, all in all, that you talk to Gianni is not lamentable
       d. *Penso che che tu parli a Gianni non sia biasimevole
          I think that that you talk to Gianni is not lamentable

(i)b and (i)d are thus ruled out by a *[CC] filter (perhaps perceptually motivated) which, unlike the *[Vinf Vinf] one proposed in Longobardi (1978, 1980), can be neutralized by an intervening parenthetical expression, like e.g. *in fondo* of (i)a; the latter sentence, which exemplifies a relative weak CED violation, can be derived via the same marked mechanism proposed in the text of extraction from infinitival subjects.

23 The fact that such an indexed *que* does not surface as *qui* must not be surprising: Kayne (1981a) points out another case of *que*, in French comparatives, which is likely to be indexed with a QP without becoming *qui*. Actually, an indexed *que* must obligatorily become *qui* only when it governs a Nominative-marked position under coindexing (see Kayne 1981a, n. 45). If the same can be said of English indexed *that* with respect to [$_c$e], it will be possible to explain why effects of the *that*-trace type are not observed in the English counterparts of our (41)b. I am indebted to L. Burzio for pointing out the relevance of this issue.

24 See Melvold (1986) for a different (but, for our purposes, equivalent) explanation.

25 The possibility of extraction from inverted sentential subjects of unergative Verbs suddenly degrades for many speakers if a lexical object intervenes between the Verb and such subjects: compare (56)a in the text with the following:

    (i)   ??Gianni, con cui ha impressionato Maria che non fosse possibile parlare
             Gianni, with whom it impressed Maria that it was impossible to talk

We will attempt no explanation for this fact and for the variation among speakers associated with it.

26 Another conceivable test, suggesting again that the Spec of inverted sentential subjects of unergative predicates cannot contain a trace, might be provided by extraction of adjuncts like *why*, which, according to various theories since Huang (1982), must leave a trace in the Spec of every CP they cross; actually such an extraction is ungrammatical, as expected under conclusion (60):

    (i)   Perchè ti impressionerebbe che licenziassero Gianni?
             Why would it shock you that they fired Gianni?

In (i) it is, in fact, impossible to construe *perchè* ('why') with the embedded clause. However, the conditions on extraction of adjuncts are often made quite severe by additional factors and they are sensitive to lexical choices in the environment, so that it is wiser to establish (60) relying on the complex but more solid evidence discussed throughout section 5.

27 Burzio's (1981) original account for the ungrammaticality of (51)b and the like was in terms of c-command. For discussion see below in the text, before examples (77). Notice that the same phenomena discussed in this section for adnominal genitive *ne* obtain in the case of *ne* with quantified NPs (see Belletti and Rizzi (1981), who claim that this *ne* pronominalizes the head of the NP or a projection of it). In our terms, this is expected if subjects of unergative Verbs are a barrier to the external government of both their head or intermediate projection and of Spec, i.e. if they are barriers to external government in general.

28 In the recent literature, instead, mention of similar data has been made in Manzini (1986), Burzio (1986), Belletti and Rizzi (1987) and Cinque (forthcoming).

29 The fact that the argument of an Adjective like *prevedibile* ('foreseeable') is an internal one is made clear by the fact that it corresponds to the object of the related verb *prevedere* ('to foresee'). A similar reasoning can be made for 'middle' Adjectives like *certo* ('certain'), whose theme appears as a complement in the so-called 'personal' construction but as the subject in the 'impersonal' one, exactly like that of a verb such as *affondare* ('to sink'):

    (i)   a. Sono certo del suo arrivo
               I am certain of his arrival
          b. Il suo arrivo è certo
               His arrival is certain

This is additional evidence that Adjectives share the ergative/middle vs unergative distinction which characterizes Verbs. For the whole question see now Cinque (forthcoming).

30 As can be seen from the examples of this section, lexical variability seems to affect the acceptability of extractions from inverted subjects. The other plausible case of extraction from Spec of NP, i.e. *combien* extraction in French, seems to pattern in an analogous way: to judge from the contrasts provided by Obenauer (1976, see p. 5 and *passim*), it appears to be sensitive to the ergative/non-ergative distinction when it takes place from an inverted subject, and to lexical choices in general.

31 For the possibility of another strategy of 'apparent' extraction from NP, see Cinque (forthcoming, ch. 3) and references cited there.

32 There is a dislocated construction in Italian which is not sensitive to islands: it is the one with a 'hanging topic' (in the terms of Cinque 1977), i.e. a simple NP, which can be resumed also by an oblique (dative or genitive) clitic, in many cases. This construction, thus, bears a great similarity to English dislocation. Italian also displays another dislocated construction (Clitic Left Dislocation, in the terms of Cinque 1984), whose properties have been shown by Cinque to resemble to a large extent those of relationships created by 'move α', i.e. it observes island constraints. We may, then, wonder on which of the two constructions the wh-phrase of sentences like (76)b is parasitic. Since such a phrase is a PP, *a priori* it should be parasitic just on the second one, Cinque's Clitic Left Dislocation. This conclusion seems to be confirmed on empirical grounds: the apparent extraction from definite NPs of the relevant kind is, in fact, ungrammatical, not just marginal, when such NPs are embedded within an island:

(i)   a. *Gianni, di cui sono partito prima che tu incontrassi il segretario
          G., of whom I left before you met the secretary
       b. *Di quale ragazzo hai chiesto a tutti quelli che conoscevano la
          sorella di venire?
          Of which boy did you ask everyone who knew the sister to come?

This fact suggests that it cannot be the 'hanging topic' construction that is involved in the marginal acceptability of (76)b, since the latter is exempt from island constraints. The pattern also confirms the clustering of properties defining the wh-constructions pointed out by Cinque.

33 The independence of the requirement of head government was implicit in the definition of government given in Longobardi (1985b), which excluded the possibility of a maximal projection functioning as a governor and was also advocated in Koopman and Sportiche (1986), Stowell (1986) and in unpublished work by O. Jaeggli. For more evidence see also Longobardi (forthcoming).

34 Thanks are due to J. Aoun for pointing out the relevance of such a consequence of the argument.

35 Unless the clitic cliticizes on Aux or V within the VP and then it raises to I along with the latter elements.

36 The same criticism does not apply, however, to the more specific D-structure constraint on which Burzio's (1986) more recent approach relies.

37 Essentially similar contrasts arise in French and Spanish, as V. Deprez and E. Torrego (p.c.) suggest, although the behaviour of French *dont*, analysed by Godard (1986), raises some further questions.

38 It is noteworthy, however, that the same marked extractability manifested for genitive wh-phrases in (85) and in Torrego's (1986) examples does not extend to the clitic *ne* or to *combien*: their extraction from a phrase in the Spec of CP always gives rise to wildly ungrammatical sentences (see also Burzio 1986, p. 35):

(i)   *Non ne ricordo quale amico ti volesse ricattare
        I of him do not remember which friend wanted to blackmail you

(ii)   *Combien dit-on de cheveux qu'il s'est arrachés? (from Obenauer 1976, p. 55)
        How many is it said of (his) hair(s) that he tore?

Although (ii) could be excluded by some version of the Doubly Filled Comp Filter, (i) is more surprising: if (85) must be analysed as a real case of extraction, then something special has to be said for clitics. It is possible that the strong locality condition which makes the trace of clitics clause-bound is necessarily computed under reconstruction of the wh-phrase into its base position. This is, in fact, what seems to happen in Italian with anaphoric expressions subject to the locality imposed by Binding Theory:

(iii)   *Gli ho domandato quale dei propri amici tu mi volessi presentare
        I asked him which of self's friends you wanted to introduce to me

(iv)   Gli ho domandato quale dei propri$_i$ libri tu le$_i$ avessi restituito
        I asked him which of self's books you had given back to her

In (iii) the third person possessive anaphor *proprio*, which has no compatible antecedent in the embedded clause, cannot take *gli* ('him') of the matrix as its antecedent, mirroring the ungrammaticality of the clitic–trace relation in (i); (iv) shows, however, that it may take an embedded dative pronoun as its antecedent 'under reconstruction'.

39 We will leave the question open of why ordinary wh-movement usually allows scope reconstruction (within certain limits discussed in Longobardi forthcoming), whereas NP-internal movement to Spec does not.

40 For the question of *that*-deletion in relative clauses see n. 60 below.

41 (Proper) government appears to be insufficient, however, as a licensing condition for an empty complementizer, as suggested by the following contrast:

(i)   ?I consider that John should leave a necessity

(ii)   *I consider [$_c e$] John should leave a necessity

At the end of section 6, we have shown in fact that proper government may cross two maximal projections in roughly analogous constructions. Thus the small clause and CP nodes presumably containing it should not prevent the empty C of (ii) from being governed by *consider*. The obvious conclusion is that *that*-deletion does not just require proper government of the empty complementizer slot but subcategorization on the part of matrix predicate (and surface adjacency with it: see, for instance, Aoun *et al.* 1987). Assuming such a subcategorization relationship to be instantiated under government, as seems to be natural, we can even dispense with stipulating that empty complementizers need to be properly governed, as opposed to, say, empty operators. This is what is expectable, actually, in frameworks like Kayne's (1983) or its derivatives, in which the need for a proper governor is made contingent, for an empty category, on the need for an antecedent, thus reducing the ECP essentially to a chain phenomenon. For relative clauses see again n. 60.

42 The Uniformity Condition, being formulated in terms of θ-marking, predicts the impossibility of idioms in the Genitive, noted by M. Baker (cf. Chomsky, 1986a, p. 219):

(i)   Heed being paid
(ii)   *Heed's being paid/*The paying of heed

It is possible that this is too strong a conclusion, at least in Italian, given the existence of the perfectly idiomatic reading of such expressions as (iii) and (iv):

(iii)   Una lavata di capo
        lit.: a washing of head (idiom: a reproach)
(iv)   Una tirata d'orecchi
        lit.: A tearing of ears (*idem*)

We may suggest, under our proposal, that the selection of the idiomatic expression by the head Noun is sufficient to govern it and thus to assign it Genitive Case. The idea that Genitive is a θ-related Case might be maintained, as a specific condition on its assignment. It must be noted, anyway, that, to a certain extent, this question is controversial: Genitive in NPs appears to be, in many cases, a 'transformed' version of Nominative and Accusative in sentences, essentially the position taken by Benveniste (1966) in his article on Latin Genitive and the insight behind the earliest generative approaches to such issues (see Lees 1960). This is particularly striking in pairs like the following:

(v)   a. Ho pagato Gianni
          I paid Gianni
       b. Ho pagato il libro a Gianni
          I paid the book to Gianni
(vi)   a. Il pagamento di Gianni
       b. Il pagamento del libro a Gianni
          The payment of the book to Gianni

Here Accusative and Genitive pattern alike, both switching from the goal to the theme. The idea of some θ-condition on Genitive assignment as opposed to Accusative assignment is, however, supported by such classic examples as the following:

(vii) a. We entered (into) the city
       b. Our entrance into/* of the city

Accusative but not Genitive can be optionally used to Case-mark a motional complement, suggesting perhaps that a θ-condition is operating on the latter Case, but not on the former.

43 Obviously, the whole approach we have taken to extraction from NP presupposes that the successive cyclicity imposed on movement of arguments of non-structural governors cannot be satisfied by adjunction to the Xmax of the head governor of the trace, thus leaving Spec as the only possible escape hatch. Such a result can be obtained in various ways; a radical solution could forbid the presence of traces adjoined to any Xmax, perhaps by some strengthening of the definition of government (on this point see Longobardi forthcoming). Another conceivable hypothesis might instead prevent adjunction to Nmax in particular. In fact, Chomsky (1986b) has already suggested that NPs (along with CPs) cannot be adjoined to, by virtue of their being arguments, a condition perhaps reducible to θ-theory, as suggested by K. Johnson (p.c.). Taken literally, such a proposal predicts that, when an NP is non-thematic, e.g. predicative, extraction should be possible without going through Spec, hence without displaying the familiar patterns discussed throughout the text. However, this is not the case. Extraction from predicative NPs (e.g. in copular constructions) has essentially the same properties as extraction from argument NPs, whenever the relevant tests can be performed; the basic opacity-like effect is exemplified in (i):

(i)   a. Il libro di Mario, di cui questa non è certo una buona
         recensione...
         Mario's book, of which this is certainly not a good review...
      b. *Il libro di Mario, di cui questa non è certo una tua buona
         recensione...
         Mario's book, of which this is certainly not a your good review...

The impossibility of non-genitive PPs undergoing extraction is confirmed by (ii) and by the paradigm (iii):

(ii)   *La polizia, da parte della quale questo è un interrogatorio di
         Gianni...
         The police, by which this is an interrogation of Gianni...
(iii) a. Questo segnale è certamente un messaggio di/a Gianni
         This signal is certainly a message of/to Gianni
      b. Gianni, di cui questo segnale è certamente un messaggio...
         Gianni, of whom this signal is certainly a message
      c. *Gianni, a cui questo segnale è certamente un messaggio...
         Gianni, to whom this signal is certainly a message...

Example (iv) shows that a genitive phrase which cannot be realized in Spec as a possessive cannot be extracted even from a predicative NP:

(iv) a. gli auguri di Gianni/buona annata
       the wishes of Gianni/a good year
   b. i suoi auguri
       his wishes (= Gianni's)
       *its wishes (= for a good year)
   c. Gianni/*Una buona annata, di cui questi dovrebbero essere gli auguri...
       Gianni/a good year of whom/which these are likely to be the wishes...

These data suggest that extraction from predicative NPs basically shares the same properties displayed by extraction from thematic NPs. Thus, θ-theory cannot directly account for the role of Spec in extraction from NP. A possible way out in Chomsky's 'Barriers' system is claiming that adjunction is impossible to any potential θ-assignee, i.e. to any category which, under certain circumstances, may receive a θ-role. This generalization of the Chomsky–Johnson proposal is likely to have a number of positive consequences: it treats on a par referential and predicative NPs; it still bars adjunction to CP and derives, additionally, another condition on adjunction proposed by Chomsky (1986b) (at least for wh-phrases): namely, that adjunction to IP is impossible. In fact IPs are likely to be able to receive a θ-role at least in the cases of raising and ECM, if CP is deleted or absent, hence they qualify as potential θ-assignees. Consider also that we suggested that extraction from NP through Spec bears some relevant similarities to extraction from PP in Germanic as analysed by van Riemsdijk (1978) (cf. Longobardi, forthcoming, for a more detailed elaboration). If this suggestion is on the right track, PPs should be added, in the 'Barriers' system, to the set of the Xmax phrases rejecting adjunction. Our proposal may perhaps derive this property as well: in fact, it is well known that some Verbs seem to contribute to the θ-marking of the NP object of their prepositional complement (cf. the different meaning of the *for*-phrase in *I bought a bone for the dog* and *I substituted a cat for the dog*). A possible approach to these facts might claim that a θ-role is assigned by the Verb to the PP and that, then, it percolates down to the NP, which is the real argument. Under this analysis PPs should be added to the class of potential θ-assignees, deriving, through the revised condition on adjunction, the obligatoriness of extraction through Spec for objects of Prepositions, hence, to a considerable approximation, van Riemsdijk's original analysis of Germanic P-stranding.

44 It is reasonable that thematic conditions will limit the scope of this rule, in particular in cases like those discussed at the end of n. 42. If PPs headed by *a* ('to') may be sometimes considered an instantiation of NPs with Dative Case, additional conditions must distinguish assignment of Genitive from assignment of Dative. On this matter see also Chomsky (1986a).

45 For a different hypothesis about the position of I, however, see Travis (1984).

46 Given the Consistency Principle we must assume that in such examples as (113)b, or also (112) in German, the recursive side of the AP is the left one, since on such a level non-consistent phrases may appear, like the head-initial PPs of (112) and (113)b; as G. Cinque (p.c.) points out, this may raise some problems, which we will not address here, with respect to X'-theory, since modifiers of the AP usually occurring in the Spec may appear after the PP complement, as the QP *più* ('more, most') does in (113)b.

47 I am indebted to H. van Riemsdijk and E. Reuland for providing me with the Dutch data. It is also worth noting that the fact the words *de berg op* form a phrase appears to be independently confirmed by the possibility of fronting it as a single constituent, as in the following example, due to E. Reuland:

(i)   De berg op klom hij
       On the mountain climbed he

48 In these terms it becomes finally plausible to relate a difference between Italian and English/French to the null subject parameter in a principled way: Rizzi (1982b) argued, in fact, that the strategy of government from Comp for the trace of an extracted subject must be unavailable in Italian, so that movement from a postverbal position turns out to be obligatory. A similar conclusion was reached also by Bracco, Brandi and Cordin (1985) and Brandi and Cordin (1986) in the study of several Italian dialects (see also Kenstowicz 1985a for Arabic dialects). As Rizzi observed, however, this fact could not be easily related to the rest of the null subject properties of the system, essentially based on K. T. Taraldsen's insight about the existence in Italian of a 'strong' I. Now we can rule out the strategy in question as a straightforward consequence of the null subject parameter if we somehow assimilate a strong I, like the Italian one, to lexical categories, in the sense relevant for Minimality (but not for the Consistency Principle), thus preventing its Spec from being governed (and Case-marked) by it and at the same time by an element external to IP. Since many Slavic languages are reported to display both grammatical violations of the Consistency Principle and grammatical extractions of agreeing NP specifiers, it is tempting to try to relate the two phenomena, as suggested by R. Kayne (p.c.). One possibility in this framework is that categories like N in Slavic do not qualify as 'lexical' or 'strong' either for the Consistency Principle or for Minimality.

49 The French construction of the type *combien ... de garçons* or *beaucoup ... de garçons* must be distinguished from the superficially analogous construction of other languages exemplified in Italian by *quanti ... dei ragazzi/di questi ragazzi*: in fact, at a closer look, several differences emerge:

(i)   First of all, in the French construction *de* is not followed by the article, a possibility excluded in Italian:
       a. *Quanti hai incontrato di ragazzi?
       How many did you meet of boys?

(ii)   Second, it is marginally possible to extract *quanti* over a wh-island in the Italian construction in question, but not in the French one, as pointed out by Obenauer (1985):

      a. ??Quanti non sai dove incontrare di questi ragazzi?
         How many don't you know where to meet of these boys?
      b. *Combien ne sais-tu pas où rencontrer de garçons?
         lit.: How much don't you know where to meet of boys?

(iii) The Italian genitive phrase can be extraposed, the French one cannot:
      a. Ho incontrato molti, ieri, dei tuoi studenti
         I met many, yesterday, of your students
      b. *J'ai rencontré beaucoup, hier, d'étudiants
         lit.: I met much, yesterday, of students

(iv) The Italian QP may apparently undergo passivization, stranding the genitive phrase:
      a. Molti sono stati interrogati degli studenti
         Many have been questioned of the students
      b. *Beaucoup a été interrogé d'etudiants
         lit.: Much has been questioned of students

(v) As suggested by the glosses, while the Italian QP agrees in gender and number with the genitive phrase, the French one does not and triggers no agreement with the past participle where this would be expected:
      a. Combien de boîtes as-tu mises dans la voiture?
         How many boxes have you put (fem. plur.) into the car?
      b. Combien as-tu mis de boîtes dans la voiture?
         lit.: How much have you put (masc. sing.) of boxes into the car?

Switching the inflectional forms of the participles of (v)a and (v)b would yield ungrammaticality. These paradigms suggest, then, that the two constructions are quite different: on the grounds of the facts in (iii) and (iv), in particular, we hypothesize that while in the French construction a real QP can be extracted from the Spec of NP, in Italian a partitive genitive phrase is extraposed out of the NP and the latter can be further wh-moved or even NP-moved to the subject position, as in (iv)a. Furthermore, being a full argument, such an NP is not subject to the strong wh-island effects typical of many non-argument wh-phrases, as e.g. in (ii)a opposed to (ii)b.

50 A readily available alternative to the hypothesis presented in the text consists of taking the Spec, and not the full NP, to be directly Case-marked by a higher Verb in French QP + *de* + N constructions, and then to assume that the whole NP may satisfy LF visibility compositionally, i.e. as an effect of all its part being Case-marked. The idea that a PF visibility condition requires a Case to appear on nominal and adjectival heads, QPs, and Determiners is the natural consequence of the *rationale* behind Vergnaud's original Case theory; i.e. extending to languages without overt Case inflections the Case requirements affecting certain categories in morphologically Case-inflected languages.

51 We will take here the not uncontroversial stand of viewing Comparative Subdeletion as an instance of wh-movement of a QP. The results so obtained provide some support for the hypothesis. A brief discussion of the issue can be found in Chomsky (1977).

52 The situation is, actually, more complex than predicted by our framework

here; we are not addressing in fact the problem of the ungrammaticality of the French counterparts of (125)a and (126)a without *de*:

(i) a. *J'ai autant de frères que Marie (a) sœurs
    b. *Jean a plus d'argent que Marie n'a amis

Such facts may motivate the further hypothesis, advocated by Battye (1988), that also empty quantified specifiers of NPs are parametrically subclassified into two types, one obligatorily requiring genitivization of the head (in French and, e.g. Genoese, a Northern Italian dialect), the other rejecting it (Italian). The latter would, of course, be licensed just by the Case conditions referred to in the text, namely in Subdeletion contexts.

53 We will not address here the question of why Italian displays such a limitation on the Comparative Subdeletion construction.

54 The relevance of the Preposition for extraction of Specifiers in Rumanian is also confirmed by the extractability of other intensifiers of APs under *de* insertion; cf., for instance, the following examples provided by C. Dobrovie-Sorin (p.c.):

(i)   Te-ai făcut teribil de inteligent
       You became terribly intelligent
(ii)   Teribil de inteligent te-ai făcut!
       Terribly intelligent you became!
(iii) Teribil te-ai făcut de inteligent!
       Terribly you became intelligent

A few other data given in Grosu (1974) seem, however, to suggest that some lexical idiosyncrasies may affect the relevant pattern.

55 A similar suggestion has been made also by L. Rizzi in a presentation given at the University of Trento in February 1987.

56 The difference between Italian and English concerning the base position of measure phrases in APs might perhaps be related to the parameter proposed in chapter 3, which orders non-internal arguments and modifiers with respect to the heads and is clearly set in opposite ways in the two languages. This would be the case if measure phrases were taken not to be projected by the head A as internal arguments (i.e. not through subcategorization) but to be selected as external semantic functions, in the sense defined for NP-modifiers in chapter 3.

57 In (139) we chose to maintain government as an obligatory relationship, using thus an 'iff'. If we use just an 'only if' definition of government, conceiving of it as a more abstract feature which may or may not be assigned by the governor to the governee, it becomes possible to introduce into the formulation of Minimality a more literal rephrasing of the Uniqueness Principle, an insight originally due to E. Reuland (1983) and K. T. Taraldsen (1984): (ii) would then read: '…β is canonically contained or lexically governed in γ'. The relevance of Case-marking for protection of Spec is here derived by the more

general principle that Case is obligatorily assigned or (transmitted via agreement) under government. Notice that we have been assuming throughout a slight ambiguity of the notion 'Case-marked'. In fact assignment of Genitive Case to a trace on the recursive side of the NP, as in Italian, for instance, does not interfere, according to our analysis, with the accessibility of an intermediate trace in Spec to external government. But Case transmission through agreement with the head seems to be more constraining: given the existence of structures like (i)a and b in Italian, it is not clear why a sentence like (ii) with the derivation suggested by the traces should be ungrammatical:

(i)   a. Ho conosciuto delle ragazze simpaticissime
        b. Ho conosciuto delle simpaticissime ragazze *t*
            I met very nice girls
(ii)   *Quanto simpatiche hai conosciuto delle *t* ragazze *t*?
            How nice did you meet girls?

Especially if Giorgi and Longobardi (chapter 3) are correct in assigning (i)b the derivation indicated, Case agreement could perhaps take place just in postnominal position, freeing the Spec position from internal government requirements. Apparently this option must be ruled out. One possibility is that Case transmitted via agreement differs from Case regularly assigned by a head in that it can only be carried along through wh-chains, and not through other chains, e.g. those of NP-internal movement (this seems to be the case with scope, for instance, as illustrated in sect. 7). This way, agreement with, involving government by, the head should take place in Spec in (i)b and in (ii), deriving the desired results. Some suggestive evidence for the proposed distinction is provided by the following paradigm:

(iii)   a. Ritengo responsabile Mario
            I hold responsible Mario
        b. Mario è/sembra responsabile
            Mario is/seems responsible
        c. **Lo ritengo Mario
            I hold it Mario
        d. Mario lo è/sembra
            Mario is/seems it
        e. Quanto responsabile dobbiamo ritenere Mario?
            How responsible should we hold Mario?
        f. Ne ritengo responsabile Mario
            I hold responsible for it Mario

It is, in fact, possible to account for the sharp contrast between (iii)c and (iii)d assuming that the predicative phrase is Case-marked directly by the copular Verb in (b) and (d), but receives Case via agreement with its subject *Mario* in (a) and (c). As a consequence of the proposed principle on movement of Case, cliticization would be blocked in (c) but not in (d). Examples like (e) show that wh-movement is possible from the same position, suggesting the mentioned difference between wh-chains and others. Finally, (iii)f shows that clitic movement is possible from inside a predicative phrase of the type in question, corroborating the hypothesis that a Case problem, and not some locality condition on clitics, rules (iii)c out. The fairly acceptable status of (iv) suggests also that every Verb subcategorizing for a small clause may, in principle, assign inherent Accusative to the predicate of the latter, but just in case the subject has been removed by NP-movement, i.e. when it does not have to be structurally Case-marked by the same Verb:

(iv)   Mario lo è sempre stato ritenuto
       Mario has always held it

The situation recalls the one postulated by Belletti and Rizzi (1988) for the case of 'psychological' Verbs, where the theme must NP-move to the subject position in order for the experiencer to receive inherent Accusative from the Verb. The proposal is confirmed by the following observation, suggested by A. Giorgi (p.c.): in some varieties of Italian the clitic *ci*, which can be considered prepositional (cf. Kayne 1975 on French *y*) or intrinsically Case-marked as oblique, may be used as a pro-predicate with a copular Verb:

(v)   Medico, Gianni non ci diventerà mai
       (A) doctor, Gianni will never become it

In the regional variety of Rome such a clitic may pronominalize the predicate of a small clause even if the matrix Verb still assigns Accusative to the subject, e.g. in structure with the Verb *fare* which keeps here an old meaning of 'estimate':

(vi)   Così stupido, non ti ci facevo proprio
       So stupid, I did not estimate you it

This is explained in the proposed framework, since *ci*, being a PP or an intrinsically Case-marked phrase, does not have to receive Case via agreement. Notice that if this explanation is correct for the non-extractability from NP of phrases agreeing in Case with the head it constitutes a further argument in favour of extraction through Spec. In fact, if direct wh-movement from the postnominal position were possible, no Case problem should arise in examples like (ii): the ungrammaticality of the latter, instead, suggests that either Case-agreement must have taken place directly in Spec, blocking external government of the trace, or a chain which would be improper (with respect to transmission of Case-agreement), as NP-internal, must have been created relating an agreement postnominal position with Spec.

58 This theorem is also likely to embody another prediction, capturing an insight originally due to Zubizarreta (1979, n. 29): consider in fact that in chapter 3, it is argued at length that the prenominal Spec position is an A′-position in Romance, but an A one in English and in other Germanic languages; consider further that a condition usually suggested to hold for chains headed by A-positions is that the position marked for Case be precisely the head of the chain (see Chomsky's (1986a) Last Resort Principle; see also Kayne 1986): the

conclusion to be drawn from the conjunction of these two axioms is that English movement to the Spec of NP must create chains where Case is assigned to or, at least, realized on the head, that is in Spec. In our framework of Minimality this means that in English extraction from NP should not occur through Spec, because Case-marking would always protect it from the required external government. Actually, it should not occur at all apart from cases of extraposition and reanalysis, essentially along the lines sketched in Horn (1974), Bach and Horn (1976), and Chomsky (1977). In other words the English pattern of extraction from NP should display deviations from the rigid scheme of Cinque's generalization: in fact, it seems that at least some violations of Cinque's generalization do arise in English in both directions:

(i)   a. a writer by whom I read many books
       b. ?*a man of whom I know the older sister

It is both the case that 'non-subjects' can sometimes be extracted, as in (i)a, and that subjects are hard to extract as in (b). The translations of these sentences yield reverse judgements in Italian, as expected. Thus, although the whole question of extraction from NP in Germanic still deserves more careful investigation, some evidence may already support the prediction suggested by our hypothesis.

59 M. Kenstowicz (p.c.) points out that the typological prediction seems to be correct also in Chadic languages like Tangale: here, in fact, no movement to the Spec of NP visibly arises and a wh-phrase which is the argument of a head Noun can never be extracted but rather induces pied piping of the whole NP.

60 The phenomenon of *that* deletion in relative clauses raises two questions with respect to our framework: first of all it suggests that government by the nominal head of a relative CP may cross this latter node, although it is not a complement (in the sense of 'internal argument') of the governor. This fact may lead to the conclusion that relative clauses and internal arguments must be grouped together, for the Minimality clause (139)c (i). This solution is rather stipulative and, perhaps, suspicious: in chapter 3 it is argued in fact that the class of attributive modifiers, of which relative clauses are part, patterns more like external arguments of Nouns than like internal ones. Another solution would consist of supposing that the Minimality clause (139)c (i) does not hold for government under coindexing, a reasonable move, since it appeals to a distinction (i.e. internal vs external arguments) which makes full sense only for lexical categories, whereas government under coindexing is the only case of definition (139)a which completely disregards the lexical properties of the governor. Either solution enables us to maintain Cinque's (1981b) and Kayne's (1981a) insight that the so-called deletion of wh-phrases in Comp (i.e. in the Spec of C) is subject to a government requirement on the part of the coindexed head of the relative clause. The second issue raised by relative *that* deletion is the following: if we want to reduce the head-government requirement constraining null Complementizers to subcategorization (to be instantiated under government) rather than to an ECP constraint (e.g. Kayne's CC), as suggested in note 41, we must stretch the concept of 'sub-

categorization' to include not only the relationship between an X^o and the heads of its arguments, but also that between the nominal projection usually called 'head' of a relative clause and the complementizer C^o technically heading the latter CP.

3   NP parametrization: the Head–Subject hypothesis

* The two authors have elaborated every part of this research together. However, as far as legal requirements are concerned, A. Giorgi takes responsibility for writing sections 1, 4, 7, 8, 9 and 11; G. Longobardi for writing the introduction and sections 2, 3, 5, 6, 10 and 12. A preliminary version of the present work was presented at the 1986 Glow Conference in Girona (Spain).

1 See also Coopmans (1984) and Hawkins (1985) for a debate on the value of the generative and typological approaches to the study of UG.

2 Among notions roughly equivalent to Chomsky's parameter, as all based on a two-term Head–Modifier opposition, are Venneman's (1974) Operator–Operand and Keenan's (1978) Function–Argument distinctions.

3 As in the previous chapters, we will continue to follow Chomsky (class lectures, 1986) in taking Spec to be a syntactically definable space and not a particular node or categorial label: more precisely, we term Spec the pre-head position of any Xmax. Descriptively, such a position is characterized in the Romance and Germanic NPs analysed in our work by the following properties:

(a)   It precedes the head

(b)   It has structural prominence (i.e. there is no pre-head branching under N', at least: see ch. 1)

(c)   It is accessible to government by an external head (under the conditions studied in detail in ch. 2)

(d)   It may be the position occupied by the elements referred to as 'Determiners' (demonstratives, articles, QPs, etc.: but see ch. 4 for discussion of an alternative)

(e)   It is on the opposite side with reference to the base position of internal arguments (the so-called non-recursive one: see ch. 2)

(f)   It is the target of most 'core' NP-internal movement rules

It is an important theoretical question whether these properties go together universally, e.g. following from one another in a principled way so as to provide a single more primitive definition of Spec. Let us examine briefly the ramifications of the question. Clearly, the coincidence of (a) and (e) is an epiphenomenon due to the head–complement nature of the languages discussed: it is analytically true that in complement–head languages like Turkish or Japanese the two notions must diverge. It is instead an empirical problem whether the other properties are a consequence of (a) or of (e). For example, Lightfoot (1979) appears to propose that a non-casual connection holds between (d) and (e). However, according to the data in Greenberg

(1966), it seems that property (d), namely the position of demonstratives and QPs with reference to the head, is parametrized in a way partially dependent on our Head–Subject parameter: it is possible, in fact, to express his generalizations (see especially the discussion of universal 18) by stating that Determiners either pattern like other non-complements under the Head–Subject parameter or precede the head Noun even in head–subject languages. Such is, for instance, the case of Romance. What seems never to arise is, thus, for Determiners to follow the Noun in subject–head languages (in this sense the postposed definite article of Scandinavian languages must be analysed as a result of cliticization, perhaps not unlike the Rumanian one, or of movement of the head N).

Property (b), namely the structural prominence of elements in Spec irrespective of their thematic interpretation, e.g. of possessives expressing an internal θ-role, certainly cannot be universally a function of the prenominal position, since in complement–head languages we must still expect internal arguments to be base-generated under N′. It is perhaps true that (b) is universally a consequence of (e), that is the node X′, constituting on a certain side the domain of internal arguments, never branches on the opposite side of the head. This would immediately follow, for example, from the principle assumed below in the text according to which N′ contains all and *only* the internal arguments of the head. That Spec accessibility to an external governor (i.e. property (c)) holds is likely to follow either from (b) (its structural prominence) or, rather, directly from (e) (its occurring on the non-recursive side). The choice is far from being totally resolved on empirical grounds. Finally, it is also plausible that lexically unselected positions able to be targets of movement can only be generated under the conditions expressed in (b), namely outside X′, the domain of subcategorization of the head, although not exclusively in Spec: (see also sect. 12). Again, this is an empirical question which needs wider and more accurate typological investigation. For the internal layering of the various elements occurring in the Spec position we refer the reader to the remarks made in note 14 below and in chapter 4.

4 In certain languages there exist morphosyntactic features which single out genitive agents and possessors, excluding internal arguments, as pointed out in Renzi (1985b). In Old French, for example, adnominal +human NPs realized Genitive Case in two different ways: agents and possessors (in the usual extended sense) used the preposition *à* or a prepositionless realization with non-nominative morphology, the so-called *Cas Régime*; NPs bearing an object function used the preposition *de* (see Foulet 1982 for details and examples). English NPs too, however, provide an empirical argument to single out thematic subjects and possessors on the one hand, vs objects on the other. In fact, Aoun *et al.* (1987) mention the fact that in such expressions as *each picture of John's*, *John's* can be understood either as the possessor or as the agent of the picture, but never as the theme; from this observation, the authors draw structural conclusions quite compatible with ours.

5 Our proposal is reminiscent of Zubizarreta's (1979) original insight about the non-A status of Spec of NP in Romance and, like hers, is also likely to capture

certain asymmetries in extraction from NP between English and Romance: for some suggestions on this point (actually, a further consequence of the Head–Subject parameter) see note 58 of chapter 2 above. NPs in languages like Turkish or Japanese display the reverse order with respect to the Romance (or Semitic) one: subject–complement–head. We do not know if there are languages whose NPs display the complement–head–subject order: were this not the case, the fact could be significant and reflect an implication between the values of the Head–Subject and the Head–Complement parameters. On subjects of NPs in another non-Indo-European language, Hungarian, see also Szabolcsi (1987).

6 Following Anderson (1984), we analyse the other occurrence of *'s* in English, namely that in *a book of John's*, as a normal prenominal Genitive of an NP with an empty N^{max-1}.

7 We could also speculate on the possibility of assigning Case to the right and carrying it along to Spec under movement. It is unclear whether this should, in principle, be allowed in Romance: the evidence is necessarily meagre, since the typically prepositional Genitive realization of Romance is only appropriate for the postnominal position; in fact it would be filtered out prenominally by the Consistency Principle formulated in chapter 2, section 9, which in Romance normally prohibits a right recursive phrase in the pre-head position of a lexical category. On a very literary stylistic level it is possible to find in Italian violations of the Consistency Principle like the following:

(i) a. ?il di lei fratello
        the of her brother
     b. la di lui madre
        the of him mother

These could be examples of Genitive Case carried along under movement from a postnominal position. However, they seem to be very isolated lexical exceptions limited to third person pronouns among all NPs in the language. More interesting is the case of Old French, where, as we know, some Genitives could be realized by the *Cas Régime*, i.e. without any preposition. Here we find a few instances of prepositionless Genitive occurring also prenominally, but limited to a small number of lexical items (see Foulet 1982, 18–19). Marginally, the phenomenon appears in Old Italian texts (see Rohlfs 1949, sect. 630 for details), in particular in fixed expressions with the word for 'God'. In modern Italian a case of prepositionless Genitive could perhaps be instantiated by the invariable items *cui* ('whose') and *altrui* ('of someone else'). For the former see also chapter 2, section 4.

8 A notable exception is represented by Tangale, according to the description provided by Kenstowicz (1985b).

9 Under Anderson's analysis accepted in note 5 above, also the *of* phrase in *a book of John's* is likely to count as heavy as the corresponding *a book of John's collection*.

10 Of course no 'heaviness' restriction appears for agents of NPs expressed through *by*-phrases: as observed in Jaeggli (1986) and in chapter 2, such

phrases display a rather adverbial behaviour and may, thus, be assumed to occur freely without a necessary chain relationship to the prenominal θ-position.

11 It is conceivable that the Scandinavian languages may be considered even more restrictive than English in the licensing conditions for postnominal subjects; see also the Norwegian data in chapter 4. For a discussion of the wide acceptability of postnominal subjects in German (and Dutch) see instead section 10 below.

12 Such a distinction between two types of Adjectives is essentially similar to the one proposed by Bolinger (1967, 1972) and resembles that made by Marouzeau (1922) between 'adjectifs déterminatifs' and 'qualificatifs' in Latin. Vincent (1985 and p.c.) also suggests the relevance of another type of distinction: namely, between Adjectives expressing 'objective' qualities, like *verde* ('green'), and those expressing 'subjective' or 'evaluative' properties, such as *elegante* and *simpatico* used in the text. For the possible consequences of the distinction on word order, see note 19 below.

13 On this point see also Demonte (1982). With some lexical choices there may sometimes arise other differences in meaning between the prenominal and postnominal position: to give just one example, the phrase *un alto ufficiale* (lit.: 'a tall officer'), in addition to being a non-restrictive variant of *un ufficiale alto* (lit.: 'an officer tall'), also has the special meaning of 'an officer high in rank' (e.g. a colonel or general), which is absent in the other order. Such distinctions do not seem to have a significant relation with the parameter here presented or the theoretical approach proposed.

14 As we mentioned before, the internal structure of the prenominal position, which we called Spec, must be rather complex: it should contain at least one position for Determiners, if they occurred within Nmax (but see on this matter ch. 4), and one for Adjectives (understood in a sense which will be further clarified in sect. 11), to say nothing here of numeral quantifiers; Adjectives, however, may occur recursively as in the following example:

(i)   l'ottima nuova segretaria di Maria
       the excellent new secretary of Maria

At least in cases like this, it appears that the Adjectives are not coordinated by asyndeton, first for intonational reasons and, more persuasively, because overt coordination of two such Adjectives turns out to be semantically not very natural:

(ii)   ?l'ottima e nuova segretaria di Maria
       the excellent and new secretary of Maria

Furthermore, the naturalness of such expressions often depends on the relative order of the Adjectives, a phenomenon perhaps reducible to considerations of semantic scope but certainly mysterious under a coordination hypothesis:

(iii) ?la nuova ottima segretaria di Maria
       the new excellent secretary of Maria

It is plausible then to postulate a structure like the following:

(iv)   [la [ottima [nuova [segretaria...]...]...]...]

This piece of structure, although base-generated in English, but partially derived by AP-preposing in Italian, is, to a certain extent, identical on the surface for the two languages.

15 Recall that the Consistency Principle prohibits, in fact, right recursion for a phrase contained as a left sister within an N-projection, in languages whose NPs project internal arguments to the right, like all the Germanic and the Romance ones. It is likely that the same principle is also responsible for the obligatory postnominal occurrence of relative clauses in Germanic, which would then behave exactly like 'heavy' APs. Recall also that the Consistency Principle does not apply to genitive phrases such as the one in (16)a, since the latter, being headed by the postpositional head *'s*, instantiates a case of (marked) left recursion, tolerated by the formulation given in chapter 2.

16 See, however, note 8 above and Kaufman (1974) for possible exceptions. Notice, on the contrary, that Greenberg's universal 25 may be understood as suggesting a tendential leftwardness of cliticization for pronominal objects.

17 There are several often-cited examples apparently contradicting the claim that referential Adjectives cannot express internal θ-roles:

(i)   a. lo sfruttamento minorile
          the juvenile exploitation
      b. il bombardamento londinese
          the London bombing

It is very plausible, however, that in such cases the referential Adjective does not bear a real internal θ-role, but rather an R-relation: *minorile* and *londinese* would be interpreted essentially as if they meant 'concerning minors' or 'concerning London', and not as expressing a thematic object; this hypothesis is confirmed by the observation that whenever there is an agent expressed through a *by* phrase, the acceptability of examples (i) immediately decreases:

(ii)   a. ?*lo sfruttamento minorile da parte delle grandi imprese
          the juvenile exploitation by big firms
      b. ?*il bombardamento londinese da parte dei tedeschi
          the London bombing by the Germans

This fact is expected precisely under the hypothesis that the phrases of (i) express no real internal θ-role, but just a looser R-relation: in fact this is what happens with genitive phrases clearly expressing R-relations. Consider, e.g., the following paradigm:

(iii)   a. Le occupazioni di Milano preoccupano il governo
          The occupations of Milan worry the government

  b. Le occupazioni milanesi preoccupano il governo
   the Milanese occupations worry the government
  c. Le occupazioni da parte degli studenti hanno rovinato l'Università
   di Milano
   The occupations by the students ruined the University of Milan
  d. Le occupazioni di Milano da parte degli studenti non sono state
   numerose
   The occupations of Milan by the students were not numerous
  e. ?*Le occupazioni milanesi da parte degli studenti...
   The Milanese occupations by the students...

(iii)a has in principle two readings: in one, it is Milan itself which is occupied (repeatedly, hence the plural) in its entirety; in this reading *Milano* appears to express the real internal θ-role of the head Noun. In the other reading, what is occupied is just a number of institutions or buildings which happen to have some relationship with Milan (most likely they *are* in Milan). In this latter reading *Milano* expresses an R-relation. The distinction is made possible here by the lexical choice of the head *occupazione* ('occupation') (with heads like *bombardamento* ('bombing'), the difference is obscured by the fact that the bombing of a proper subpart of London is interpretatively non-distinct from 'bombing London'). Now, it is clear that (iii)b only preserves the second meaning, already implying that Adjectives can only express external roles. Consider also what happens in (c) and (d): (c) shows that the use of a *by* phrase is normally possible, but (d) suggests that it entails the special restriction announced above: in fact (d) can only mean that Milan itself, as a whole, has been occupied, namely the first reading of (iii)a. The generalization seems to be that when a *by* phrase is inserted, and a potential 'direct' argument is overtly present, the head cannot be 'intransitivized' and such an argument *must* be understood as bearing the internal θ-role. Accordingly, (iii)e, where the Adjective counts as a direct argument (for reasons mentioned in ch. 2, sect. 3), becomes ungrammatical, exactly like (ii)a and b, thus supporting our general approach.

18 It might be proposed (see Kayne, 1981b) that a prohibition against the mismatch of categorial features (AP/NP) applies as a condition on chains (generally) to rule (18)b out. However, this would be both too weak, since it would not generalize to cases like (19)a and too strong, because Pesetsky (1982) has provided examples where the condition of categorial identity with the antecedent seems not to apply to variables. An analogous conclusion with respect to the French Leftward-*Tous* rule is pointed out in Cinque (1986).

19 This hypothesis will receive straightforward independent support in section 12 from the analysis of contrasts such as:

(i) a. la restituzione di se stessa$_i$ a Maria$_i$
   the restoration of herself to Maria
  b. *la restituzione propria$_i$ a Maria$_i$
   the restoration self's (possessive) to Maria

A possible objection is instead raised by the observation that the linear order normally holding between a referential Adjective expressing an external θ-role and a regular internal argument is exactly the opposite of the one expected on structural grounds. In fact, the Adjective, although supposedly higher in structure, always precedes the PP realizing an internal argument:

(ii) a. l'invasione tedesca del Belgio
         the invasion German of Belgium
      b. *l'invasione del Belgio tedesca
         the invasion of Belgium German
      c. l'ultimatum cinese all'India
         the ultimatum Chinese to India
      d. *l'ultimatum all'India cinese
         the ultimatum to India Chinese

This surface pattern, however, seems to result quite naturally from independently motivated constraints and operations. First of all, consider that, as for the grammaticality of (ii)a and c, the case is not different from others, whose properties have been discussed in chapter 1. Consider, for instance, the following examples:

(iii) a. la descrizione di Marco Polo della Cina
          the description of Marco Polo of China
       b. i regali del Khan a Marco Polo
          the presents of the Khan to Marco Polo

In chapter 1, Giorgi has argued that the internal arguments of NPs may be stylistically extraposed to the right of an external one, while preserving structural properties which show their relation to an N'-internal position. This explains the *possibility* of the order found in (ii)a and c; the reason for its *obligatoriness*, i.e. for the ungrammaticality of (ii)b and d, must then be sought in some surface condition normally requiring that Adjectives occur next to the head Noun. Such a condition seems to be independently manifested by the fact that even in cases where a non-referential Adjective cooccurs postnominally with an external argument of the head, it is this latter which must obligatorily follow:

(iv) a. i dipinti meravigliosi di Leonardo
         lit.: the paintings wonderful of Leonardo
      b. *i dipinti di Leonardo meravigliosi
         lit.: the paintings of Leonardo wonderful

Notice also that at first sight the same condition seems to be respected in a mirror-image fashion in English (*Leonardo's wonderful paintings* vs *wonderful Leonardo's paintings*), although it is not clear that a true generalization is to be found here, since a prenominal English genitive phrase also has the function of Determiner.

20 Literary Italian displays very occasional exceptions to this generalization in fixed expressions using the words *regio, reale* ('royal') or *pontificio* ('pontifical'):

(i) a. regio decreto
     royal decree
     b. Reale Accademia delle Scienze
     Royal Academy of Sciences
     c. Pontificio Ateneo Salesiano
     Pontifical Salesian Athenaeum

The origin of such fixed expressions may perhaps be found in borrowings from Germanic (this is particularly plausible for the prenominal adjectival phrase *Imperiale Regio* ('Imperial Royal'), an obvious calque from German *Kaiserlich und Königlich*), or must be due to Latin influence. In Latin, in fact, owing perhaps to its wider freedom of surface order, referential Adjectives, like genitive phrases, may appear superficially either on the left or the right of a head Noun. Limiting ourselves to the data observed in Meillet-Vendryès (1968, p. 587), we may cite the following examples:

(ii) a. erilis filius (Plaut. Most. 83 et alibi)
      the son of the master
      b. vinum dominicum (Petr. Sat. 31)
      the wine of the master

However, the highly detailed study by Marouzeau (1922) argues convincingly that in first-century BC Latin the normal position for referential Adjectives, possessives and all sorts of genitive phrases was the postnominal one and that prenominal occurrences were a product of contrastive focus on the fronted phrase. His analysis strongly suggests, then, that Latin was basically an NOS language too (contrary to what seems to be assumed in Hawkins (1983, p. 331), who, however, does not consider Marouzeau's results), with the addition of a relatively free scrambling rule, fronting contrastive or salient information, sometimes also at a distance from the original position. The similarity between Latin, as described by Marouzeau, and modern Romance languages is also accentuated by the fact that also in Latin predicative Adjectives appear to be restrictive, especially on the right of the head Noun, and appositive when prenominal, and determiner-like expressions such as demonstratives and quantifiers seem to basically occur prenominally.

21 N. Chomsky (p.c.) and N. Vincent (p.c.) suggested we should also try to reduce the different distribution of the restrictive/appositive reading under the proposed parameter: in fact, the patterning of the restrictive reading (only postnominal in Romance, prenominal in English) appears to mirror that of referential Adjectives. It could be proposed that the restrictive reading of an Adjective is always quasi-referential, in the sense of denoting the set of all elements out of which the one denoted by the head Noun is taken. So, *un*

cavallo bianco ('a white horse'), in the restrictive interpretation, would be understood essentially as a horse of the set of the white horses. The restrictive AP would, thus, be a referential expression holding a non-thematic relation to the head, most likely an external semantic function in the sense relevant for the Head–Subject parameter. This approach, which needs much deeper investigation and argumentation, might, then, lead to the suggested reduction.

22 French appears to be slightly more restrictive than Italian or Spanish in allowing preposing of non-referential APs. For instance a literal translation of (31)b does not seem to be as acceptable. Of course, it is perfectly compatible with our general claims that additional language-specific restrictions may be found on the rule of Romance which preposes non-referential APs to Spec. According to traditional grammarians, like Grevisse (1975), such restrictions might even be considered of phonological nature.

23 For some discussion of this fact, especially focusing on Spanish, see Demonte (1982, in particular pp. 467–8) and the references cited there. Vincent (1986) also notices that 'objective Adjectives' (see n. 12 above) occur more naturally in postnominal position in Italian, while subjective ones tend to precede the Noun. This factor contributes to explaining intriguing additional word-order tendencies in Italian NPs, without completely overlapping with the explanation for the behaviour of referential Adjectives that we provide in the text; the reason is that 'objective' APs, e.g. colour ones, only have a preference for the postnominal position, which for referential Adjectives is instead obligatory; the following examples represent an informative minimal pair:

(i)　a.　le verdi montagne svizzere
　　　　the green mountains Swiss
　　b.　*le svizzere montagne verdi
　　　　the Swiss mountains green

24 An A like *diffuso* ('widespread') often displays incompatibility with an overt external argument, as in the following example:

(i)　　la (*nostra) diffusa paura di una guerra
　　　(*our) widespread fear of a war

However, it cannot be classed among referential Adjectives, since it may occur prenominally as in (i), and under modification:

(ii)　　la diffusissima paura di una guerra
　　　the very widespread fear of a war

The incompatibility with an overt subject argument cannot, then, be attributed to the θ-criterion. For a discussion of the properties of *widespread* in English see Grimshaw (1986).

25 A necessary premise to any comparative analysis of Germanic and Romance Noun compounds is that the latter are much rarer than the former. Compounding seems to be essentially productive in Germanic but lexically conditioned in a severe way in the Romance languages. It is possible that such a situation is another, indirect, consequence of its linear parametrization. In

fact, the structure of Romance compounds, being head initial, is likely to favour the clash of two general tendencies holding in all Indo-European languages: first, that the inflectional features of a compound (gender, number) must occur on the head of such a compound; second, that the inflectional features of a word are morphologically realized as the final part (ending or morphological head in Williams's 1980 sense) of this word. This situation, which directly qualifies structures like *capo/-i settore* ('department head/-s') as marked, one way or another, never arises in Germanic.

26 Among the external semantic functions performed by compound modifiers and intuitively distinct from the R-relation expressed in traditional *tatpurusa* examples we must again include the predicative one, which seems to hold e.g. between *frog* and *man* in a compound like *frogman*; we can so account for the well-behaved parametrization of such cases (cf. Italian *uomo rana* ('frogman') lit.: *man frog*).

27 The uniqueness requirement singles out a rather restrictive notion of 'argument', since it clearly does not apply to referential Adjectives which may cooccur with genitive NPs, both bearing an R-relation to the head (multiple assignment is in fact a typical option for such a non-thematic functional role):

(i)   John's German car

However if (41)a–(42)a and (50) constitute a true linguistic generalization, Italian possessives must be distinguished from referential Adjectives, which they may resemble (see sect. 11), as subject to the Uniqueness Requirement. It is possible that the latter applies to expressions which are 'arguments', in the sense of having specified referential features, like number and person (see n. 52 below), or that referential As do not count for it, since they could always be optionally incorporated into the head N (see ch. 4, sect. 7 below).

28 It is impossible, unfortunately, to test directly the behaviour of Scandinavian languages with respect to the parametric property discussed in this section: in fact, it is most often the case that the only way to express a postnominal agent is by means of a preposition, like Norwegian or Swedish *av*, which has, among others, the meaning of English *by* and is currently used to express the passivized agent both in sentences and nominals. In English, in fact, the structures with the *by* phrase are acceptable, showing that its presence does not necessarily require the presence of a trace in Spec constituting a violation of the Argument Uniqueness Requirement proposed above. Notice that these observations also suggest, then, an additional argument in favour of Jaeggli's (1986) hypothesis that the *by* phrase within NPs may actually function as an adjunct and not as an argument (see Longobardi, 1985b, and ch. 2 of this vol., for further evidence).

29 The sentential counterpart to (52)b is grammatical:

(i)   The ship was destroyed to collect the insurance

The control of PRO can be assumed to be performed here by the passive morpheme EN of the Past Participle, acting as an essentially arbitrary argument along lines suggested by Jaeggli (1986) and Roberts (1987) (see also

Chomsky 1986a). A case like (52)b, instead, parallels the ungrammaticality of (ii), a kind of example first pointed out by Manzini (1980; see Chomsky 1981, p. 143; 1986a):

(ii)   *The ship sank to collect the insurance

30 See section 12 for an argument that even in potentially 'passive' NPs like *la distruzione della nave* (*da parte di NP*) ('the destruction of the ship (by NP)') the genitive phrase *della nave* ('of the ship') does not string-vacuously raise from its N′-internal position to occupy the one of the external argument.

31 Notice that such a $[_{NP}e]$ position of Romance can only be empty, because if it were lexically filled, it would require a realization of Genitive Case and, thus, under possessivization of the internal argument, it would trigger a violation of the Possessivization Principle discussed in chapter 2.

32 Williams's argument is based on the acceptability of sequences like (i):

(i)   yesterday's destruction of the ship to collect the insurance

However, in (i) there is no reason to assume that *yesterday's* competes with the subject argument under the Uniqueness Requirement, thus obliterating a pronominal empty category. In fact, in section 6, we have argued that only one *argument* may occur in Spec; but *yesterday* can be interpreted as an adverbial expression, which does not necessarily exclude the empty subject. This appears to be confirmed by the perfect grammaticality of a phrase like (ii), contrasting with (41)a in the text:

(ii)   yesterday's phone call of the woman I am trying to date

In Italian, as well, such adverbs seem to receive Genitive Case, although on the right side of the head Noun:

(iii)   la distruzione della nave di ieri
          the destruction of the ship of yesterday

Since in English Genitive can be assigned into Spec, the form in (i) should not be surprising. Notice also that in the cases in question, the control of the PRO subject of the purpose clause cannot be effected by the so-called 'event', a possibility suggested by H. Lasnik for examples like the following:

(iv)   the sinking of the ship to start the war

In fact, while it is conceivable to say that the sinking of a ship started a war, it is impossible for the destruction of a ship to collect an insurance. The subject of the latter kind of predicate must obviously be animate and the clear intuition about the meaning of (i) is that it is identical with the agent of the destroying.

33 That syntactically unrealized arguments cannot control or bind has been argued also in Rizzi (1986).

34 Notice, with respect to examples like (63), that cases of backward control, both in sentences and in Noun Phrases, may dispense with the c-command requirement, an option forbidden for binding of anaphors. This fact reinforces

the conclusion that a pronominal empty category is present as subject of the NP, bridging the relationship between *Mario* and the anaphor.

35 The impossibility of a proper binding relation between *Mario* and the anaphor in (63) must be only imputed to lack of prominence on the part of *Mario* and not to the opacizing effect of *my*, at least in the case of *sé* and *propria*; the latter in fact, as long-distance anaphors, may skip the locality effects induced by an intervening subject. For a detailed analysis of the relevant aspects of the Italian anaphoric system see Giorgi (1983; ch. 1 of this vol.).

36 The reading of the possessive as an internal argument is impossible with the plural of *conoscenza* and of some of the other items used in the examples of the text:

(i)   le sue conoscenze
        his/her notions (lit.: knowledges)

However, this does not affect our argumentation, since in the plural *conoscenza* does not take a genitive internal argument at all:

(ii)   le conoscenze degli uomini
        the notions (lit.: knowledges) of men

The genitive phrase in (ii), in fact, can only be understood as the subject. If an internal argument is to be expressed, it is embedded in a real PP:

(iii)   le conoscenze sugli uomini
        the notions (lit.: knowledges) about men

Finally, in the plural, the subject argument cannot be expressed through a *by* phrase:

(iv)   ?*le conoscenze da parte degli uomini
        the knowledges by men

In sum, the plural *conoscenze* appears not to have the argument structure and the properties of the corresponding singular, but rather those of Nouns denoting material products, e.g. *libro*:

(v)   a. il suo libro
            his/her book
       b. il libro di Maria
            Maria's book
       c. un libro su Maria
            a book about Maria
       d. *il libro da parte di Maria
            the book by Maria

37 N. Chomsky (p.c.) brings to our attention the persistence of the contrast when a *by* phrase is expressed:

(i)   a. the knowledge of algebra by the students
       b. *algebra's knowledge by the students

Such pairs may lead to the conclusion that the expression of a *by* phrase can be compatible with the presence of an empty subject in Spec, although it should be noticed that it is not compatible with an overt one:

(ii)   *their knowledge of algebra by the students

Alternatively, it is possible to understand Jaeggli's 'Affectedness Constraint' in a slightly more abstract way, rephrasing it so as not to always require an empty subject for Nouns like *knowledge*:

(iii)   If a complement of X is unaffected, the external θ-position, if present, can never be dethematized.

Now, (i)a would clearly be allowed since no subject NP category would be present, but (i)b and (ii) would be ruled out by some version of the θ-criterion, essentially like (iv)a and b:

(iv)   a. *Algebra knows *t* by the students
         b. *They know algebra by the students

However, we must add that some evidence that an empty subject NP is *always* present in these nominals can be found in chapter 4 below.

For a different judgement on (i)a, see Rappaport (1983), cited also in Zubizarreta (1986).

38 Shifting the burden of the explanation for the 'Affectedness' phenomena from the interpretation of the object to the question of the θ-role assigned to the subject creates the expectation that the thematic properties of the latter may play a role in defining the class of Nouns forbidding the possessivization of the object. In this sense, such a move may represent an empirical advantage. It seems, in fact, that, unaffectedness of the object being equal, the agentivity of the subject θ-role may improve the acceptability of possessivization:

(i)   a. ?the thief's description by the witness
         b. *the thief's sight by the witness

Many speakers seem to find (i)a better than b, and in Swedish and Norwegian it appears that possessivization of the object is generally well tolerated with 'description':

(ii)   Johans beskrivning
         Johan's description

In (ii) in fact, *Johans* is ambiguous between the agent and theme readings.

39 We will leave the question open as to how to identify the members of such a class on an independent (perhaps semantic) basis.

40 An argument in favour of the existence within NPs of instances of *di* which do not realize possessivizable Genitive Case may come from the following consideration, pointed out to us by A. Cardinaletti (p.c.): although adnominal possessivizable *di* phrases usually express arguments which are marked for Accusative or Nominative in the corresponding verbal structure, there are some arguments which are introduced by *di* both in NPs and VPs:

(i)   a. Ho convinto tutti della (= di + la) mia innocenza
          I persuaded everyone of my innocence
      b. la convinzione della mia innocenza
          the persuasion of my innocence

Such a *di* phrase cannot be possessivized even when it is the only argument of the head Noun:

(ii)   la sua convinzione
          *its persuasion; his/her persuasion

This may suggest that possessivization and realization by means of a structural Case in the corresponding verbal structure are related phenomena. If this is correct, the insight could be captured by claiming that *di* in examples (i) is a 'real' Preposition, in the sense defined in chapter 1. Accordingly, we should expect it to project a node defining the c-domain of its argument; some evidence for this can be discovered by adopting the binding tests used by Giorgi in chapter 1, for instance Burzio's test on the binding of *ciascuno*:

(iii) a. (?)Ho convinto quegli studiosi di una teoria ciascuno
          I persuaded those scholars of a theory each
      b. *Ho convinto di quelle teorie uno studioso ciascuno
          I persuaded of those theories a scholar each

41 We may thus put forward the hypothesis that the analysis provided in this section holds consistently for Continental West Germanic. We ignore whether Frisian patterns here with Continental West Germanic or rather like English.

42 In German the shift of a 'heavy' restrictive AP to the postnominal position is usually forbidden:

(i)   *ein Mann treu(er) der Frau, die er seit langem liebte
          a man faithful to the woman, whom he had long loved

An appositive AP seems instead to be acceptable after the NP of which it is predicated, with the head A uninflected, a characteristic of NP-external predicative Adjectives in German:

(ii)   dieser Mann, treu(*er) der Frau...
          this man, faithful to the woman...

It is reasonable, thus, to suspect that these are cases of APs occurring outside the NP, perhaps as secondary predicates, or even outside the regular two dimensional syntactic structure, in the spirit of what was suggested for appositive relatives in Cinque (1981b). Perhaps the same analysis is conceivable for the sporadic cases of postnominal Adjectives in Middle High German (see Behaghel's 'Satzlehre' in Paul-Mitzka 1966). The fact that regular restrictive APs cannot be shifted to the right in German, even when they are in violation of the Consistency Principle (see ch. 2), must be taken as a confirmation of the need for a 'functional' motivation of rightward AP movement; in fact, APs in German can be found with right- or left-complement recursion, as in the following example from Haider (1987, p. 19):

(iii) a. Stolz auf sich war sie schon immer
          Proud of herself she has always been

b. Auf sich stolz war sie schon immer
   Of herself proud she has always been

In the pre-head position of an NP, although the right-recursive order is correctly excluded by the Consistency Principle, the left-recursive one is, predictably, grammatical:

(iv) a. *eine stolze auf sich Frau
        a proud of herself woman
     b. *ein treuer der Frau, die er seit langem liebte, Mann
        a faithful to the woman whom he had long loved man
(v) a. eine auf sich stolze Frau
        lit.: a of self proud woman
     b. Ein der Frau, die er seit langem liebte, treuer Mann
        A man faithful to the woman who loved him long

On NP-modifiers in German see also Toman (1986).

43 That *von* in NPs is a realization of Genitive Case and differs from *von* in the regular prepositional usages (which are wider than in the case of English *of*, or Italian *di*) is suggested by a difference in contraction properties: the regular Preposition contracts with the masculine or neuter singular definite article to yield *vom* from *von dem*; but *von* in NPs does not.

44 There exist in German some cases where the Genitive *-s* is used as an apparent phrase ending or postpositional morpheme, e.g. in complex proper names like *Karl Friedrichs* or *Wolfgang von Goethes*, and in coordinations such as *Otto und Marias*. These instances seem to distinguish the German Genitive marker also from real Case endings as exemplified by Latin or other ancient Indo-European dialects. It may be suggested, however, that in German such an *-s* is a word-final (i.e. head-final) affix, and that coordinations and complex proper names of the type mentioned above are dominated by a single head node, i.e. constitute a N^0 category.

45 To be precise, it is possible to hypothesize that the structure of German (or of Dutch), as far as this part of syntax is concerned, is the result of two stylistic varieties, such that prenominal Genitive is productively part of the system in the more literary one and essentially forbidden (apart from proper names and expressions like *wessen*, *dessen* ('whose')) in the other, more current and modern. This latter variety would be the source for the phenomena in which German differs from English and Scandinavian, according to the explanation proposed in this section. On the nature of Genitive Case in German and on adjacency requirements on its occurrence, see also Haider (1987).

46 A Case different from Genitive, but somehow realized on possessivized NPs, namely Dative, can instead regularly appear on the left in certain categorial varieties of German, in the context of a peculiar 'doubling' construction:

(i)   dem Hans sein Buch
        lit.: the + Dat Hans his book
        Hans's book

Such a construction provides the opportunity of a minimal linear contrast with a closely corresponding structure in French:

(ii)   son livre à lui
        lit.: his book to him
        his book

To account for these constructions in our framework, the minimal assumption is that in both languages the possessive can occur cliticized on the head Noun, being in a chain with its A-position, where it is doubled by a Dative NP. The different linear position of the latter is now a straightforward consequence of the values of the Head–Subject parameter in Germanic and Romance.

47 If Chomsky (1986a) is right in claiming that Genitive assignment is a consequence of θ-marking in NPs, referential Adjectives must be assigned such a Case at an abstract level, without obviously realizing it (see also ch. 2 above). As a consequence, the kind of Case-marking which is rightward (and pulls to the right θ-marking as well) should be the realization and not assignment. It is perhaps simpler to claim that θ-marking is obligatorily associated with Genitive-marking only when it affects nominal expressions (not for APs or sentences), and that both Genitive assignment and realization go to the right in German along with θ-marking. This slight departure from Chomsky's literal proposal seems to be more in the spirit of his idea of relating inherent Case-marking to θ-assignment.

48 A classic example of the theoretical fruitfulness of the study of 'intermediate' cases in parametric variation is provided by Brandi and Cordin's (1981, 1986) analysis of pro-drop phenomena in northern and central Italian dialects.

49 For the structure of NPs in Greek see also Horrocks and Stavrou (1987).

50 Another possible exception mentioned by Hawkins (1985) is Guajajara, an Indian language of South America, which is alleged to be VSO, NA and Gen N, thus violating (92)b. However, Bendor-Samuel (1972) gives several orders for Guajajara sentences, including OV, and provides examples of locative expressions which seem to be easily interpretable as postpositional phrases. Thus, it is not inconceivable that internal arguments of N may be base-generated to the left and that Genitive Case is also exclusively assigned in the same direction, forcing external nominal arguments to undergo preposing in order to be Case-marked. This way, the Guajajara NP would just be the mirror image of the Dutch and German one, as we have analysed it.

51 For discussions of related methodological questions see also Drachman (1985) and Coopmans (1984).

52 More precisely, our hypothesis is that in all the languages considered here possessives are non-distinct from genitive NPs, at least at some interpretatively relevant level (D-structure and/or LF), in addition to being either Determiners or Adjectives at a more superficial level. Italian possessives, for example, differ systematically from regular APs in a number of respects, in part already exemplified in the text:

(i)   They can bind anaphors and pronouns
(ii)   They can bind traces

(iii)   They can always control; referential APs, on the contrary, seem to be able to control in Italian, but only very marginally if the features of the controller are overtly manifested in the controlled infinitival VP, e.g. on a participle:

    a. il tentativo cinese di resistere all'invasione giapponese
       the Chinese attempt to resist the Japanese invasion
    b. il tentativo cinese di essere ammess*i* alle Olimpiadi
       the Chinese attempt to be admitted (masc. plur.) to the Olympics

All these properties may be related to their lack of intrinsic features mentioned under point (iv) below:

(iv)   They are doubly specified with respect to number: namely they have a singular/plural ending agreeing with the head Noun, like all Adjectives, plus an intrinsic number expressing the cardinality of the entity they denote (*mio* vs *nostro* 'my' vs 'our'). There is no way, however, of ever knowing whether *tedesco* ('German') refers to one or more Germans (or German states).

53 By the term 'possessives' we refer here mainly to pronominal items like *mio*, *my*, *mon*, not focusing on expressions like English *John's*, which can easily be taken to be NPs, realizing Genitive through a PP headed by the dummy postposition *'s* (see ch. 2). The latter, which have no equivalent in Romance as a consequence of the value of the Head–Subject parameter, are, however, subject to the same possessivization Principle discussed in chapter 2, and seem to occur as Determiners in the sense of having roughly the meaning and the distribution of the definite article and of pronominal possessives. C. Lyons (1986) proposes a parametric distinction quite similar to ours, treated, however, in terms of structural positions rather than categorial ones. Although the node labelling assumed by Lyons should perhaps be slightly modified in the light of some results of these chapters, it seems to us that Lyons's assumption about a structural correlate of our categorial distinction is straightforwardly correct: see our note 56 below and the alternatives discussed in chapter 4. We consider less uncontroversial, however, Lyons's attempt to attribute to Latin possessives also a Determiner status when they occur prenominally, as a consequence of the assumption that *meus liber* would have been unequivocally understood as definite, i.e. as 'my book', never as 'a book of mine', when in non-predicative position.

54 Third person plural possessives, in literary Catalan and some of its northern spoken varieties, preserve an old 'weak' form *llur*, plur. *llurs* ('their'), which seems to behave rather as a Determiner, unlike the other members of the paradigm. Most spoken varieties, however, replace *llur* by the singular form *seu*, which appears to be an Adjective, as in Italian. More sporadically such alternations are found also in other persons (see Badia i Margarit 1984 and n. 63 below).

55 An apparent difficulty for our categorial hypothesis could be raised by the fact that a possessive cannot be coordinated with a true Adjective, but only with *di* + NP phrases (see Belletti 1978, and Giorgi, ch. 1):

(i)   a. *la casa mia e bella
           the house my and nice
      b. la casa mia e di Gianni
           the house my and of Gianni

This might suggest that possessives are always PPs or genitive NPs. However, it seems that the identity requirement on coordination is essentially interpretative rather than strictly categorial; consider the following data:

(ii)   il libro mio e di Moravia
         the book my and of Moravia
(iii)   un libro bello e di valore
         a book nice and of value (valuable)
(iv)   *l'annessione tedesca e improvvisa dell'Austria
         the German and sudden annexation of Austria
(v)   l'occupazione nostra e tedesca della Jugoslavia
         our and German occupation of Yugoslavia

Example (ii) can both mean 'the book which has been written by me and Moravia', or 'the book owned by me and Moravia', but it cannot mean 'the book which I own and Moravia has written' (or vice versa). This suggests that exact semantic identity is required. Example (iii) shows that once such identity is observed, identity of categorial specification is unnecessary. Furthermore, (iv) shows that categorial identity is also insufficient: in the cases where a non-possessive Adjective plays an argument role, it cannot be coordinated with a true predicative Adjective, exactly as in (i)a. Example (v), instead, confirms the expectation that a possessive and a non-possessive Adjective can be coordinated under identity of thematic function. This allows us to maintain that possessives have a surface categorial specification as Adjectives or Determiners, even if they display argumental interpretative properties.

56 See note 14 above. According to what is suggested there, Nmax could be initially rewritten, in Italian or English, roughly as follows (but for arguments that D may occur outside Nmax and the consequences of this assumption see ch. 4 below):

(i) $N^{max} \rightarrow DP\ N^{max-1}$
(ii) $N^{max-1} \rightarrow (AP)\ N^{max-1}$

Rule (ii) provides for the recursion suggested by sequences of non-coordinated Adjectives in prenominal position. Obviously, such APs cannot be already lexically filled at D-structure in Romance, according to our hypothesis of section 3, but they can in Germanic. Actually, linear ordering of prenominal possessives and regular Adjectives is not completely neutral (but this is also true of sequences of two or more non-possessive Adjectives), so that some further, perhaps stylistic, conditions should be introduced: most often a possessive precedes another Adjective, but the opposite order, though stylistically more *recherché*, is by no means impossible, especially with superlatives:

(iii) il mio bel libro
    the my beautiful book
(iv) a. i primi suoi scritti
    the first his writings
  b. un ottimo suo articolo
    a very good his article
  c. il più bel suo libro
    the most beautiful his book

In postnominal position Italian possessives precede predicative Adjectives (unless they are particularly stressed), as the referential ones do (see n. 19 above):

(v) a. l'opera sua più bella
   the work his most beautiful
  b. *l'opera più bella sua
   the work most beautiful his
  c. l'opera dantesca più famosa
   the work Dantesque most famous
  d. *l'opera più famosa dantesca
   the work most famous Dantesque

57 The exception is represented by certain common kinship names, when they occur unmodified in the singular:

(i) Mio padre ha telefonato
   My father called up

but not:

(ii) a. *Mio vero padre...
   My real father...
  b. *Mia sorellina...
   My little sister...
  c. *Miei cugini hanno telefonato
   My cousins called up

58 Notice that in Italian determinerless NPs in the plural, or with an uncountable head, have a wider range of occurrences: it looks as if there existed an empty plural/uncountable Determiner with a basically existential meaning (see also Benincà 1980 and Torrego 1984 for some discussion):

(i) a. E' un po' di tempo che non frequento biblioteche
   It is a while that I do not attend libraries
  b. Mangio spesso patate/pesce
   I often eat potatoes/fish

In English and other Germanic languages, plurals with no overt Determiner are also licensed with the interpretation as generic universals, as in (ii):

(ii)   a. Dogs bite
       b. Men are mortal

Since such a possibility seems absent in Romance, it might be typologically related to the pattern following from the Head–Subject parameter, but no theoretical link emerges clearly; typologically similar facts are found with titles preceding proper personal names in referential (non-vocative) usages:

(iii) a. Mister Jones (has arrived)
       b. Doktor Schmidt (ist angekommen)
(iv)   a. (E'arrivato) *(il) dottor Bianchi
       b. (Ha llegado) *(el) señor Muñoz

Some French titles already incorporate a possessive (i.e. a Determiner: *monsieur, madame*, etc.), so that the contrasts with Germanic must be sought in examples like the following:

(v)   a. President Reagan has just arrived
       b. *(Le) Président Reagan vient d'arriver

The analysis of null Determiners needs, anyway, much further investigation.

59 Such a necessity appears to be suspended, instead, in languages with no article at all, like Latin or Slavic. The whole question deserves detailed analysis.

60 In (116)a *questo* is probably not a real predicate, but rather a referential argument, the 'semantic' subject of predication, according to the theory of identificational copular sentences developed in Longobardi (1983). If this is the case, (116)a reduces to the same kind of examples as (116)b, but the line of reasoning is unaffected. There are also other Determiners which appear in predicative and gapped contexts unavailable to *my* in English, but it is unclear whether they always constitute real instances of Ds:

(i)   a. I ragazzi sono molti/tre
           The boys are many/three
       b. Tre sono venuti
           Three have come

It is possible, in fact, to show that such elements, in addition to being Determiners, may also be differently categorized, so as to constitute sometimes lexical projections, most likely APs. In fact, *molti* and cardinals may also occur in prenominal position along with a Determiner, hence as a sort of AP:

(ii)   i molti/tre amici di Mario
           the many/three friends of Mario

It is true that, unlike regular Adjectives, cardinals hardly occur in postnominal position, but this property is unlikely to be dependent on their being also categorized as Determiners; in fact, it extends in many cases to other numerical Adjectives, like ordinal ones, which do not share the Determiner status:

(iii) a. *i figli tre
          the children three
       b. *il figlio terzo
          the child third
       c. *Terzo figlio è nato
          Third child was born

61 The feature [±strong] should also be assigned to Spanish definite articles such as *el* which unlike the [−strong] ones of most other languages considered may also occur with empty nominal heads:

(i)   el de Juan
       the one of John

An analysis of the question along very similar lines can be found in Brucart and Gràcia (1986).

62 A [+strong] Determiner could perhaps be identified in Italian as well, examining the demonstrative *quello* ('that'), which often cannot occur in prenominal position where it is replaced by the weaker *quel*:

(i)   quel ragazzo/*quello ragazzo
       that boy

However, the proposed feature assignment faces an apparent difficulty since the form *quello* is obligatorily restored in some phonologically restricted environments, i.e. before vowels (with truncation) and certain initial consonant clusters:

(ii)   a. quello stupido
          that stupid
       b. quell'animale
          that animal

This morphophonological alternation is found also with other Determiners and Adjectives, such as *uno/un* ('a') or *bello/bel* ('beautiful'), *buono/buon* ('good'), and in all these cases the first form, in addition to occurring as a conditioned aliomorph of the second in prenominal position, is homophonous with the one occurring in all the strong positions. Two observations suggest, in any event, that we have to do with real [+strong] forms, which only by chance happen to be homophonous with one allomorph of the [−strong] one: the first is that the same alternation is found with the definite article (*lo/il*) where it may not have distributional content, since both allomorphs are exclusively [−strong] in Italian. The second, more important, is that in the masculine plural the two forms of *quello* are not homophonous any longer: *quegli/quei* is the alternation for the [−strong] form, and *quelli* is the exclusively [+strong] one. In the domain of Adjectives exactly the same is true of *begli/bei* with respect to *belli*.

63 In the previous stages of French, however, *mien* displayed the full distribution of a [+strong] or even [±strong] Adjective (see also Foulet 1982). A similar situation must have arisen in the history of Catalan (see Badia i Margarit 1984), where even now, in some restricted expressions, the archaic weak form can be found as a Determiner beside the more current [±strong] adjectival form of the Italian type: cf. *mon germà/el meu germà* ('my brother'). Lyons (1986) convincingly argues that a sort of weak/strong possessive distinction must also have existed in colloquial Latin in areas remote from the present domain of Romance languages.

64 We have no obvious explanation for the non-equally acceptable status of **el amigo mio* ('the friend mine') with the definite article and the postnominal possessive Adjective: it is plausible, however, that it is functionally related to the possibility of using the simpler *mi amigo* ('my friend').

65 Such a raising of *di* + NP phrases to the 'higher' subject position could perhaps be not completely excluded, but only quite marginal. This assumption would account for the less severe unacceptability noted in the control cases of (131) and (132), with respect to the corresponding sentential examples (in the text the difference was marked by using '?*' and '*' respectively). Following Chomsky's (1986a) distinction between Case assignment and Case realization, it is possible to assume that Genitive is only assigned, but not necessarily realized in the case of the object in the internal position, the realization being performed in the higher one. The Last Resort Principle would then apply to Case realization, not to Case assignment. Actually this seems to be the intended account in Chomsky (1986a) for English *Rome's destruction t*. The reason why such an example is perfectly grammatical, while in Italian raising of the object of an NP to the postnominal subject position is at best very marginal, must then be sought in the fact that in English the realization of Genitive is different for internal and external positions (*of* insertions vs *'s* insertion). The situation would then become analogous to that of Italian possessives, which may raise to the postnominal higher A-position, as confirmed by examples like the following:

(i)   (?)L'assunzione loro dopo essere stati esaminati...
      The hiring their after being examined...

Following the proposal made in chapter 2, section 3, we may assume that Italian possessives and English genitive phrases which end up in Spec are already marked at D-structure by a special Case feature, +Gen +Poss, which is unrealizable under N'. The Last Resort Principle should then be so understood as to completely disallow A-movement from positions of automatic Case realization (as non-distinct from assignment, e.g. for the object of an active transitive verb), to permit A-movement from positions where Case (at least the particular one assigned) is unrealizable, and to rule highly marginal A-movement from positions where the assigned Case could optionally be realized (the case of +Gen−Poss under N').

66 Given that no Argument Uniqueness Requirement seems to apply in postnominal positions (see sect. 6), we may wonder whether it is not possible

to use for control the position corresponding to the possessor. This way, a possessive object could raise to an A-position outside N' without interfering with the presence of an empty pronominal subject. However, it is highly implausible that this option may exist: in fact it was argued in chapter 1 that a possessor phrase cannot bind into the argument frame of the head Noun essentially for opacity reasons; it is conceivable that the same reasons may forbid control from the possessor position into an adverbial adjunct of the head Noun, if Nouns selecting a possessor position and compatible with the relevant type of adverbial clause exist at all.

67 If the reasons given in note 12 above for the '?*' status of (136)a are correct, then the full ungrammaticality found in (137)c is exactly what should be expected.

68 Against Nominative transmission through a chain, however, see Belletti (1988).

69 We will not analyse here other inversion options of French which are not shared by English and could be relevant to our discussion: e.g. the possibility of Heavy NP Shift from tensed subject positions, pointed out in unpublished work by V. Deprez, to whom we are much indebted for discussion.

Another manifestation of postverbal subjects in French which finds no correspondence in English could be, under Sportiche's (1988) theory of floating Quantifiers, the contrast in the position of *all/tous* in the following sentences:

(i) a. *They have called all
     b. Ils ont téléphoné tous

See Sportiche (1988) for the analysis of Q-floating presupposed by these suggestions.

70 If an analogous assumption can be motivated for the non-Nominative Case assigned in causative constructions, it will become tempting to treat in terms of the Head–Subject parameter the well-known contrast between English and French/Italian exhibited by *I made John call/leave* vs *Ho fatto telefonare/partire Gianni*. The issue has a number of ramifications which it would be impossible to consider here.

4   Null pronominals within NPs and the syntax of DPs

* Although all parts of this work were elaborated jointly by the two authors, A. Giorgi takes responsibility for the Introduction and sections 1, 2 and 4, and G. Longobardi for sections 3, 5, 6 and 7.

1 That Italian PRO can have a split antecedent even under obligatory control was pointed out in Giorgi (1983):

(i) a. Gianni$_j$ ha proposto a Maria$_i$ di PRO$_i$ raggiungerlo a Casablanca
       Gianni proposed to Maria to join him in Casablanca
     b. Gianni$_j$ ha proposto a Maria$_i$ di PRO$_j$ raggiungerla a Casablanca
       Gianni proposed to Maria to join her in Casablanca

c. Gianni$_j$ ha proposto a Maria$_i$ di PRO$_{j+i}$ partire insieme per Casablanca
Gianni proposed to Maria to leave together to Casablanca

In this case, both *Gianni* and *Maria*, taken separately, are possible controllers, as shown by the distribution of pronouns in the subordinate clause. If one of them is not a possible controller, the grammaticality of the split antecedent reading decreases:

(ii) a. Gianni$_j$ ha incoraggiato Maria$_i$ a PRO$_{*i+j}$ partire insieme per Casablanca
Gianni encouraged Maria to leave together to Casablanca

2 In the relevant examples, it is impossible to exclude the arbitrary reading of PRO and of the anaphor it binds, because in Italian it is always admitted in cases of non-obligatory control, provided that the morphological ending is masculine plural. This is the reason why we included the asterisk on *se stessi* in parentheses.

With respect to the impossibility of a split antecedent with anaphors, consider the following examples:

(i) a. *Gianni$_i$ ha restituito Maria$_j$ a se stessi$_{i+j}$
Gianni restored Maria to themselves
b. Gianni ha restituito Maria$_i$ a se stessa$_i$ (con una lunga terapia psicoanalitica)
Gianni restored Maria to herself (with a long psychoanalytic therapy)
c. Gianni$_j$ ha restituito Maria a se stesso$_j$ (con il suo affetto paziente)
Gianni restored Maria to himself (with his patient love)

The impossibility of (i)a shows that, even if both elements are possible antecedents for the anaphor, they cannot be taken together. On the other hand, this reading is available for pronouns:

(ii) Gianni$_i$ ha restituito Maria$_j$ alla loro$_{i+j}$ famiglia (con il suo affetto paziente)
Gianni restored Maria to their family (with his patient love)

3 *Insieme* ('together') is subject to a kind of binding requirement, in that it must have a local c-commanding antecedent. Consider the following examples:

(i) a. *Gianni e Maria$_i$ sperano che io pensi di PRO$_i$ partire insieme per Casablanca
Gianni and Maria hope that I think to leave together to Casablanca
b. I genitori di Franco e Teresa partiranno insieme per Casablanca
The parents of Franco and Teresa will leave together (the parents/*Franco and Teresa) to Casablanca

Furthermore, *insieme* cannot take a split antecedent, as suggested by the following contrast:

(ii)   a. Gianni$_j$ ha portato i suoi fratelli$_i$ insieme$_{i+j}$ al cinema
            Gianni took his brothers together to the movies
        b. *Gianni$_i$ ha portato suo$_i$ fratello insieme$_i$ al cinema
            Gianni took his brother together to the movies

(Further discussion of the antecedent requirements for *together* can be found in Chomsky (1986a).) The use of *insieme* in our examples in the text is thus further proof concerning the presence of an empty pronominal controllable by split antecedents. If this were not the case, in fact, the requirements of *insieme* would be violated.

4   A possible further argument for the existence of an empty subject within NPs was suggested by Higginbotham (1980, n. 11, p. 690). He points out that the 'gate' function typical of PRO with respect to weak crossover in sentences seems to have a counterpart within NPs, constituting therefore an indirect test for the presence of PRO in such contexts. Consider the following examples (from Higginbotham 1980):

(i)   Devotion to his$_i$ country is expected of every soldier$_i$

If there is a PRO subject of the NP in this example, it will contribute to overcome the expected weak crossover violation, exactly as it does within infinitival subject clauses. Higginbotham also points out that, according to this hypothesis, in (ii) the bound interpretation should be less acceptable:

(ii)   The queen's devotion to his$_i$ country inspires every soldier$_i$

His intuition confirms this prediction. In Italian we essentially find the same pattern as that pointed out by Higginbotham:

(iii)   a. La devozione al suo$_i$ paese contraddistingue ogni soldato$_i$
            Devotion to his country is typical of every soldier
        b. ?*La devozione della regina al suo$_i$ paese incoraggia ogni soldato$_i$
            The queen's devotion to his country encourages every soldier

Example (iii)a is, in fact, better than (iii)b (however, see Hoji (1986) for a different view concerning these phenomena).

5   Example (24) is considered marginal by some speakers. Such a judgement seems to be due to the fact that, for the same speakers, a nominal argument with *ordinare* ('order') is marked with respect to a sentence.

6   Some Verbs require obligatory control only of a PRO subject of an embedded sentence. Others strongly favour control also on the subject of a complement NP, although the lexical choice of the head of the latter and that of the matrix tense may also affect the result. At first sight, *ordinare* ('order'), *decidere* ('decide'), *pensare* ('think') obligatorily control the PRO subject of a sentence as well as the subject of a NP, as shown in the text in examples (24) and (25). On the other hand, *volere* ('want'), *amare* ('love'), *odiare* ('hate') and *esortare* ('encourage') do not impose an obligatory control requirement on the subject of an NP, as shown in examples (26) and (27). It is unclear whether the bipartition is due to different and poorly understood control properties, or to the degree of semantic compatibility with the generic context necessary to license the arbitrary reading.

7 With respect to the control properties of PRO, the infinitive preceded by the article in Italian behaves like a NP (see Salvi 1985):

(i) a. Gianni odia il conoscere se stesso/se stessi$_{arb}$
     Gianni hates knowing himself/oneself
     b. Gianni odia conoscere se stesso/*se stessi$_{arb}$
     Gianni hates knowing himself/oneself

A tentative explanation of the behaviour of these infinitives in general could be achieved by the claim that such constructions are projected out of an infinitival INFL specified as [+N] and taking a regular VP as its complement. Thus, INFL and its projections would have the structure and properties typical of the N system, while maintaining a verbal structure inside them, as pointed out by Salvi.

8 The reconstruction effect must also extend to A-chains (see also below in the text) in order to account for the analogous behaviour displayed by participial modifiers as in the following example:

(i) La sorella di Gianni non apprezza la conoscenza di *se stesso* da lui raggiunta
     Gianni's sister does not appreciate the knowledge of himself attained by him

Example (i) is likely to contain an NP trace as the object of the participle, somehow related to *la conoscenza di se stesso* ('the knowledge of himself'). The phrase structure of these examples is not completely clear, but their reconstruction properties might be compatible, e.g., with an analysis in the spirit of Vergnaud's (1974) head-raising proposal for relative clauses.

9 Examples like (34) appear to raise some difficulties for an analysis of reconstruction phenomena in terms of NP-structure (see van Riemsdijk and Williams 1982). For other approaches to reconstruction, see also Cinque (1982), and Barss (1986).

10 A more minimal comparison of infinitives and NPs is marginally available even using appositive relative clauses also with the latter; some (equally marginal) reconstruction effects arise with NPs, in fact, also in the appositive reading typical of the following examples:

(i) a. ?Gianni pensa che la conoscenza di se stessa, che Maria non
     intende comunque perseguire, sarebbe un obiettivo difficile
     Gianni thinks that knowledge of herself, which Maria however
     does not want to pursue, would be a difficult goal
     b. ?Gianni apprezzerebbe una maggiore conoscenza di se stessa, che
     Maria invece non intende perseguire
     Gianni would appreciate a better knowledge of herself, which
     Maria instead does not want to pursue

11 One could wonder whether, in those lexically conditioned cases where control is obligatory even with NPs, reconstruction is also inhibited. Consider, thus, the following example, with the lexical choice of (24)b:

(i)   *Gianni ha deciso la consegna di se stessa alla polizia che Maria
         voleva evitare
         Gianni decided the delivery of herself to the police which Maria
         wanted to avoid

This sentence is ungrammatical because the subject of the NP headed by
consegna ('delivery') cannot be identified with *Maria*, therefore leaving the
anaphor unbound, but can only be *Gianni*. This fact appears to confirm that
the D-structure control strategy can only be taken when no obligatory control
requirement holds at S-structure.

12 Recall, however, that in chapter 3, section 9, it has been argued that *fear* and
   knowledge belong to two different classes of unaffecting Nouns, distinguished
   in terms of Case properties. On the question of Affectedness, it was noticed by
   Rizzi (1986) that the object of *fotografare/fotografia* ('(to) photograph')
   counts as affected, contrary to semantic expectations. However, the subject of
   such an item, unlike that of *fear*, or *knowledge*, is understood as an agent, not
   as an experiencer: now, as we proposed in chapter 3, on the grounds of
   Jaeggli's (1986) suggestions, it is precisely the nature of the subject θ-role
   which is likely to be most relevant in defining the syntactic class in question.

13 The contrast of (39)a with (42) can also be reproduced with respect to principle
   C violations; cf. the relevant interpretations of the following:

(i)   a. Una migliore conoscenza di Gianni avrebbe giovato molto alla sua
            carriera
            A better knowledge of Gianni would help his career very much
         b. Quelle vecchie fotografie di Gianni hanno giovato molto alla sua
            carriera
            Those old pictures of Gianni helped his career very much

14 The non-obligatoriness of expletive subjects in NPs follows, as we suggested,
   from the lack of a predicative maximal projection; their impossibility is
   probably due to the fact that they fail to be licensed either as arguments or as
   subjects of predication. In fact, it seems to be a widely supported generalization
   that expletives arise only in positions where they are required. In addition to
   that, if expletives require Case, they are independently excluded within NPs by
   Chomsky's (1986a) Uniformity Condition, which prohibits the assignment of
   an inherent Case such as Genitive to phrases which are not arguments of the
   head.

15 As suggested in chapter 1 (sect. 6), an opacizing empty subject seems to
   become obligatory within any NP when the agent is somehow expressed in the
   sentence, e.g. through a relative clause; this may explain the ungrammaticality
   of the following:

(i)   *Gianni mi ha mostrato i ritratti di se stesso in divisa che Maria
         gli aveva fatto a Modena
         Gianni showed me the portraits of himself in a uniform that Maria
         had taken of him in Modena

16 We are thus led to the prediction that with Nouns other than those of the unaffecting class, the parallelism between control with designated antecedents in clauses and NPs may break down. This is perhaps correct in sentences like the following, although the judgements are not very clear:

    (i)   a. *Gianni$_i$ ha chiesto a Maria di fotografare se stesso$_i$ in divisa
                Gianni asked Maria to photograph himself in a uniform
           b. (?)Gianni ha chiesto a Maria una fotografia di se stesso in divisa
                Gianni asked Maria a picture of himself in a uniform

Example (i)a is clearly possible because in such a structure the PRO subject of the infinitive must be controlled by *Maria*, which is incompatible with the masculine feature of the reflexive. But (i)b appears to be grammatical in an unspecified interpretation of the agent of *fotografia*. Such an interpretation cannot be induced by an arbitrary PRO, always possible in NPs: otherwise its presence would prevent *se stesso* from referring back to *Gianni*, its only feature-compatible antecedent.

17 Recasting a result arrived at in chapter 2, section 5 into this new terminology, we could propose that only c-government may cross a maximal projection, affecting the Spec of the latter.

18 Given such a formulation of the government requirement in the binding conditions, we may also expect the existence of a PRO with the function of possessor. In fact, according to the evidence discussed in the previous chapters, also the function of possessor seems to be assigned outside N′. This possibility does not face immediate counter-evidence, but is also difficult to prove, mainly because of the binding properties of possessors discussed in chapter 1 (sect. 6). If, however, it turned out that PRO possessors do not exist, this could be attributed to the fact that PRO is usually related to a θ-grid (cf. the non-existence of infinitival PRO with expletive functions).

19 Notice that the formulation given in the text would allow for PRO as the subject of I also in a tensed sentence. However, this option is probably independently excluded because PRO would then be subject of AGR, violating the well-known, and poorly understood, constraint against + anaphoric expressions as subjects of AGR. Another problem is how to allow PRO to occur in the Spec of NP in the Germanic languages without being c-governed by an external governor in the light of the results given in chapter 2. One possibility is that an abstract agreement-like relationship optionally holds with the head Noun protecting PRO from receiving external government.

20 It is hard, however, to prove empirically the existence of a *pro* object within APs. In fact, the latter hardly admit of two internal arguments and probably no case exists where such arguments are potentially coreferential, so as to permit a binding test. Other tests used by Rizzi (1986) are difficult to apply within APs as well as within NPs, because of the unclear status of processes like small-clause predication inside such phrases. The complementary question may also arise, i.e. whether PRO can appear within VP as a subject: an answer in the affirmative was proposed by Kayne (class lectures MIT, autumn 1986).

21 In note 31 of Rizzi (1986), L. Burzio is credited for an important suggestion,

which would amount to reducing the freer relation order of direct and indirect complements in Italian VPs (with respect to the English one) to the licensing of an expletive object *pro*; the latter might function as a resumptive position for a shifted direct object. If Burzio's suggestion can be worked out, in the light of our proposal in this section, it can naturally apply to explain the equally free order of internal arguments inside NPs, discussed in chapter 1.

22 It is, of course, also possible to have the nominalization corresponding to (56), which is equally grammatical (as well as equally stylistically 'cumbersome'):

    (i)   La riconciliazione di se stessi con se stessi...
               The reconciliation of oneself with oneself...

23 The tendency to disjointness found in (i) between the surface subject theme and the understood agent is probably to be attributed to the disjointness properties of the -EN morpheme which discharges the latter θ-role (see Roberts 1987):

    (i)   Gianni è stato riconciliato con se stesso/Maria/...
               Gianni was reconciled with himself/Maria/...

Since no -EN morpheme occurs in nominalizations, the phenomenon is correctly predicted not to arise there, exactly as in middle verbal constructions.

24 See ch. 3 for detailed discussion of the argument structure in NPs and especially sec. 2 of the Appendix for the status of the subject position as a target of movement.

25 The brackets including the diacritics of (61) are due to the acceptability of such examples with the PRO of the adverbial controlled by the understood agent of the capture, rather than by *Gianni*. This interpretation is possible, although irrelevant, throughout the paradigm: it is, however, important because it suggests that a PRO subject bearing the external θ-role can also occur with lexical items like *cattura* which are inherently 'passive', i.e. can never express such a θ-role by means of an overt genitive phrase (see Cinque 1980, 1981; see also ch. 2). Thus the property of being inherently passive for an N cannot be traced back to interpretative reasons, i.e. to θ-theory, but perhaps to Case-theoretic reasons.

26 Since dative $a + NP$ phrases are able to function as binders in Italian, as pointed out by Giorgi (1986, and this vol., ch. 1), we may wonder whether understood dative complements show this sign of syntactic activity. Rizzi (1986) shows that this appears to be the case with Verbs in Italian (but not in English):

    (i)   Uno psicoanalista esperto può restituire se stessi
               An expert psychoanalyst may restore oneself

(Indeed we even find these sorts of example fully acceptable, not just marginally so, as suggested by Rizzi.) Rizzi argues, then, that an arbitrary *pro* can occur in Italian also as an indirect object of V. Now, the situation is, once more, analogous within NPs, as expected under the approach suggested in the text:

(ii)   La restituzione di se stessi effettuata da un esperto psicoanalista
può dare giovamento
The restoration of oneself effected by an expert psychoanalyst may
be profitable

The existence of a dative empty category *pro* within NPs allows us to test our hypothesis of the text that the non-arbitrary cases of an understood direct object, like examples (59), represent instances of PRO, not of *pro*. Consider, in fact, that dative internal arguments should be unable, since unmarked for Genitive, to raise to the subject position outside N', and, thus, to be realized in the form of PRO. Given the usual assumptions, understood datives must then be expected to be only arbitrary, refusing control. Although the judgements are delicate and it is not easy to construct a pragmatically plausible example, the prediction seems to be borne out by the interpretation of sentences like the following:

(iii) a. *La restituzione del proprio$_i$ patrimonio, decretata dal giudice dei
minori, ha molto giovato alla carriera che Maria$_i$ si prefiggeva
The return of self's property, decreed by the minors' judge, helped
very much the career that Maria was planning for herself
       b. La restituzione al proprio$_i$ ambiente familiare, decretata dal giudice
dei minori, ha molto giovato alla carriera che Maria$_i$ si prefiggeva
The return to self's family environment, decreed by the minors'
judge, helped very much the career that Maria was planning for
herself

In both these examples, the agent of *restituzione* is most naturally understood as different from *Maria*, and the possessive anaphor *proprio* cannot be directly bound by *Maria*, which is too deeply embedded to bind, though not to control. Thus, binding between *Maria* and *proprio* must be mediated by a controlled empty pronominal within the NP. Now, as expected, this is possible in (iii)b, where such an understood binder is a direct internal argument, hence may raise and surface as control PRO. In (iii)a, the only potential binder would be the understood indirect (dative) argument, but it cannot be controlled by *Maria*, confirming that only raising to the subject position as PRO permits control. A structure like (iii)a is obviously acceptable with *proprio* interpreted arbitrarily, hence bound by a normal arbitrary *pro*, as in the following example:

(iv)   La restituzione del proprio patrimonio è sempre un evento
fortunato
The return of self's property is always a lucky event

27 On the differences between English, Italian and other languages with respect
to the categorization of possessives, see chapter 3, section 11.
28 In addition to PRO, also another empty category is likely to occur in the Spec
of an NP with an overt Determiner, namely the trace of extracted genitive
phrases in Romance, according to the analysis proposed in chapter 2.

29 The two constraints could actually be generalized into a universal Doubly Filled Spec Filter, requiring that at most one maximal projection occur in the Spec of every XP. However, in order for this generalization to be achieved, it is necessary to adopt the DP structure of (69)b above (to remove Determiner Phrases from the Spec of NP) and perhaps to assume that an A like *German* in *my German car* does not head a maximal projection or can anyway be incorporated into the head Noun at the relevant level of representation. It would also be necessary to find some proviso to account for cases like (65)a above.

30 See also, on this point, Torrego (1988).

31 In principle, also typological evidence could help decide between (69)a and b. Consider, in fact, the abstract case of a demonstrably consistent Spec/complement/head language: here structure (69)a would predict a [D[...N]] order, but (69)b would suggest [[...N...]D]. However, we have not yet been able to actually pursue this line of investigation.

32 Possessive pronouns in English would now be less different from phrases like *John's*: both types of phrases would be marked by a semantic feature [+det], as a consequence of their particular way of realizing the abstract Genitive Case.

References

Abney, S. (1986), Functional Elements and Licensing, ms., MIT, Cambridge MA.
(1987), The English Noun Phrase in its Sentential Aspect, PhD dissertation, MIT, Cambridge MA.

Anderson, M. (1979), Noun Phrase Structure, PhD dissertation, University of Connecticut.
(1984), Prenominal Genitive NPs, *The Linguistic Review*, 3, 1–24.

Aoun, J. (1985), *A Grammar of Anaphora*, MIT Press, Cambridge MA.

Aoun, J. and Y. Li (1987), Syntax of Quantifier Scope, ms., University of South Carolina.

Aoun, I., N. Hornstein, D. Lightfoot and A. Weinberg (1987), Two Types of Locality, *Linguistic Inquiry*, 18, 537–77.

Aoun, J. and D. Sportiche (1982), On the Formal Theory of Government, *The Linguistic Review*, 2, 211–36.

Azoulay, A. (1978), Article défini et relations anaphoriques en français, *Recherches Linguistiques*, 7.

Bach, E. and G. Horn (1976), Remarks on 'Conditions on Transformations', *Linguistic Inquiry*, 7, 265–99.

Badia i Margarit, A. (1984), *Gramàtica històrica catalana* (2nd edn), Tres i Quatre, València.

Baker, M. (1985), Incorporation as a Theory of Grammatical Function Changing, PhD dissertation, MIT, Cambridge MA.

Barss, A. (1986), Anaphoric Chains, PhD dissertation, MIT, Cambridge MA.

Battye, A. (1988), Reflections on Nominal Quantification in Three Romance Varieties, ms., University of York and University of Venice.

Belletti, A. (1978), Strutture coordinate e possessivi, *Rivista di Grammatica Generativa*, 3, 1.
(1988), The Case of Unaccusatives, *Linguistic Inquiry*, 19, 1–34.

Belletti, A. and L. Rizzi (1981), The Syntax of NE: Some Theoretical Implications, *The Linguistic Review*, 1, 117–54.
(1988), Psych-verbs and θ-theory, *Natural Language and Linguistic Theory*, 6, 291–352.

Bendor-Samuel, D. (1972), *Hierarchical Structures in Guajajara*, Summer Institute of Linguistics Publications, Norman, OK.

Benincà, P. (1980), Nomi senza articolo, *Rivista di Grammatica Generativa*, 551–63.

Benveniste, E. (1966), *Problèmes de linguistique générale*, Gallimard, Paris.

Bolinger, D. (1967), Adjectives in English: Attribution and Predication, *Lingua*, 18, 1–34.

(1972), *Degree Words*, The Hague, Mouton.

Borer, H. (1984), *Parametric Syntax*, Foris, Dordrecht.

(1986), I-subjects, *Linguistic Inquiry*, 17, 375–416.

Bouchard, D. (1984), *On the Content of Empty Categories*, Foris, Dordrecht.

Bracco, C., L. Brandi and P. Cordin (1985), Sulla posizione di soggetto in italiano e in alcuni dialetti dell'Italia centro-settentrionale, in L. M. Savoia and A. Franchi De Bellis (eds.), *Sintassi e morfologia della lingua italiano d'uso*, Bulzoni, Rome.

Brandi, L. and P. Cordin (1981), Dialetti e italiano: un confronto sul parametro del soggetto nullo, *Rivista di Grammatica Generativa*, 6, 33–88.

(1986), From Two Italian Dialects to Null Subject Parameter: Null Subjects, Subject Clitics and Inversion, ms., Scuola Normale Superiore, University of Trento. Now in O. Jaeggli and K. Sapir (eds.) *On the Null Subject Parameter*, Kluwer, Dordrecht.

Bresnan, J. (1976), Evidence for a Theory of Unbounded Transformations, *Linguistic Analysis*, 2, 353–93.

Brucart, J. and L. Gràcia (1986), I sintagmi nominali senza testa, *Rivista di Grammatica Generativa*, 11, 3–32.

Burzio, L. (1981), Intransitive Verbs and Italian Auxiliaries, PhD dissertation, MIT, Cambridge MA, 184–221.

(1986), *Italian Syntax: a GB Approach*, Reidel, Dordrecht.

Chomsky, N. (1970), Remarks on Nominalizations, in R. Jacobs and P. Rosenbaum (eds.), *Readings in English Transformational Grammar*, Ginn and Co., Waltham MA.

(1975), *Reflections on Language*, Pantheon, New York, 71–132.

(1977), On Wh-movement, in P. Culicover, T. Wasow and A. Akmajian (eds.), *Formal Syntax*, Academic Press, New York.

(1980), On Binding, *Linguistic Inquiry*, 11, 11–46.

(1981), *Lectures on Government and Binding*, Foris, Dordrecht.

(1982), *Some Concepts and Consequences of the Theory of Government and Binding*, MIT Press, Cambridge MA.

(1986a), *Knowledge of Language*, Praeger, New York.

(1986b), *Barriers*, MIT Press, Cambridge MA.

(1988), Some Notes on Economy of Derivation and Representation, ms., MIT, Cambridge MA.

Cinque, G. (1977), The Movement Nature of Left Dislocation, *Linguistic Inquiry*, 8, 397–412.

(1980), On Extraction from NP in Italian, *Journal of Italian Linguistics*, 5, 47–99.

(1981a), Sulla nozione di soggetto di SN in italiano, *Cultura Neolatina*, 41.

(1981b), On the Theory of Relative Clauses and Markedness, *The Linguistic Review*, 1, 247–94.

(1982), Constructions with Left Peripheral Phrases, Connectedness, Move α and ECP, ms., University of Venice.

(1984), Clitic Left Dislocation in Italian and the Move α Parameter, ms., University of Venice.

(1985), Aggettivi ergativi e non ergativi, paper presented at the 'Incontro di Grammatica Generativa', Rome.

(1986), Bare Quantifiers, Quantified NPs and the Notion of Operator at S-structure, *Rivista di Grammatica Generativa*, 11.

(1988), On *si* Constructions and the theory of *arb*, *Linguistic Inquiry*, 19, 521–81.

(1990), Ergative Adjectives and the Lexicalist Hypothesis, *Natural Language and Linguistic Theory*, 8, 1–39.

(forthcoming), *Types of A′ Dependencies*, MIT Press, Cambridge MA.

Coopmans, P. (1984), Surface Word-order Typology and Universal Grammar, *Language*, 60, 55–69.

Delfitto, D. (1986), Per una teoria dello *scope* relativo, *Rivista di Grammatica Generativa*, 9/10, 215–63.

Demonte, V. (1982), El falso problema de la posición del adjectivo; dos análisis semánticos, *Boletín de la Real Academia española*, 62, 453–85.

Drachman, G. (1985), Language Universals: the Two Approaches, *Folia Linguistica*, 12.

Emonds, J. (1976), *A Transformational Approach to English Syntax*, Academic Press, New York.

Ernout, A. and F. Thomas (1972), *Syntaxe Latine* (6th edn), Klincksieck, Paris.

Evans, G. (1980), Pronouns, *Linguistic Inquiry*, 11, 337–62.

Fiengo, R. and J. Higginbotham (1981), Opacity in NP, *Linguistic Analysis*, 7, 395–422.

Foulet, L. (1982), *Petite syntaxe de l'ancien français*, Champion, Paris.

Fukui, N. and M. Speas (1986), Specifiers and Projections, *MIT Working Papers in Linguistics*, 8, 128–72.

Giorgi, A. (1983), Toward a Theory of Long Distance Anaphors: a GB approach, *The Linguistic Review*, 3, 307–61.

(1986), The Proper Notion of C-command and the Binding Theory: Evidence from NPs, in S. Berman, J. Choe and J. McDonough (eds.), *Proceedings of NELS* 16, University of Amherst, MA, 169–85.

(1987a), On the Notion of Complete Functional Complex: some Evidence from Italian, *Linguistic Inquiry*, 18, 511–18.

(1987b), Prepositions, θ-marking and C-command, paper presented at the 'Groningen Round Table on Long-Distance Anaphors', Groningen.

Godard, D. (1986), French Relative Clauses with *dont*, in J. Guéron, J. Y. Pollock and H. Obenauer (eds.), *Grammatical Representation*, Foris, Dordrecht.

Gràcia, L. (1986), La teoria temàtica, PhD dissertation, University of Barcelona.

Graffi, G. (1980), Universali di Greenberg e Grammatica Generativa, *Lingua e Stile*, 15, 371–87.

(1987), Soggetto strutturale e soggetto tematico, paper presented at the 'Convegno di Grammatica Generativa', Trento.

Greenberg, J. (1966), Some Universals of Grammar with Particular Reference to the Order of Meaningful Elements, in J. Greenberg (ed.), *Universals of Language*, MIT Press, Cambridge MA, 73–113.

Grevisse, M. (1975), *Le Bon Usage* (10th edn), Duculot, Gembloux, Belgium.

Grimshaw, J. (1986), Nouns, Arguments and Adjuncts, ms., Brandeis University.

Grosu, A. (1974), On the Nature of the Left Branch Condition, *Linguistic Inquiry*, 5, 308–19.

Gruber, J. (1965), Studies in Lexical Relations, PhD dissertation, MIT, Cambridge MA.

Guéron, J. (1986), Inalienable Possession, PRO-Inclusion and Lexical Chains, in J. Guéron, J. Y. Pollock and H. Obenauer (eds.), *Grammatical Representation*, Foris, Dordrecht.

Haider, H. (1987), Die Struktur der deutschen NP, ms., Universities of Vienna and Stuttgart.

Hawkins, J. (1982), Cross-category Harmony, X-bar, and the Predictions of Markedness, *Journal of Linguistics*, 18, 1–35.

(1983), *Word Order Universals*, Academic Press, New York.

(1985), Complementary Methods in Universal Grammar: a Reply to Coopmans, *Language*, 61, 569–87.

Hellan, L. (1986), Reference to Thematic Roles in Rules of Anaphora in Norwegian, ms., University of Trondheim.

Higginbotham, J. (1980), Pronouns and Bound Variables, *Linguistic Inquiry*, 11, 679–708.

(1983), Logical Form, Binding and Nominals, *Linguistic Inquiry*, 14, 395–420.

(1985), On Semantics, *Linguistic Inquiry*, 16, 547–93.

Hoji, H. (1986), Empty Pronominals in Japanese and the Subject of NP, in J. McDonough and B. Plunkett (eds.), *Proceedings of NELS 17*, University of Amherst, MA.

Horn, G. (1974), The Noun Phrase Constraint, PhD dissertation, University of Massachusetts, Amherst.

Hornstein, N. (1977), S and the X-bar Convention, *Linguistic Analysis*, 3, 137–76.

Horrocks, G. and M. Stavrou (1987), Bounding Theory and Greek Syntax: Evidence for Wh-movement in NP, *Journal of Linguistics*, 23, 79–108.

Huang, J. (1982), Logical Relations in Chinese and the Theory of Grammar, PhD dissertation, MIT, Cambridge MA.

Jackendoff, R. (1972), *Semantics and Cognition*, MIT Press, Cambridge MA.

(1977), *X-bar Syntax: a Study of Phrase Structure*, MIT Press, Cambridge MA.

Jaeggli, O. (1986), Passive, *Linguistic Inquiry*, 17, 587–622.

Kaufman, E. (1974), Navajo Spatial Enclitics, *Linguistic Inquiry*, 5, 507–33.

Kayne, R. (1972), Subject Inversion in French Interrogatives, in J. Casagrande and B. Saciuk (eds.), *Generative Studies in Romance Languages*, Newbury House, Rowley, MA, 70–126.

(1975), *French Syntax: the Transformational Cycle*, MIT Press, Cambridge MA.

(1981a), ECP Extensions, *Linguistic Inquiry*, 12, 93–133 (now in Kayne 1984).

(1981b), On Certain Differences between English and French, *Linguistic Inquiry*, 12, 349–71 (now in Kayne 1984).

(1981c), Unambiguous Paths, in R. May and J. Koster (eds.), *Levels of Linguistic Representation*, Foris, Dordrecht, 143–83 (now in Kayne 1984).

(1983), Connectedness, *Linguistic Inquiry*, 14, 223–49 (now in Kayne 1984).

(1984), *Connectedness and Binary Branching*, Foris, Dordrecht.

(1986), L'Accord du participe passé en français et en italien, *Modèles Linguistiques*, 7, 73–89.

Kayne, R. and J. Y. Pollock (1978), Stylistic Inversion, Successive Cyclicity and Move NP in French, *Linguistic Inquiry*, 9, 595–621.

Keenan, E. (1978), Language Variation and the Logical Structure of Universal Grammar, in H. Seiler (ed.), *Language Universals*, G. Narr, Tübingen.

Kenstowicz, M. (1985a), The Null Subject Parameter in Modern Arabic Dialects, in *Proceedings of NELS* 14, Amherst University, Amherst MA.

(1985b), The Phonology and the Syntax of Wh-expressions in Tangale, *Studies in the Linguistic Sciences*, 15, 2.

Keyser, J. and T. Roeper (1984), On the Middle and Ergative Constructions in English, *Linguistic Inquiry*, 15, 499–505.

Koopman, H. (1984), *The Syntax of Verbs*, Foris, Dordrecht.

Koopman, H. and D. Sportiche (1982), Variables and the Bijection Principle, *The Linguistic Review*, 2, 139–60.

(1988), Subjects, ms., University of California at Los Angeles and University of South Carolina.

Koster, J. (1978), Why Subject Sentences Don't Exist, in S. J. Keyser (ed.), *Recent Transformational Studies in European Languages*, MIT Press, Cambridge MA, 53–64.

(1984), On Binding and Control, *Linguistic Inquiry*, 15, 417–59.

Larson, R. (1988), On the Double Object Construction, *Linguistic Inquiry* 19, 335–91.

Lasnik, H. (1976), Remarks on Coreference, *Linguistic Analysis*, 2, 1–22.

Lasnik, H. and A. Barss (1986), A Note on Anaphora and Double Objects, *Linguistic Inquiry*, 17, 347–54.

Lasnik, H. and M. Saito (1984), On the Nature of Proper Government, *Linguistic Inquiry*, 15, 235–89.

Lees, R. B. (1960), *The Grammar of English Nominalizations*, Mouton, The Hague.

Levin, B. and M. Rappaport (1986), The Formation of Adjectival Passives, *Linguistic Inquiry*, 17, 623–61.

Lieber, R. (1983), Argument Linking and Compounds in English, *Linguistic Inquiry*, 14, 251–85.

Lightfoot, D. (1979), *Principles of Diachronic Syntax*, Cambridge University Press, Cambridge.

(1982), *The Language Lottery*, MIT Press, Cambridge MA.

Longobardi, G. (1978), Doubl-inf, *Rivista di Grammatica Generativa*, 3, 2.

(1980), Remarks on Infinitives: a Case for a Filter, *Journal of Italian Linguistics*, 5, 101–55.

(1983), Le frasi copulari in italiano e la struttura della teoria sintattica, *Annali della Scuola Normale di Pisa*, 13, 4.

(1985a), Connectedness, Scope and C-command, *Linguistic Inquiry*, 16, 163–92.

(1985b), The Theoretical Status of the Adjunct Condition, ms., Scuola Normale Superiore di Pisa.

(1986), In Defence of the Correspondence Hypothesis: Island Effects and Parasitic Constructions in LF, ms., Scuola Normale Superiore di Pisa.

(forthcoming), *Movement, Scope and Island Constraints*.

Lyons, C. (1984), Genitive Case and Definiteness, paper presented at the 'Groningen Round Table on Indefiniteness'.

(1986), On the Origin of the Old French Strong–Weak Possessive Distinction, *Transactions of the Philological Society*, 1–41.

Manzini, M. R. (1980), On Control, ms., MIT, Cambridge MA.

(1983a), On Control and Control Theory, *Linguistic Inquiry*, 14, 421–46.

(1983b), Restructuring and Reanalysis, PhD dissertation, MIT, Cambridge MA.

(1986), Phrase Structure and Extraction, paper presented at GLOW, Girona.

Marouzeau, J. (1922), *L'Ordre des mots dans la phrase latine: les groupes nominaux*, Champion, Paris.

May, R. (1977), The Grammar of Quantification, PhD dissertation, MIT, Cambridge MA.

Meillet, A. and J. Vendryès (1968), *Traité de grammaire comparée des langues classiques*, Champion, Paris.

Melvold, J. (1986), Factivity and Definiteness, ms., MIT, Cambridge MA.

Milner, J. C. (1982), *Ordres et raisons de langue*, Seuil, Paris.

Obenauer, H. G. (1976), *Etudes de syntaxe interrogative*, Tübingen, Max Niemeyer.

(1978), A-sur-A et les variables catégorielles: comment formuler les transformations transcatégorielles?, in University of Quebec, Montreal. *Syntaxe et sémantique du français, Cahier de linguistique*, 8.

(1985), On the Identification of Empty Categories, *The Linguistic Review*, 4, 153–202.

Ouhalla, J. (1988), Movement in Noun Phrases, paper presented at the LAGB Meeting, Durham, UK.

Paul, H. and W. Mitzka (1966), *Mittelhochdeutsche Grammatik* (20th edn), Max Niemeyer, Tübingen.

Perlmutter, D. (1978), Impersonal Passives and the Unaccusative Hypothesis, in *Proceedings of the Fourth Annual Meeting of the Berkeley Linguistic Society*, University of California, 157–89.

Pesetsky, D. (1981), Complementizer–Trace Phenomena and the Nominative Island Condition, *The Linguistic Review*, 1, 297–343.

(1982), Paths and Categories, PhD dissertation, MIT, Cambridge MA.

Pollock, J.-Y. (1989), Verb Movement, UG, and the Structure of IP, *Linguistic Inquiry*, 20, 365–424.

Postal, P. M. (1971), *Crossover Phenomena*, Holt, Rinehart and Winston, New York.

Radford, A. (1988), *Transformational Grammar*, Cambridge University Press, Cambridge.

Ramat, P. (1986), *Introduzione alla linguistica germanica*, il Mulino, Bologna.

Rappaport, M. (1983), On the Nature of Derived Nominals, in L. Levin, M. Rappaport and A. Zaenen (eds.), *Papers in Logical Functional Grammar*, Indiana University, Linguistics Club, Bloomington IN, 113–42.

Reinhart, T. (1976), The Syntactic Domain of Anaphora, PhD dissertation, MIT, Cambridge MA.

(1983), Coreference and Bound Anaphora: a Restatement of the Anaphora Questions, *Linguistics and Philosophy*, 6, 47–88.

(1987), Specifier and Operator Binding, in E. Reuland and A. ter Meulen (eds.) *The Representation of (In)definiteness*, MIT Press, Cambridge MA, 130–67.

Renzi, L. (1985a), L'articolo zero, in L. M. Savoia and A. Franchi De Bellis (eds.), *Sintassi e morfologia della lingua italiana d'uso*, Bulzoni, Rome, 271–88.

(1985b), *Nuova introduzione alla filologia romanza* (with the collaboration of G. Salvi), Il Mulino, Bologna.

Reuland, E. (1983), Governing -*ing*, *Linguistic Inquiry*, 14, 101–36.

Riemsdijk, H. van (1978), *A Case Study in Syntactic Markedness*, Foris, Dordrecht.

Riemsdijk, H. van and E. Williams (1981), NP Structure, *The Linguistic Review*, 1, 171–217.

Ritter, E. (1986), NSO Noun Phrase in a VSO language, ms., MIT, Cambridge MA.

Rizzi, L. (1982a), *Issues in Italian Syntax*, Foris, Dordrecht.

(1982b), On Chain Formation, ms., University of Calabria.

(1986), Null Objects in Italian and the Theory of *pro*, *Linguistic Inquiry*, 17, 501–57.

Roberts, I. (1987), *The Representation of Implicit and Dethematized Subjects*, Foris, Dordrecht.

Roeper, T. (1984), Implicit Arguments and the Projection Principle, ms., University of Massachusetts, Amherst MA.

Roeper, T. and M. Siegel (1978), A Lexical Transformation for Verbal Compounds, *Linguistic Inquiry*, 9, 199–260.

Rohlfs, G. (1949), *Historische Grammatik der italienischen Sprache und ihrer Mundarten*, vol. II, *Formenlehre und Syntax*, Francke, Bern.

Ross, J. (1967), Constraints on Variables in Syntax, PhD dissertation, MIT, Cambridge MA.

(1969), On the Cyclic Nature of English Pronominalization, in D. Reibel and S. Schane (eds.), *Modern Studies in English*, Prentice Hall, Englewood Cliffs NJ, 187–200.

Rothstein, S. (1983), The Syntactic Forms of Predication, PhD dissertation, MIT, Cambridge MA.

Rouveret, A. (1980), Sur la Notion de proposition finie, gouvernement et inversion, *Langages*, 60, 75–107.

Rozwadoska, B. (1986), Thematic Restrictions on Derived Nominals, ms., University of Massachusetts, Amherst MA, University of Wroclaw, Poland.

Ruwet, N. (1972a), Comment traiter les irrégularités syntaxiques: contraintes sur les transformations ou stratégies perceptives?, in N. Ruwet, *Théorie syntaxique et syntaxe du français*, Seuil, Paris, 252–886.

(1972b), A Propos d'une classe de verbes 'psychologiques', in N. Ruwet, *Théorie syntaxique et syntaxe du français*, Seuil, Paris, 181–251.

Safir, K. (1984), *Syntactic Chains*, Cambridge University Press, Cambridge.

(1987), The Syntactic Projection of Lexical Thematic Structure, *Natural Language and Linguistic Theory*, 5, 561–601.

Saito, M. (1984), Some Asymmetries in Japanese and their Theoretical Implications, PhD dissertation, MIT, Cambridge MA.

Salvi, G. (1985), L'infinito con l'articolo, in: L. M. Savoia and A. Franchi De Bellis (eds.), *Sintassi e morfologia della lingua italiana d'uso*, Bulzoni, Rome, 243–68.

Sells, P. (1986), Coreference and Bound Anaphora: A Restatement of the Facts, in S. Berman, J. Choe and J. McDonough (eds.), *Proceedings of NELS 16*, University of Amherst, MA.

Shlonsky, U. (1988), Government and Binding in Hebrew Nominals, ms., University of Haifa.

Sportiche, D. (1988), A Theory of Floating Quantifiers and its Corollaries for Constituent Structure, *Linguistic Inquiry*, 19, 425–49.

Steriade, D. (1981), On the Derivation of Genitival Relatives in Romance, ms., MIT, Cambridge MA.

Stowell, T. (1981), Origins of Phrase Structure, PhD dissertation, MIT, Cambridge MA.

(1986), Null Antecedents and Proper Government, in S. Berman, J. Choe and J. McDonough (eds.), *Proceedings of NELS 16*, University of Amherst, MA, 476–93.

Szabolcsi, A. (1987), Functional Categories in the Noun Phrase, in I. Kenesei (ed.), *Approaches to Hungarian*, Jate Szeged.

Taraldsen, T. (1978), *On the NIC, Vacuous Application and the That-Trace Filter*, Indiana University Linguistics Club, Bloomington IN.

(1984), Some Phrase Structure Dependent Differences between Swedish and Norwegian, *Working Papers in Scandinavian Syntax*, 1.

(1989), Sintagmi Nominali in norvegese, Paper presented at 'Convegno di Grammatica Generativa', Bologna.

Toman, J. (1986), Transparent Heads, Inheritance and Normal Form, ms., University of Regensburg.

Torrego, E. (1984), Determinerless NPs, ms., University of Massachusetts, Boston MA.

(1986), Empty Categories in Nominals, ms., University of Massachusetts, Boston MA.

(1988), Evidence for Determiner Phrases, ms., University of Massachusetts, Boston MA.

Travis, L. (1984), Parameters and Effects of Word Order Variation, PhD dissertation, MIT, Cambridge MA.

Venneman, T. (1974), Theoretical Word Order Studies: Results and Problems, *Papiere zur Linguistik*, 7, 5–25.

Vergnaud, J. R. (1974), French Relative Clauses, PhD dissertation, MIT, Cambridge MA.

Vincent, N. (1986), La posizione dell'aggettivo in italiano, in H. Stammerjohann (ed.), *Proceedings of the Conference 'Tema–Rema in Italiano'*, G. Narr, Tübingen, 181–95.

Williams, E. (1977), Discourse and Logical Form, *Linguistic Inquiry*, 8, 101–39.

(1980), Predication, *Linguistic Inquiry*, 11, 203–38.

(1982), Another Argument that Passive is Transformational, *Linguistic Inquiry*, 13, 160–3.

(1985), PRO and the Subject of NP, *Natural Language and Linguistic Theory*, 3, 297–315.

Zubizarreta, M. L. (1979), Extraction from NP and a Reformulation of Subjacency, ms., MIT, Cambridge MA.

(1985), The Relation between Morphophonology and Morphosyntax: the Case of Romance Causatives, *Linguistic Inquiry*, 16, 247–89.

(1986), Levels of Representation in the Lexicon and in the Syntax, ms., University of Tilburg and University of Maryland.

Index